VOCATIONAL EDUCATION & TRAINING

The Northern Territory's history of public philanthropy

VOCATIONAL EDUCATION & TRAINING

The Northern Territory's history
of public philanthropy

DON ZOELLNER

Australian
National
University

PRESS

Published by ANU Press
The Australian National University
Acton ACT 2601, Australia
Email: anupress@anu.edu.au
This title is also available online at press.anu.edu.au

National Library of Australia Cataloguing-in-Publication entry

Creator: Zoellner, Don, author.

Title: Vocational education and training : the Northern Territory's
            history of public philanthropy / Don Zoellner.

ISBN: 9781760460990 (paperback) 9781760461003 (ebook)

Subjects: Vocational education--Government policy--Northern Territory.
            Vocational education--Northern Territory--History.
            Occupational training--Government policy--Northern Territory.
            Occupational training--Northern Territory--History.
            Aboriginal Australians--Vocational education--Northern Territory.

Cover design and layout by ANU Press. Cover photograph: 'Northern Territory Parliament House main entrance' by Patrick Nelson.

This edition © 2017 ANU Press

Contents

List of figures

Foreword

This book represents a balancing act in drawing together the widely scattered elements of the history of vocational education and training in the Northern Territory—somewhat reminiscent of one of those circus performers with a series of plates spinning on the top of sticks. The first plate balances the temptation to offer a general critique of all government actions as opposed to the limitations of this specific research effort and the evidence associated with vocational training. It seems plausible that one might find that the large health and education agencies with thousands of public employees and large amounts of capital infrastructure might respond to ministerial direction quite differently from that discussed here. On the other hand, sport, recreation and land development might be more similar. Alternatively, there is an important, principled separation between the minister and the police and law courts that might suggest different explanations of Cabinet actions.

Plate two in our analogy offsets presenting an accurate, accessible story against the mind-numbing suite of acronyms and systematic complexity for which the sector has become infamous. The third plate poises a theoretical explanation of government ministers behaving as wealthy philanthropists against the desire to create something more than a pure chronology of events. Finally, plate four seeks parallels between the relative roles of government agencies/public institutions/private concerns and the ambitions of those who are elected to public office.

There is also an attempt to describe the tone and atmosphere surrounding many of the major events contributing to the story of vocational education and training since the early 1970s. These have been gathered from interviews with many of the key participants, verbal and written reports tabled in the ubiquitous meetings held to give direction to policy and practice, handwritten notations in the margins of archival materials and my personal participation in some of the major activities.

While every attempt has been made to carefully attribute as many references as possible, there are crucial contextual matters described in this book that do not exist on the public written record. Nevertheless, they help to explain ministerial behaviour and cannot be ignored for the sake of accuracy—possibly plate five spinning away!

Finally, this book is the latest in a series of journal articles and conference presentations that build upon the findings of research I conducted as part of my Doctor of Philosophy studies during 2010–13 into how the Australian vocational education and training system works. In the Northern Territory, there is unprecedented access to the political process and to the ministers of government, senior public servants and industry leaders, allowing for novel explanations of their behaviour to be researched. Of course, while recording the history of vocational education and training itself in a single volume helps to tell the Territory's story, the counter-balanced purpose is to stimulate debate and further explore *how* this has all come about in order to create the potential for better policy-making in the future.

It might seem odd for an account of the training system to have virtually no reference to students or teachers. However strange, that is the way the scheme has been conceived and constructed—students are to be processed and assessed against competency standards that have been designed to be more or less teacher proof. That is yet another story.

Don Zoellner

Acknowledgements

This account of vocational education and training would not have been possible to produce without the assistance of four very important institutions and their staff. The Northern Territory Library, the Northern Territory Archives Service, the National Archives of Australia (Darwin) and the Charles Darwin University Library. Each holds a remarkable repository of materials that have provided much of the content upon which this book is based. Their staff members have been unfailingly helpful and genuinely sought to understand my intentions and assist with my every request, regardless of how odd.

There are literally dozens upon dozens of former work colleagues, business people, industry representatives, government employees, ministerial staffers and the ministers themselves who have been exceedingly generous with their time, receptive to questions and who have provided frank recollections about the continued development of the Northern Territory's vocational education and training system.

In addition, I have been encouraged and supported by Professor Rolf Gerritsen's dry wit and rigorous attention to detail. His personal experience of Northern Territory Government operations and of broader national socioeconomic policy were highly useful in testing the application of a theory of philanthropic behaviour as an explanatory factor in determining ministerial actions. I would also like to acknowledge the ongoing support of my colleagues at Charles Darwin University's Northern Institute and in particular the encouragement of the Director, Professor Ruth Wallace.

Finally, it is also important to recognise the many tens of thousands of Northern Territory residents and their teachers who have been targeted for improvement and made subject to ministerial philanthropy—even if it happened unknowingly! Without their participation and continued patronage, none of the events described here would have taken place.

1

Setting the scene

The Northern Territory occupies the central northern portion of the Australian continent. Geographically, it is the third biggest jurisdiction in the nation but it has the smallest population of all the mainland states and territories at almost a quarter of a million residents. In 2014, about half of these people lived in the capital city, Darwin, while the remainder were widely scattered across the territory. The climate ranges from the monsoonal savannahs of the far north to arid rangelands in the south central areas. These conditions have traditionally been viewed as challenging for many European economic and social development endeavours. On the other hand, the entire Northern Territory landscape has an ancient and varied Indigenous history dating back many millennia, and this heritage continues to influence many of the political and economic decisions made at both local and national levels regarding the governance and future aspirations of this still-frontier province. While Aboriginal matters will feature prominently in this account of how governments have made use of vocational education and training in the Northern Territory, this is essentially a story about the impact of European social, economic, bureaucratic and political practices in a remote and sparsely populated region. The history of today's Charles Darwin University and its position as the Territory's largest provider of vocational training is not the primary object of this story as its development is well documented by Berzins and Loveday (1999) and more recently added to by Webb (2014).

Taking a lead from Heatley (1979, pp. 10–11), the political history of the Northern Territory can be roughly divided into five major time spans:

- pre-1863 era of discovery and abortive European settlement;
- South Australian administration 1863–1911;
- early Commonwealth control 1911–46;
- late Commonwealth control from the post–World War Two period to 1978; and
- era of self-government from 1978 to the present.

Each of these time periods will be considered in turn in order to develop the central proposition that structures this narrative—vocational education and training has been, and continues to be, deployed as a tool of governments to achieve desired social and economic outcomes. It will also be argued that elected government ministers have utilised vocational education and training as a philanthropic intervention into the lives of Northern Territory residents. As a corollary, if one wishes to understand the decision-making process used by ministers and, consequently, how the training system works, knowledge of philanthropy and its related behaviours will provide a highly productive perspective.

Schervish (1998, p. 600) describes philanthropy as 'the social relation of care in which individuals (and groups) respond to the moral invitation to expand the horizons of their self-interest to include meeting the needs of others'. The defining characteristic of philanthropy is the type of social signals it responds to rather than its institutional characteristics. In analysing the behaviour of Northern Territory Government ministers, the focus will concentrate upon a specific style of philanthropy—the distinctive contributions that are made by the very wealthy (Schervish, Herman & Rhenisch 1986). The Northern Territory ministers have control of the more than $100 million each year that is spent on vocational education and training (Productivity Commission 2014, Table 5A.1) and they determine how to redistribute this substantial sum to organisations and individuals to provide both private and public benefit. The phenomenon described here is not a case of simple political patronage or pork-barrelling; it is much more complex and has a positivist moral goal of improving society by managing the behaviour of the citizens who elected the minister in the first place.

Furthermore, it will be proposed that interested parties can more effectively influence the policy-making and distribution of public funds allocated to vocational education and training if they understand how philanthropists think and act rather than traditionally focusing solely upon the operations of bureaucracies. It will be contended that decisions about the financial and programmatic elements of vocational education and training in the Northern Territory are made by a minister who is elected to serve as the philanthropist of the public's combined resources. Highly successful ministers have not allowed public servants to dominate their own finely tuned political instincts and knowledge of their electorates in determining how the public largesse is distributed. While the various government agencies have an important role to play in shaping the success or failure of any particular training program, their place in the decision-making process is subordinate to the minister. Because the national training system is complex and highly bureaucratised, most participants and stakeholders in vocational education and training attempt to prompt policy direction and, more importantly, resource allocation through institutionalised processes. This narrative proposes that while it is necessary to deal with the multitude of training committees, departments, reviews, providers, licensing/registration boards, commissions, authorities and regulators, that alone is not sufficient to understand how vocational education and training operates and which considerations make the most impact upon ministerial decision-making.

In order to truly shape the highly politicised vocational education and training agenda, an alternative construction of how the system actually works is required—one where the Northern Territory Government minister with responsibility for training operates as a wealthy philanthropist. Even though the munificence displayed and enacted by the minister uses public rather than private resources, the people of the Northern Territory expect, indeed demand, this type of behaviour. Ministers and governments that are not perceived to be responsively philanthropic in their behaviour are punished at election time and replaced with a set of ministers who are more closely attuned to the intensely personal lifestyle aspirations of the miniscule electorates that return the 25 members of the Northern Territory Legislative Assembly every four years. The repeated re-election of the Country Liberal Party for the first 26 years of self-government and the 11 years of Labor rule that followed demonstrates the success of ministers minding the social and economic interests of the electorate. As described by Weller and Sanders (1982, p. 40), 'because of electoral susceptibility, nothing is too small or trivial for a Northern Territory minister'. Heatley (1998, pp. 73–74) observes that incumbency in a seat offers a strong positive advantage for an elected Member of the Northern Territory Legislative Assembly for 'those who attend to constituency duties diligently' while those who are perceived as 'not being sufficiently attentive' face electoral oblivion.

With the introduction of European styles of governance into the Northern Territory, two idiosyncratic Australian political traits have guided the development of vocational education and training. As described by Hancock (Manne & Feik 2012, p. 2), Australians have a distinctive and peculiar expression of their individualism characterised by reliance upon the state—an entity that is seen as a 'vast public utility' for the satisfaction of needs. In describing the responsiveness of Northern Territory Government ministers to pressure groups and local electoral attitudes, Heatley (1979) proposes that this reliance on public resources has become the 'epitome' of the Territory's political culture. Notwithstanding, the Northern Territory experience is only the provincial expression of a much more pervasive national ambivalence towards economic development that pays homage to free market principles while simultaneously expecting governments to intervene for the public good and generally prevent market failure.

Australian governments generally support market-based approaches, but this has been tempered by a domestic form of 'colonial socialism' (Butlin, Barnard & Pincus 1982, p. 13) characterised by the use of public interventions to attract financial capital and labour in support of private interests. In addition, social and some economic developments have been achieved through direct market participation by government bodies in areas such as banking, railways, air travel and essential services provision. Throughout the twentieth century, 'a variety of private interests were able to attract discriminatory benefits from public business in a way and to a degree that would not have been possible had these undertakings been conducted privately' (Butlin, Barnard & Pincus 1982, p. 341). When these benefits were combined with the early adoption of non-market mechanisms to redistribute national wealth through a variety of social welfare entitlements such as universal education, invalid pensions, old-age pensions, unemployment benefits and health programs, Australia from 1908 had become 'something of a social laboratory in the Western world' (Butlin, Barnard & Pincus 1982, p. 337). As will be shown, many commentators believe that with the 1911 Commonwealth assumption of responsibility for the Northern Territory, this social experimentation could be conducted without fear of political consequences or even superficial public debate.

A second attribute has developed in conjunction with the expectation of government support for private interests. National, state and territory governments are preoccupied with concerns about how to manage the population through the physically least coercive means. Foucault proposed that the whole purpose of government is 'the conduct of conduct' in advanced market democracies (Burchell, Gordon & Miller 1991, p. 48). The Australian Public Service Commission (2007, p. 5) unequivocally claims that 'public policy is most concerned with attempting to change citizens' behaviour'. The Commission has found that in formulating good public policy it is necessary to move beyond rational choice models where a simple calculation of costs and benefits will determine a person's behaviour. More subtle considerations are required that take into account the scarcity of a product or service. If citizens perceive that ministers can furnish an unlimited supply of vocational training, for example, it is unlikely to be highly valued and comes to be expected as a 'free service' in the absence of price signals in a competitive market. In addition, most citizens heavily discount future costs or benefits when compared to immediate expenses and advantages (Australian Public Service Commission 2007, p. 12). This bastion of public policy also subscribes to the idea that those who live in the direst social and economic circumstances apply an especially high discount rate, making it less likely they will voluntarily make longer-term investments in their own health, welfare or education. In these circumstances, the demands for a philanthropic intervention are all but irresistible to those ministers who have sought and accepted responsibility for managing society.

Because vocational education and training is frequently deployed as part of the solution to almost every social and economic problem facing governments of advanced market democracies (Zoellner 2013b, p. 65), it is a particularly well-suited public policy tool that gives effect to this type of public philanthropy. More pragmatically, training is one of the few major policy areas that remain in the control of various state and territory governments when compared to the Commonwealth Government's financial and legislative clout. The political battles over control of vocational education and training have featured prominently in the relationships between the federal, state and territory governments since

World War Two (Tannock 1975; Whitelock 1973). In describing funding disputes associated with the establishment of a national training system in 1990, the Northern Territory Department of Education Secretary stated:

> The Commonwealth is quite blatantly using its financial power to bludgeon States into accepting those resource agreements or risk the funding being given to other States and Territories. It seems likely that this process will continue unless there is a concerted action by all States/Territories to resist. The trend will continue if the States compete against each other and the Commonwealth is able to play one off against the other (Northern Territory Archives Service 1985–1990).

In February 1992, the Commonwealth Government offered to fully fund a new national vocational education and training system as part of the Prime Minister's economic statement *One Nation* (Goozee 2013, p. 353). Although this course of action was rejected by the various state and territory leaders, it paved the way for a compromise solution to the perceived problems of national consistency of training content, levels of qualifications and funding arrangements as part of a much broader agenda of micro-economic reform that included a strong emphasis upon increasing the level of private sector competition faced by government agencies. The various governments settled upon the creation of the Australian National Training Authority to guide national efforts in the training arena. While this Authority no longer exists, having been disbanded in August 2005 by the Commonwealth Government, it ensured that many of the features of the current national training system were established in pursuit of nation-wide standards, recognition of qualifications, labour mobility and more market-driven provision of training by both public and private training organisations.

The Northern Territory was at the forefront of adopting and enacting the policies associated with the broader reform that was to be driven through the newly formed Council of Australian Governments. In May 1992, the Northern Territory Chief Minister, Marshall Perron (1992, pp. 2–3), linked vocational education and training to:

> increased cooperation among governments in the national interest, reforms to achieve an integrated, efficient national economy, and a single national market; and continuing structural reform of government and review of relationships among governments.

Perron went onto describe the specific vocational education and training agreements that had been reached by the national, state and territory leaders. These included a major increase in the level of vocational education and training provision with a national priority given to reducing youth unemployment, further national reform that included increased competition, the introduction of quality systems and national recognition of qualifications. Unsurprisingly, matters of funding and administrative arrangements were 'yet to be resolved' (Perron 1992, p. 14).

This was a fairly easy set of commitments for Perron to take to the national heads of government meeting because in February of the same year his Education Minister, Shane Stone (1992), had already announced a 'new era in vocational education and training' for the Northern Territory. The major features of Stone's statement to the Legislative Assembly included greater devolution of operational decision-making to local industry and colleges (coupled with increased centralisation of funding and policy decisions through the establishment of the Northern Territory Employment and Training Authority), government funding for both public and private providers, competency-based training, recognition of prior learning mechanisms, national standards for providers as well as recognition of interstate qualifications. In reflecting upon his time as Minister for Education and Training and a cooperative attitude towards the Australian Government minister, Stone states, 'John Dawkins and I worked well at Ministerial Council level and our mutual commitment and interest in a national training and vocational education structure paid handsome dividends for the Territory' (Martin & Dewar 2012, p. 95).

In its 1997 review of the commitment of the various state and territory governments to microeconomic reform, the Industry Commission (1998, pp. 133–139) described the Northern Territory as a 'national leader' in the reform of vocational education and training. One detailed analysis of public policy-making in Northern Territory vocational education and training concluded that, when compared to other jurisdictions, local ministers have had the relative luxury of being able to focus upon policy and funding. This is because the Northern Territory has never operated its own public training system in the format of a government agency and has achieved even greater policy flexibility by referring its quality compliance functions to the national regulator (Zoellner 2013a).

In fact, the histories of the gradual incorporation of training into a national system and the constitutional/political advancement of the Northern Territory demonstrate considerable congruence as parallel case studies of federalism at work, particularly since the mid-1970s. Before embarking on this journey that will plot the centrality of training as a tool of ministerial philanthropy in pursuit of the social and economic development of the Northern Territory, a brief characterisation of current vocational education and training sets the scene for that which has gone before.

The Northern Territory Government's Department of Trade, Business and Innovation describes vocational education and training as one of the strategies being used to achieve social, economic and environmental sustainability. Vocational education and training is highly valued because it provides skills and knowledge that enable an economic citizen to pursue lifelong learning resulting in continued and gainful employment. Training became formally organised in southern Australian colonies in the mid to late nineteenth century with the establishment of adult education in the form of schools of mines, mechanics institutes, university extension courses, workers' educational associations and so forth. Industrial unions also became involved in the early twentieth century when instruction was mostly directed at male apprentices in manufacturing industries. This training was controlled by the states and eventually resulted in 'confusion of institutional eccentricity' represented by the chronically disparate state training systems producing neither the number of skilled workers nor the right skills for a national economy facing a global trading market driven by rapid advances in technologies (Whitelock 1974, p. 269).

In spite of Prime Minister Curtin rejecting the Duncan Review's 1944 recommendation for a national adult education system on the grounds of expense and not wishing to engage in a political battle with the state premiers (Whitelock 1973, p. v), by 1974 national economic problems had become so acute that the demand for the provision of Commonwealth funding to a training sector identified as Technical and Further Education became impossible to ignore (Goozee 2013, pp. 126–127). The various state-based systems came to be identified by the nationally accepted acronym TAFE, which also served as a generic reference to formal training that was provided through the allocation of public funds from state and Commonwealth Government sources in response to the Kangan Review (Australian Committee on Technical and Further Education 1974). As the Northern Territory was still under the control of a Commonwealth Government that was concentrating on developing the Darwin Community College, local needs for training infrastructure and operating funds were not considered by the Kangan Committee as there was no TAFE system in existence in the jurisdiction.

As described previously, by 1992 the Commonwealth, state and territory governments agreed to establish a national training system to deliver vocational education and training. The term Technical and Further Education now symbolised the institutions and bureaucracies of the large public state-based systems. Government funds have been progressively directed towards both publicly owned and private providers since that time while formal training, and its recognition at one of 10 levels of national qualifications, has been adopted by most major occupational categories and is available to both genders. The national training system is characterised by high levels of industry strategic direction, nation-wide regulation of standards and the centralised determination of industry-specific competencies in training packages produced by the Industry Skills Councils/Skills Service Organisations or contained in nationally accredited courses. The Northern Territory established a 'quasi-market' in vocational education and training in which individuals paid for about 10 per cent of the total training effort and the government-supported arm's-length public institutions, such as Charles Darwin University and Batchelor Institute of Indigenous Tertiary Education, for another 55 per cent of the training delivered in 2012. The remaining 35 per cent of public funding in the Northern Territory was allocated to private training organisations (National Centre for Vocational Education Research 2013a, Table 15).

This national training system has evolved into an extraordinarily complex arrangement (Australian Workforce and Productivity Agency 2013, p. 118). Vocational education and training, as it currently exists, can only be enacted through the cooperation between a state or territory government and the Commonwealth Government. In order to 'do' the national training system, federal policy and funding establishes the general structures and directions. These include registration of training providers, the Australian Qualifications Framework and the collection and dissemination of nationally consistent data through the National Centre for Vocational Education Research. The actions of various state and territory governments allocate the people, locations, buildings, programs and tactics that react to centralised guidance in unpredictable and idiosyncratic ways reflecting the political economy in each jurisdiction. Contestations at the interface between national policy-setting and local operational management ensures a lack of consistency across jurisdictions and never-ending skirmishes over who ultimately pays for training (McDowell et al. 2011). Instead of presenting a barrier to high levels of ministerial discretion in the use of the vocational education and training, the complexity of the national system provides politicians and bureaucrats with an extraordinary amount of flexibility in the development of public policy because they can pick and choose from a variety of theoretical perspectives related to markets and the possibility of market failure, microeconomic reform, colonial socialism and the role of government in 'conducting the conduct' of the citizenry.

The next chapter will turn to the nature of philanthropy and the motivations that guide the decisions made by those who behave in a 'generous' manner. Each of the chapters that follow will explore the tension between the predominant Australian rhetoric of a capitalist free market and the seemingly insatiable desire on the part of citizens for government involvement and action in vocational education and training. Some ideas have remained strong through this historical journey, while a handful has fallen out of public favour. Others have disappeared, only to resurface many years later. Viewing the Northern Territory's development of vocational education and training through the alternative lens of philanthropic behaviour will produce both an inclusive historical account of the sector for the first time, as well as a novel proposition of how the system actually operates.

2

Philanthropic behaviour

This chapter describes the special characteristics and activities associated with 'public philanthropy' prior to commencing the historical account of the development and uses of vocational education and training in the Northern Territory. The benevolent behaviour of the Northern Territory ministers who have had responsibility for training since self-government in 1978 (full local responsibility for education and training was formally obtained in July 1979) is considerably more nuanced and purposeful than simplistic acts of charity or patronage for favoured individuals or organisations. Ministerial direction of training policy, programs and large sums of money provides a non-coercive form of social control that is targeted at the socioeconomic development of the jurisdiction and its inhabitants. Furthermore, the use of public philanthropy, a bipartisan technique mobilised by whichever political party forms government, is explicitly accepted and even expected by the population. The importance of the relationship between the electorate and the minister, who seeks to be entrusted with temporary control of the public's munificence, cannot be over emphasised.

Following the explanation of some general observations about philanthropy, specific Australian characteristics that modify and contextualise its enactment are described. The actions of the super-rich or wealthy philanthropists will then be joined to a consideration of the types of behaviour exhibited by ministers acting as wealthy public philanthropists and their unwavering commitment to 'improving' society through the specification of economic goals.

Philanthropy 'conjoins a resolute sentiment of sympathetic identification of others, a thoughtful discernment of what needs to be done and a strategic course of action aimed at meeting the needs of others' (Schervish 1998, p. 600). It is not defined by volunteerism and is not alone in attending to the public good. The distinctive features of philanthropy lie in the kinds of signals it pays attention to in 'deciding what needs of which people' are heeded in order to improve society (Schervish 1998, p. 600). In the Northern Territory, the generation of these signals is intensely personal—most ministers are usually greeted with their given name and they individually come to know each of the major participants in the training system. Successful ministers are constantly testing the pulse of the electorate and specialise in minutiae because no decision is insignificant when calculating the potential electoral consequences (Weller & Sanders 1982).

Brody (1987) believes that many contemporary democratic states have replaced the need for and taken over the role of private philanthropy in the name of providing universal services, as a right of citizenship, in order to increase the general welfare. These activities are funded by progressive rates of taxation. The early twentieth-century Australian experience described by Lyons (2001, pp. 100–102) demonstrates a 'nationalisation' of many so-called 'third sector' non-profit organisations as they accepted increased tax-payer funding and additional government regulation that accompanied gaining access to the public purse. Following World War Two, a lasting legacy of this additional government support was a decline in private philanthropy. For example, Brennan (1994) provides a detailed account of this phenomenon in the childcare sector. Over several decades, community interest in the development of preschool-aged children shifted from the philanthropic provision of kindergartens designed to instil middle-class values into poverty-stricken nineteenth-century working-class children to an economic and productivity calculation of the cost of providing Commonwealth Government childcare subsidies in the twentieth century. Government action was instigated by an economically driven agenda to increase workforce participation and respond to elements of a much broader feminist agenda according to Brennan (1994). The eventual departure from not-for-profit provision of childcare was rather an easy move since 'Australian giving is shaped by its historical and political leanings towards the welfare state'; also, citizens believe that government has a rightful place in the provision of public philanthropy as a collective responsibility springing from the peculiar Australian brand of egalitarianism that accepts some market-driven behaviours (McDonald & Scaife 2011, pp. 315–321). Wolf (1989, p. 30) observes, 'Most public policy decisions are usually even more concerned with distributional issues (namely, who gets the benefits and who pays the costs) rather than efficiency issues (namely, how large are the benefits and costs)'.

Philanthropy is a form of social behaviour that provides a direct, rather than indirect, expression of social involvement via the redistribution of wealth. Donors offer money, time and ideas for specific programs that they then seek to control. Philanthropy always has something to do with power and the direction of society with a particular focus on the maintenance of society as a social system. 'Philanthropists show personal initiative, triggered by strong commitments to the goals they want to support. They are not obliged to give; instead they are willing to give' (Schuyt, Bekkers & Smit 2010, p. 4). In addition, 'the concept of philanthropy has been modified in accordance with the evolution of societies, economics and politics, particularly, the role of the state' (Daly 2012, p. 548). Governments have embraced public philanthropic behaviour as they have simultaneously deployed more centralised managerial styles of governance. The increased provision of public resources to both private and non-profit organisations, contracted to operate specified programs, allows ministers and senior bureaucrats to concentrate upon policy and funding decisions (Zoellner 2013a). With the benefit of hindsight and due to the unique historic pattern of constitutional development, it can be shown that the Northern Territory Government has applied the principles now known as 'new public management' to vocational education and training even before the phrase became fashionable in the 1980s. The net result has been described by Dollery and Wallis (2003, p. 31) as 'philanthropic paternalism' through which the affluent philanthropic donors may impose their own preferences on the operations of voluntary and non-profit organisations that have been contracted to deliver services on behalf of governments.

According to Coutsoukis (1999, p. 3), the focus on managerial approaches to public giving is more frequently aligned with setting and measuring quantifiable impact that does good for the community. However, public philanthropy is never an exclusively strategic intervention into social control and improvement because of community emergencies, non-strategic community needs, other government priorities and pressure to participate in popular causes (Coutsoukis 1999, p. 6). In spite of Australia's general acceptance of neo-classical economics where the ideal is a free market, government financial intervention is a widely used mechanism to protect against or deal with cases of market failure (Lyons 2001, p. 199). For vocational education and training in the Northern Territory the dangers of market failure are ever-present due to remoteness, small populations giving rise to 'thin markets', a tiny economic base reminiscent of a developing country and only a handful of training providers. Australians generally, and Northern Territorians specifically, expect government ministers to be actively involved when it comes to training the potential workforce.

There is an unstated acceptance on the part of both ministers and the public that the primary objective of giving behaviour is the creation of social value and not personal gain on the part of politicians (Daly 2012, p. 546). The Northern Territory's deployment of vocational education and training as a tool of government mostly conforms to the ethical arguments for greater equity identified by Lyons (2001, p. 105):

- modern market economies induce extremes of income and poverty that can be ameliorated by redistributive policy interventions;
- people do not always behave in their own interests; and
- increased training provides more equal economic opportunity.

The strong emphasis on corporate managerialism that accompanied the widespread adoption of new public management practices into Australian governments guided and simultaneously narrowed the range of behaviours available to government ministers. The major feature of this style of management means that the operations of government are facilitated through contractual arrangements between an agent and the principal (Hill & Hupe 2002, p. 110). In Northern Territory vocational education and training, the mundane activities of teaching, assessing and reporting on skills acquisition are conducted by a variety of public and private training providers (agents) that are responsive to government bodies that in turn are answerable to a minister (principals) for contractually specified outputs, quality processes and the provision of information and data in nationally determined formats. The incorporation of new public management into the fledgling Northern Territory Government operations in conjunction with self-government in 1978 has not hindered the minister's capacity to operate as a philanthropist, but it has aligned the way they operate with an identifiable sub-group of philanthropists. This cluster has been described as the wealthy (Schervish, Herman & Rhenisch 1986) or even as the super-rich (Hay & Muller 2013).

Once an elected member of the Legislative Assembly takes on the role of the minister with responsibility for training, their professional and personal lives become much more complicated. In order to be re-elected and project a positive image of government, they must maintain the intimate relationship with their electorate. On the other hand, they have gained jurisdiction-wide and national responsibilities that cannot be ignored and, if cleverly managed, can be turned to the financial advantage of the Northern Territory and the chance of further electoral success. As previously described, the importance of maintaining touch with the local constituency cannot be overemphasised in the tiny Northern Territory electoral divisions—each having around 5,000 registered voters in 2012. Just a few hundred voters changing their support for a particular candidate can result in quite large statistical swings. Having reiterated the omnipresence of parochial considerations, the object of attention now turns to the role that the local member assumes when entering Cabinet and ministerial office.

Because vocational education and training has been made operational in the Northern Territory through the agent–principal contractual arrangements associated with new public management, the local minister is in a political 'sweet spot'. With the risk of failure, the messiness of day-to-day operations and human resource management all contracted away, the minister can focus upon policy and funding (Zoellner 2013a). Obviously, with a large sum of money at his or her disposal, the minister of the day can gain the support of Cabinet colleagues to determine what programs, organisations and individuals are to be subsidised with public dollars. More subtly, and possibly even more importantly, the minister interacts with constituents on the basis of all care but minimal operational responsibility. The minister can receive complaints from disgruntled members of the public and display genuine empathy and sympathy. Equally, he or she can be successfully lobbied to finance the alleged training needs of particular industry sectors or even individual businesses. For example, the ministerial files of the first Chief Minister of the Northern Territory, Paul Everingham, and his Minister for Education, Jim Robertson, bulge with written requests for vocational education and training facilities; these include the establishment of the Gillen House hospitality and tourism training building in Alice Springs (instead of Darwin), the establishment of the Community College of Central Australia and supporting the agricultural industry by the establishment of a Katherine Rural Education Centre (Northern Territory Archives Service 1977–1979). As will be shown later, each of these extensive lobbying efforts was successful.

In support of the local electors and potential campaign donors, ministerial staff frequently query training providers at quite detailed levels in order to provide the minister with information, invariably referred to as 'good news stories' that can be used to demonstrate that the minister has 'done something' on behalf of citizens. Having access to around $100 million each year, pursuing a specific socioeconomic policy agenda and being insulated from operational responsibilities serves to position the minister as a wealthy philanthropist. He or she can intervene as much or as little as is felt to be politically advantageous and exert significant amounts of control over the behaviour of the population in terms of the quantities of training and the areas of the economy that are going to be allocated public funding to improve the skills base. Archer (2012), for example, has described the gradual decrease in public financial support for the arts community that has forced many Australian tertiary education and training programs to either close completely or drastically reduce their scale of operations. The Northern Territory also demonstrates this judgemental process with its gradual removal of public funding for the Adult and Community Education providers culminating in no allocations being made since 2010 (National Centre for Vocational Education Research 2014, Northern Territory Table 15).

The trappings of ministerial office further reinforce the image of a well-heeled patron guiding vocational education and training. The ministerial suites are located on the top floor of the Northern Territory Parliament House and command sweeping views of Darwin Harbour. Ministers are delivered into the basement of the building in chauffeur-driven sedans and use a private lift to convey them to their offices. Constituents wishing to complain to, lobby or hold discussions with the minister must enter the building through an airport-style security checkpoint in the main street-level entrance and then be escorted to the suite. Once there, a number of ministerial officers and advisors are seen to be busily tending to the business of executive government. Depending upon the perceived status of the visitor and their relationship with the minister, the meeting venue can either be in a well-appointed, windowless meeting room or in the minister's wood-panelled office with its expansive panorama that is visible from the equally sprawling handmade wooden desk. For most visitors, the meeting is also attended by an advisor who makes notes and often poses questions on behalf of the minister. Cups of coffee and tea are freely available as a symbol of ministerial generosity. The minister's diary is permanently overcommitted and various minders will ensure that meetings do not run over time or even end meetings quite abruptly with veiled references to emergencies or crucial matters of state suddenly arising. The net effect of this process is that the visitor is left with the impression that they have been very lucky to have gained direct access to the minister and privileged to be able to present their case to this very important and resource-laden person. Of course, the foregoing describes a stereotypic characterisation of the conduct of the very wealthy as well.

Figure 1. Paul Henderson, minister, second from right, and guests on the fifth-floor balcony of the Northern Territory Parliament House, 2005.
Source: Creator Northern Territory Government Photographer. PH0730/2184.
Northern Territory Government Photographer Collection, Northern Territory Library.

It has been theorised that the distinctive contribution of affluence to philanthropic behaviour 'is that wealth affords individuals the means for moving from being simply consumers of the social agenda to being producers of it' (Schervish, Herman & Rhenisch 1986, p. 9). Philanthropy of the wealthy contributes to this productive function by redistributing resources to individuals and organisations to cater for expressed needs and to achieve their goals:

But the fact remains that the most telling characteristic of philanthropy when conjoined to wealth is its potential to actively create the public agenda by directly producing the institutions capable of achieving that public agenda. Through concerted philanthropic efforts, the wealthy, for good or for ill, for progressive or conservative ends, actually produce (rather than simply run or influence) the organisational world at the cutting edge of society (Schervish, Herman & Rhenisch 1986, pp. 10–11).

It has been long recognised that for certain groups of individuals and social institutions, socially necessary outcomes have not been provided by the untrammelled workings of the market economy. Philanthropy has, in some areas, replaced the market as a means to meet social and economic needs (Schervish, Herman & Rhenisch 1986, p. 6).

While some of the theorisation about the philanthropic behaviour of the wealthy is relatively recent, acknowledging the productive activities that arise from the coincidence of wealth and a specific agenda is not new. The Rockefeller Foundation in the United States is credited with the creation of the social sciences as a university-level field of study during the inter-war period (Patterson 2001, p. 73). For example, John D Rockefeller, having personally founded the University of Chicago in 1892, used his various foundations to spend more than US$50 million in the 1920s and 1930s directed at:

making the social sciences more scientific in order to promote social and economic stability, to eliminate subjective studies of social phenomena and to develop more effective methods of social control (Patterson 2001, p. 73).

The Rockefeller Foundation's influence reached all the way to Australia by funding the development of an anthropology program at the University of Sydney to be focused 'especially in colonial practices and the social management of natives' (Patterson 2001, p. 73). Given the prominence of racial considerations in Australian public policy in the inter-war period, it is easy to understand this particular endowment. We will return to the theme of race in the following chapters.

Hay and Muller (2013) have offered a more recent analysis of the giving behaviours of the group they call the 'super-rich' that results in 'super-philanthropy'. They believe that this new philanthropy links wealth with an attitude of responsibility that is also bound to public policy. Donors tend to support familiar people and organisations and their impact 'helps shape as well as contribute to causes' (Hay & Muller 2013, p. 6). These wealthy philanthropists tend to target problems rather than institutions by supporting specific solutions. They also want to have a part in shaping the social and economic institutions of a region that is 'manifested in community polity and civic commitment' (Hay & Muller 2013, p. 7). Sara Blakely, the founder of the company that makes and sells the wildly successful undergarments called 'Spanx', states that philanthropy is part of her company's culture. Having made 'the world a better place, one butt at a time', she now wishes to do the same 'one woman at a time' by supporting women allowing them to 'prosper, invent, be educated, start their own businesses and run for office' (Blakely 2013). In her 'giving pledge' that is inspired by the Bill & Melinda Gates Foundation and the actions of Warren Buffett, this highly successful business woman describes how she will use her wealth to promote American market capitalism and enhance the role played by female entrepreneurs (Blakely 2013). As a wealthy philanthropist, Blakely intends to solve problems of gender inequality through the provision of formal education and business support designed to increase the economic participation and success of women in advanced market democracies.

Before turning to the specific characteristics of Northern Territory ministers and their use of vocational education and training, there is a final consideration in the historical development of the wealthy philanthropist—linking their favoured projects to the actions of a democratically elected government. For this we return to the activities of the Rockefeller Foundation and one of its early sub-entities, the Laura Spelman Rockefeller Memorial. This memorial fund was established by John D Rockefeller, Senior, in 1918 in memory of his wife and it eventually consolidated with the Rockefeller Foundation in 1929. This fund supported health initiatives around the world as well as providing the initial finance for the establishment of the various social sciences as respected academic disciplines (Fisher 1983). The major goal was the creation of 'the objective knowledge that could result from scientific research [that] could in turn lead to greater *social control*' (Fisher 1983, p. 210, emphasis in original).

Throughout the 1920s and 1930s the efforts of these foundations were directed at supporting individuals and organisations that would produce social science research deemed to be useful in ordinary practical affairs and 'that could be directly utilised to increase social control' as an alternative to the rise of both communism and fascism in Europe

(Fisher 1983, p. 213). In response to the policy elite's widespread concern over the possible demise of liberal democratic capitalism due to the prolonged economic depression, the Rockefeller Foundation sponsored scientific research that would improve living standards in order to maintain social order. It was envisaged that these outcomes would be achieved through the operation of an 'efficient democracy' whose actions were guided by centralised control and coordinated planning (Fisher 1983, p. 223). As we have seen, these are similar to the intended benefits attributable to new public management.

Up to this point, it has been demonstrated that wealthy philanthropists are active in the production of programs and institutions that promote their own views about how to improve the social and economic characteristics of society and even the world. There is little evidence that the super-rich 'pursue a crudely self-interested public agenda or single-handedly accomplish it' (Schervish, Herman & Rhenisch 1986, p. 10). In fact, wealthy philanthropists frequently intervene to either complement market mechanisms or even to replace the market as a means to fulfil social and economic needs (Schervish, Herman & Rhenisch 1986, p. 6). It has also been contended that when acting in their Cabinet capacity, Northern Territory Government ministers display behaviours that are similar to the wealthy. This conduct is sanctioned by the voting public in part due to the Australian culture of egalitarianism that does not celebrate wealth or individual financial achievement (McDonald & Scaife 2011, p. 314). Helping behaviour is viewed as an Antipodean group norm that 'will emphasise collective responsibility, specifically, government responsibility' for the alleviation of social problems (McDonald & Scaife 2011, p. 315). Northern Territory Government ministers are guided by both a mandate and an expectation to take charge of the collective wealth, that is the public purse, and do good things with it. The use of new public management principles further supports the philanthropic nature of ministerial behaviour in vocational education and training by distancing the politicians from direct personal responsibility for the problems of daily operational matters, while still allowing them to claim success when the expected outputs are achieved. Through the use of extensive planning, budgeting and reporting mechanisms, ministers can direct support to individuals, businesses and institutions they believe are best placed to contribute to the social and economic development of Australia's most sparsely settled political jurisdiction.

Following the lead of Gordon (1991, p. 3), the remainder of this chapter is based upon a specific way of thinking about the practice of government—one that pays more attention to the routines and performance of government and less attention to its institutions. Such a rationality, focused upon the 'how' of government, relies upon two inter-related propositions. The first is that the aim of modern government is to guide the development of individuals in such a way as to also foster a general improvement of the state (Gordon 1991, p. 10). The other allows for the governance of the population through the use of expert systems and knowledge that can identify problematic individuals and groups in society who display a combination of characteristics that can be deemed to present a significant, albeit involuntary, risk to themselves or the community (Gordon 1991, p. 45). For example, in a 2004 study into the use of vocational education and training as a pathway to employment in the Northern Territory, 'five employment disadvantaged groups—youth, people with disabilities, long term unemployed, mature aged people and people from a non-English speaking background' were singled out for special consideration as being at risk of adding to the unemployment figures (Falk et al. 2004, p. ix).

In the Northern Territory, these challenging groups frequently include Indigenous people and have also been further refined to include the unskilled, the geographically isolated, unemployed youth, women, young people who leave school before year 12, single mothers, those on welfare benefits, convicted criminals, the disabled and those with low levels of literacy and numeracy. These sets are frequently represented as having become problematic due to market failure that can be addressed by non-market interventions such as philanthropy. For example, the high level of unemployment benefits directed at residents who live in remote Indigenous communities is frequently attributed to the absence of market economies that can provide local employment opportunities and the unintended outcomes of public policy to do with award rates of pay, the financial year budget cycles used by governments, new technologies and unionism (for example see Shimpo 1985, p. 47).

The accumulated public wealth held by government and directed by the minister provides the means to produce the social agenda and the institutions capable of implementing the programs that support the intended improvements to society. Possibly the most prominent example of this behaviour in the Northern Territory was the creation and support of the various institutions that have become Charles Darwin University.

The Northern Territory Government prioritised the local provision of higher education in the face of implacable opposition of Commonwealth funding agencies, isolation, small population and reputational concerns on the basis that this institution was required to allow for the social, cultural and economic development of the jurisdiction (Harris 1987). Although not a single member of the Northern Territory Cabinet at that time held a university degree, their value system envisaged a crucial developmental role for an institution that could offer the entire range of recognised qualifications ranging from Certificate One to Doctor of Philosophy.

This vision was succinctly summarised by the Chief Minister, Paul Everingham, in his speech to open the 1978 Northern Territory Teachers Federation annual conference at Kormilda College in Darwin. In keeping with the new government's efforts to make a fresh start in all matters, Everingham described the Territory's envisaged education structure would be 'an integrated system of education and training, universally available and lifelong, helping the people of the Northern Territory to develop and mature as individuals and participate in the development of their society' (Northern Territory Archives Service 1977–1979, p. 2). And the classic Australian reliance upon colonial socialism for the provision of skills and capital only encouraged this fledgling government to make use of the ministerial role of wealthy philanthropist. The outcome positioned vocational education as an integral contributor to economic and social improvements in the Northern Territory.

The Rockefeller Foundation's (Fisher 1983, p. 208) contribution to the creation of a new brand of intellectual—the technical expert who brings objectivity and academic science to bear on socioeconomic problems—in the context of efficient democratic government, furnishes ministers with specialised professionals who can implement practical methods of social control. In a similar pattern to the creation of foundations that distanced objectified philanthropic activities from the individual capitalists and allowed for an appearance of the dispassionate search for knowledge and societal improvement, the development of government agencies, inhabited by these technical experts, fulfils the same role. When this institutionalised distance is combined with Australian egalitarianism's expectation of active government, ministerial action becomes de-personalised, that is, any minister can be the philanthropist. It also deploys supposedly technical-rational expert programs (guaranteeing accountability for the use of public funds) and is responsive to the 'real needs' of the community that have been calculated from extensive information gathering activities. In the face of repeated market failure in the Northern Territory and the many problematic groups of citizens, the minister's behaviour is aligned with that of wealthy philanthropists in yet another manner. The very rich philanthropists are driven by personal initiative and clear goals to improve the public good as a result of their voluntary contributions (Schuyt, Bekkers & Smit 2010, p. 4).

Figure 2. Paul AE Everingham, Member of the Legislative Assembly.
Source: Creator Unknown. PH0120/0035, N Gleeson Collection, Northern Territory Library.

This sentiment is clearly expressed in the reflections of several former chief ministers of the Northern Territory. The fourth government leader in the Territory, Marshall Perron describes, 'Before I left politics I wanted to actually do something significant for society, something that changed peoples' lives' (Martin & Dewar 2012, p. 85). His successor, Shane Stone, concurred because he was guided into government 'to serve the community' (Martin & Dewar 2012, p. 95). 'I wanted to make a difference' was the response of the sixth Chief Minister, Denis Burke, when asked why he wanted to occupy the top office (Martin & Dewar 2012, p. 122). He went on to also add a long-familiar note of caution to future aspirants, 'Don't lose touch with the concerns of the ordinary voter—they put you there and they can easily remove you' (Martin & Dewar 2012, p. 139). Former Commonwealth bureaucrat Don Russell's (2014, p. 20) long experience is that 'all political careers end badly and to answer the question what did it all mean, you have to have done things that left the nation a better place'. The act of standing for public office requires an extraordinary commitment of personal energy and concern for society, particularly in the deeply intimate political environment of the Northern Territory.

In his analysis of Australian 'third sector' organisations, Lyons (2001, p. 98) describes how citizens will form non-profit and cooperative organisations to either 'provide a service or advocate a cause for themselves and their family or for others'. He believes the introduction of new public management encouraged the governments to increase funding to non-profits 'to provide a further range of social services' (Lyons 2001, p. 103). This has allowed non-profit organisations to thrive/survive because for governments 'giving grants is always less expensive than providing services directly' (Lyons 2001, p. 108). Equally importantly, these third sector organisations have become the repository of much technical and professional expertise that is required to exercise social control as governments have distanced themselves from service provision in order to concentrate on policy and funding matters. Lyons (2001, pp. 141–183) concludes that public sector bureaucracies can be seen in a similar position to a philanthropic trust or foundation. They both have developed systems to manage giving behaviour such as submission writing, planned accountability measures, quasi-vouchers and competitive tenders in some areas. In a political sense, it is also much easier for ministers to support and subsidise formally constituted organisations that simultaneously serve the interests of multiple community members while providing a relatively efficient single point of contact for ministerial officers and government agencies. In addition, non-profit organisations provide a formal structure for receiving public funds that can be seen to protect the investment from personal greed or incompetent self-management skills on the part of individual recipients.

Having described the type of actions that are associated with the philanthropy of the wealthy, it is now time to turn to the motivations that guide the behaviour of this class of philanthropist. As proposed by Schervish (1998, pp. 600–601), a defining characteristic of philanthropy is the type of social signals to which it responds. Those who have access to an accumulation of resources that are well beyond their immediate needs and those of their children invariably wish to define a social agenda and shape the political, economic and cultural relations that are given form through the operations of the economy and the state (Schervish, Herman & Rhenisch 1986, p. 4). The giving behaviours of the wealthy philanthropists described earlier (the Rockefeller Foundation, the Bill & Melinda Gates Foundation, the Spanx philanthropy board and the Northern Territory Government) are directed by a desire to support a capitalistic free-market economy while reducing the impact of market failure. This economic system allowed the wealthy to gather the resources to redistribute in the first place and they are sensitive to signals of dysfunction that threaten the continued existence of this form of political economy. Measures that purport to demonstrate the alleviation of poverty, reduction of lawlessness and decreased social and, relevantly, educational inequality determine the course of action taken by the wealthy who give. This has resulted in 'greater emphasis being given by philanthropists on strategic beneficence intended to bring about specific change' (Hay & Muller 2013, p. 8). In Ostrower's (1995) intensive study of over 100 wealthy philanthropists, a strong preference to support educational and cultural endeavours to achieve social goals was demonstrated. The wealthy organise giving in order to control the timing and size of gifts and to vary who gets what over time because they wish to shape 'the conditions and institutional frameworks within which we live' (Hay & Muller 2013, p. 4).

This concern with the welfare of the entire population has its origins in the very first descriptions of the workings of the capitalist economy. The eighteenth-century father of capitalism, Adam Smith, described 'fellow feeling—a natural sense of identification with other human beings' (Herman 2003, p. 196). Fellow feeling, according to Smith, leads to moral judgements on the 'motivating passions' that guide peoples' behaviours towards others and the general functioning of economic society. As a result of this moral grounding, Smith believed that the rich would willingly redistribute their wealth to 'advance the interest of the society' (Herman 2003, p. 199). With social welfare and economic interests conjoined, the pursuits of the wealthy and the functioning of democratic states have developed into 'campaigns for citizenship [that] link demands for certain political and legal rights with projects to reform individuals at the level of their personal skills and competencies' (Barry, Osborne & Rose 1996, p. 1). In this context, vocational education and training becomes an attractive philanthropic practice of government because 'it matches the resources of the giver to the needs of the recipient through a social relation that is directly mobilised and governed by force of a morally armed entreaty' (Schervish 1998, p. 601). Citing Bratchell, Chard (1983, p. 19) describes the role given to further education (the same as vocational education and training in Australia) in the United Kingdom prior to World War Two: 'it was driven by a strong sense that it was a sort of a charity provided with a degree of social awareness and separate from educational considerations'.

The freedom of citizens in democratic states such as the Northern Territory is not anarchy and requires regulated responsible behaviour. 'The disadvantaged individual has come to be seen as potentially and ideally an active agent in the fabrication of their own existence' as a result of the choices they make in free market social and economic spheres (Rose 1996, p. 59). Partly because of the Rockefeller introduction of technical-rational strategies into the social sciences, those requiring assistance are rendered thinkable by authorities and experts in such a manner 'that their difficulties appear amenable to diagnoses, prescription and cure' (Rose 1996, p. 53). The use of such expertise allows government to move beyond arbitrariness and to gather intelligence on those citizens deemed in need of assistance to improve their place in 'a market governed by the rationalities of competition, accountability and consumer demand' (Rose 1996, p. 41). For Rose (1996, pp. 39–43), modern democratic governments have translated 'general political programs—efficiency, prosperity, productivity—into ways of exercising authority over places, people and activities' and the wealthy philanthropists join governments by deploying expert knowledge to contribute to the exercise of this 'form of moral and technical authority'.

Philanthropy and public policy become inextricably bound as they are both reactive to signals that are morally coloured and responsive to levels of socioeconomic dysfunction. Citizens with rights and responsibilities must be encouraged to make appropriate choices to remove the inequities they experience. And in order to address these threats and impediments to democratic capitalist state functionality, wealthy philanthropists frequently have represented the problem faced by the disadvantaged as one of a lack of access and opportunity. An unquestioning acceptance of arguments linking economic success to matters of equitable access can cause the organisations that deliver training on behalf of the Northern Territory Government to arrive at some unique perspectives on the expected behaviour of residents. In describing his work as a lecturer at Batchelor Institute of Indigenous Tertiary Education, Thorpe (2005) reports on the training provided to the many Indigenous prisoners serving time in Territory gaols. He proposes that a spell inside is a good thing as it promotes superior access to training and much-improved rates of attendance than is achievable on remote locations. Thorpe then reframes the conception of the prison as a 'community' in order to justify the application of vocational programs that were initially conceived to increase Indigenous self-management and community development and keep individuals out of the 'corrections centres'.

More specifically, the lack of access to health and education services is frequently singled out for attention because poor health, low levels of skills and illiteracy are statistically linked to reduced opportunity in employment and/or entrepreneurial success in the mainstream economy. Wealthy philanthropists have taken a particular interest in the improvement of these two areas. Possibly the highest global profile philanthropy of the super-rich is conducted through the Bill & Melinda Gates Foundation. This body is made up of four divisions with one dedicated to understanding how to best target the substantial resources of the foundation. The Global Health Division 'aims to harness advances in science and technology to save lives in developing countries' while the Global Development Division 'aims to identify and fund high impact solutions' to help 'people lift themselves out of poverty and build better lives' in situations where 'healthcare and education can be unaffordable luxuries' (Bill & Melinda Gates Foundation 2014). The final division describes its work as follows:

> In the United States, our primary focus is on ensuring that all students graduate from high school prepared for college and have an opportunity to earn a postsecondary degree with labour-market value (Bill & Melinda Gates Foundation 2014).

However, the Gates Foundation interest in providing solutions to health and education problems is hardly new. In his description of the work of the Rockefeller Foundation, Fosdick (1989, p. x) reports that health and education were singled out for special attention based upon the Rockefeller family's 'moral force of Christian vision' combined with the 'intellectual rigour of modern scholarship'. He goes on to describe how the task facing the foundation's interest in improved access to opportunities for the poor was:

> to reform society through the application of new techniques and forms such as scientific research, bureaucratic management and professional organisation to the issues of the day (Fosdick 1989, p. x).

The wealthy philanthropists align with the majority of educational theorists who position education as the 'great equaliser' and key to promoting social mobility (Bacchi 2009, p. 205). Education and training, rather than being perceived as tools of economic domination (Freire 1996), are consequently portrayed as the mechanisms that reduce social distinctions and give the poor a leg up on the economic ladder. The history of the Northern Territory's vocational education and training system, as will be repeatedly demonstrated throughout the rest of this story, has been totally dominated by the unquestionable belief that inadequate access to education and training has hindered social, cultural and economic development. Equality with the rest of the national population will be achieved by providing Territorians with access to similar education and training opportunities that are available 'down south'. As previously described, the establishment of a university based in the Northern Territory was justified on these grounds. The provision of access and opportunity also lend themselves to philanthropic action because the projects can be quantified and symbolised. Schervish (1998, p. 601) believes that the predominant means of communication in philanthropy is 'the symbolic medium of words and images'. This, of course, is also the business of politicians. As pointed out by Bacchi (2009, p. 32), 'giving meaning to concepts is what politics is all about. We invest a concept with a particular meaning in order to give shape to particular political visions'. In the case of the Northern Territory, this means the development of an advanced market democracy in which citizens behave as economically responsible choice makers who look to government for financial assistance to provide access to vocational education and training.

The need to record and report on the quantity of schools and training facilities, numbers of students and apprentices, the levels of qualifications issued, competencies demonstrated, teachers and instructors employed, locations where training takes place, dollars allocated to particular industry sectors and so forth is widely accepted. As a culmination and celebration of all of this activity, ministers proudly preside over a range of awards ceremonies that symbolise all that is good with achievement in vocational education and training and the government's contribution to social and economic improvement. The minister's actions in providing and applauding increased access and opportunity is yet another example of the modern manifestation of 'colonial socialism' expected from governments who play a 'vital role in encouraging business' by supplying skilled labour and capital through systems of universal, lifelong education and building its supporting infrastructure (Lyons 2001, p. 99). Even the seemingly minor reduction in public philanthropy and government support for access to education and training can flare into a full-blown political bunfight in the Northern Territory. In an effort to reign in expenditure in 1985, the Northern Territory Government decided to introduce a charge for students using school buses. In an editorial entitled *The right bus*, the major Darwin newspaper of the time opined:

> A political issue with the potential to do the Tuxworth Government enormous damage is school bus fares. It has struck a very raw nerve in a population long used to the benevolent arm of government in the Northern Territory (Editor 1985, p. 6).

The supposedly dire consequences of ministers choosing to reduce government public philanthropy described above takes this account of the behaviours and motivations of wealthy philanthropists full circle. It has been established that Northern Territory Government ministers with responsibility for vocational education and training are guided by the same social and economic determinants of behaviour as are wealthy philanthropists. The society they envisage is democratic, gives citizens regulated choices and is built upon free-market capitalism kept in check though non-market mechanisms to protect against market failure and maintain the idiosyncratic Australian form of colonial socialism. Education and training are seen to provide the skills and knowledge to both support the economic development of the jurisdiction and also provide individual pathways to a better life and social equality through employment. Place and context matter because of the developing frontier-inspired regional values 'manifested in community polity and civic commitment' (Hay & Muller 2013, p. 7).

The importance to the minister of building and maintaining relationships with his or her local electorate has also been described in terms of avoiding political extinction at the next election. A minister also has yet another set of factors that guides behaviour as public philanthropist. Empirical studies on giving behaviour have identified the characteristics that are most important in the initiation of giving behaviour of the wealthy. For those who wish to influence ministerial decisions about which individuals and organisations are to be subsidised with public largesse, a working knowledge of the full range of things that influence would-be philanthropists is crucial to success or failure. Schervish et al. (1998, pp. 1–2) have demonstrated that 'factors inducing identification of the self with the needs and aspirations of others' have the most impact upon philanthropic behaviour. Communities of participation, defined by the networks of formal and informal relationships of the giver, are 'by far the cluster with the strongest statistical relationship' to giving behaviour. Their multivariate analysis demonstrates that identification models outweigh one's ways of thinking, the existence of ample resources, youthful experience, socioeconomic urgency and direct requests for resources. Quite simply summarised, the 'identification model remains central; association breeds identification and identification breeds charitable giving' (Schervish, Coutsoukis & Havens 1998, p. 13). This statistical correlation supports the findings of a relatively large project that interviewed dozens of the super-rich to determine what motivated their giving behaviour. They 'typically thought in terms of personal considerations, social and familial networks and identifications and attachments to different organisations' based upon an 'underlying ideological framework that informs their understanding of philanthropy as a social institution' (Ostrower 1995, p. 113).

In describing the self-identity of the members of the Northern Territory's unique Country Liberal Party, who were repeatedly re-elected following self-government for nearly a quarter of a century, Heatley (1998, p. 34) notes that the party is an uncomfortable place for 'committed ideologues' because 'instrumental reasons—the opportunity to gain preferment for political office or to further business interests—are paramount'. Heatley labels the Country Liberal Party, now known simply as the Country

Liberals, as 'pragmatic and non-doctrinal' and that many associate the party with 'their own sense of Territory identity'. Weller and Sanders (1982, p. 40) quote one Northern Territory minister, 'there is no feeling of distance from the electorate among ministers', indeed as one put it, 'we are just ordinary Territory blokes, we just happen to be in this position'. 'But they know that to remain in their position they have to respond to the demands of those other ordinary Territorians' (Weller & Sanders 1982, p. 41). The most important determinant of giving behaviour, self-identification as a true Territorian, can be viewed as a major factor influencing a minister's longevity in office in the Northern Territory.

As part of a large international study into the drivers of giving behaviour, the Australian focus group results demonstrated that in addition to perceptions of the trustworthiness of the recipient 'people generally donate to charities that fit with their self-image' (Polonsky, Shelley & Voola 2002, p. 74). The former Northern Territory Chief Minister and Minister for Education and Training, Paul Henderson (universally known as 'Hendo'), became somewhat legendary in vocational education and training circles due to the repetitious telling of his training as an apprentice ship-fitter (for example, Martin & Dewar 2012, p. 176). This was his way of building rapport and identifying with both those in training and their employers. Other findings from this study found that for the recipients of philanthropic donations 'building stronger relationships with existing donors is an important part of raising funds' because 'the donors need to feel a sense of ownership with the charity's objectives and aims' (Polonsky, Shelley & Voola 2002, p. 77):

> The most emphasised perceptual reaction was the fit of the charity with the donor's self-image. This is important because it means that charities have to develop messages that are congruent with the donor's self-image (Polonsky, Shelley & Voola 2002, p. 78).

However, there is also value in de-personalising the philanthropic relationship. The establishment of the Rockefeller Foundation, for example, was partially done to distance the individual family members from allegations of self-interested socioeconomic hegemony (Fosdick 1989). While a Northern Territory minister certainly needs to 'know' the recipient, the association between the two 'is directly mobilised and governed by force of a morally-armed entreaty' operating within an economic and political environment (Schervish 1998, p. 601). The Northern Territory Government agencies and their bureaucratic processes serve the same role as private philanthropic foundations by mediating the relationship between the minister and the recipient. This is a delicate balancing act and requires highly honed political awareness and very acute attention to detail on the part of the expert public servants who work in the government agencies. Philanthropy is a reciprocal social connection where the needs of recipients 'present a moral claim to which donors may choose to respond' and the need is not the object, rather 'the object is persons in their need' (Schervish 1998, p. 601). Even though ministers can identify with a group in the community and then decide to support them with the provision of publicly subsidised vocational education and training, this relationship has another distinctive characteristic: 'the recipient of charitable donations is usually absent from the context in which the donation is made' (Bekkers & Wiepking 2007, p. 3). In the Northern Territory, this phenomenon of giving is put into practice through the use of resource agreements. These are contracts used by the government department (principal) to 'purchase' a certain number of qualifications or training hours from the training provider (agent). The individual student learner, target of the public subsidy, is not part of the financial transaction. While it is not uncommon for the minister to eventually meet some of those in training at the ubiquitous awards evenings, workplace visits or during 'good news' photo opportunities staged in training facilities, the recipient is completely absent from the philanthropic decision-making process.

The philanthropy of the wealthy is not about interpersonal relationships and behaviour. Even though philanthropy takes place within the context of electoral relationships, the goals are not personal as the benefits are to go to 'generalised others' and the well-being of society (Schuyt, Bekkers & Smit 2010). While the Northern Territory minister will frequently know and identify with the target of government munificence, the motivation for using vocational education and training is to benefit society in general. Even the economically conservative former Commonwealth Minister for Employment, Education, Training and Youth Affairs Dr David Kemp (1998) acknowledges the need for government action in order to increase access and opportunity: 'Public funding of vocational education and training is directed at the public good, including general skill development and meeting skill needs of industry and business'. The personal and working lives of Northern Territory Government ministers are governed by a constant balancing act between the intimate nature of their electorate, the desire to improve society and the necessity to fairly and wisely use the public resources with which they have been entrusted. The role of wealthy philanthropist is both demanding and potentially rewarding for those who seek to manage society through the use of vocational education and training.

Each of the following chapters describes a particular time period and demonstrates how philanthropy through vocational education and training has been deployed in the Northern Territory as a result of European intervention into this remote and problematic part of the Australian continent. Tracing the ephemeral nature of the institutions used by the public authorities in the name of social and economic development will provide the context to exemplify how governments have gone about their business and produced ministers who act as wealthy philanthropists. Each chapter commences with a significant constitutional and political milestone that marks the Northern Territory's journey towards becoming a state-type entity on a nearly equal footing as the original states— created by the federation of six British colonies in 1901 to establish the Commonwealth of Australia as a constitutional monarchy.

3

Prior to 1911: European discovery and South Australian administration of the Northern Territory

The first of five time periods that will be used to structure this account of the development and deployment of vocational education and training in the Northern Territory covers the era when European explorers initially intruded upon the ancient Aboriginal tribal lands and culminates with the colony of South Australia gaining control of the jurisdiction.

Great Britain took possession of the northern Australian coastline in 1824 when Captain Bremer declared this section of the continent as part of New South Wales. While there were several abortive attempts to establish settlements along the tropical north coast, the climate and isolation provided insurmountable difficulties for the would-be residents. Similarly, the arid southern portion of this territory proved to be inhospitable and difficult to settle. As part of an ongoing project of establishing the borders of the Australian colonies, the Northern Territory became physically separated from New South Wales when the Colonial Office of Great Britain gave control of the jurisdiction to the Government of the Colony of South Australia in 1863 (The Parliament of the Commonwealth of Australia 1974, p. 83) following the first non-Indigenous south to north crossing of the continent by the South Australian-based explorer John McDouall Stuart in the previous year.

On the political front, in 1888 South Australia designated the Northern Territory as a single electoral district returning two members to its Legislative Assembly and gave representation in the Upper House in Adelaide. Full adult suffrage was extended by South Australia to all Northern Territory white residents in 1890 that demonstrated an explicit and purposeful disenfranchisement of the much more numerous Asian and Aboriginal populations. With Federation in 1901, Northern Territory citizens with voting rights had representation in both houses of Federal Parliament, but this situation would change in 1911 when South Australia relinquished responsibility for the Northern Territory to the Commonwealth due to the heavy financial burden of managing this remote and challenging region.

During this period of British Colonial rule in the central north–south corridor of the Australian continent, much of the contemporary understanding about how a civilised society should operate was being conceptualised in terms of race and Victorian middle-class philanthropy. Price (1949, p. 122) reports that the domestic philanthropic movements in 1830s England were able to engineer policy and programs of government that were intended to apply 'justice, humanity, civil rights and religion to colonial natives'. This development came about in response to the high levels of physical coercion and extreme levels of violence that characterised the tactics used by British colonists and their interactions with the original populations of various parts of the burgeoning empire. The establishment of colonial South Australia by so-called 'free settlers' during this same time period imported these philanthropic notions into Australia:

> Missions, and plans for political and social improvement were to be encouraged, and the Australian Aboriginals were to be provided with hunting reservations until such time as they became interested in agriculture. Missionary enterprise was to be the basis of this new endeavour (Price 1949, pp. 123–124).

This style of philanthropy contributed to a South Australian policy of integration of Aboriginal inhabitants of the colony allowing for the preservation of language and cultural values in the face of the imported social and economic system. In his master's degree thesis, 'A history of the education of full-blood Aborigines in South Australia: With references to the Northern Territory', Hart (1970, p. 29) reports that in the earliest days of European settlement in South Australia, the Lutheran missionaries had become aware of 'the need for a vocational training in skills that would gain Aborigines a livelihood in the new society'. He goes on to note that specific training experiments were commenced on the missions in 1850. From these imported and humble philanthropically inspired beginnings, a lasting legacy of using vocational education and training in pursuit of social and economic goals was introduced into the Northern Territory. In the pursuit of integration of Aboriginal people into mainstream society 'the principles of providing both a general education for children and an on-the-job vocational training for youths, with satisfying employment for all adults, could well be copied on some reserves even today' (Hart 1970, p. 41). This prophetic description of the intended role for vocational education and training still reflects a widely held view in policy circles.

In terms of European settlement, the first permanent township of Palmerston, later renamed Darwin, was established on the north coast in 1869. In the southern parts of the Northern Territory, South Australia began selling pastoral rights to intending settlers shortly after acquiring control in 1863. European incursions into the Northern Territory were further enabled with the establishment of the Overland Telegraph Line, which was completed in 1872. Connecting Adelaide with Darwin, this line provided Australia's first fast communications link with the rest of the world via an undersea cable to the Indonesian archipelago. The various repeater stations that were established through the centre of the Northern Territory facilitated non-Indigenous settlement in this remote part of the continent.

Figure 3. Charlotte Waters Telegraph Station, near the South Australian border, included a store and post office.
Source: Creator Unknown. PH0057/0002. John Blakeman Collection, Northern Territory Library.

Following the extension of pastoral interests, the Lutheran missionaries moved into the Northern Territory in 1877 with the establishment of the Finke River Mission at Hermannsburg, some 130 kilometres to the west of the present town of Alice Springs. This was done to cater for the perceived needs of the local Aboriginal tribes and as a broadening of privately funded Lutheran missionary operations in the far north of South Australia. In an 1880 report on the activities that were conducted at Hermannsburg, it is described that:

> The missionaries seized the opportunity to begin education when the people congregated for rations. Gradually the Aranda people gained confidence and came to settle near the mission. Men were employed in the garden or as the shepherds or in mustering cattle and the women and girls in house work, sewing, knitting and weaving wool from the sheep into blankets (Hart 1970, p. 73).

In summarising the impact of the Lutheran missionaries from the 1860s until World War One, Hart (1970, pp. 69–70) demonstrates the uneasy policy transition from outright coercive violence to philanthropic intention that used education and training, leading to employment, as one of its primary tools to improve the socioeconomic welfare of others:

> During the fifty years of its existence when Aborigines in the northern part of the state and in the Northern Territory were being shot down like crows and dispossessed of their lands without recompense, the work of the Lutheran mission shows a genuine concern for the Dieri people. The remnants of the tribe now living around Maree speak with real affection and gratitude for the missionaries. However limited the education and training, those who received it were able to fit successfully into work on other stations or into the mission at Finnis Springs started later by the U. A. M. [United Aborigine's Mission].

In the final decade of South Australia's political and economic responsibility for the Northern Territory, the provision of education and training was seldom treated as a high priority due to the long distances from Adelaide and the small European population. The first primary school was opened in Palmerston (now Darwin) in 1877, but closed shortly thereafter as the teacher was declared to be insane, and by 1911 there were schools on the gold-mining fields at Pine Creek and Brock's Creek in addition to the reopened school at Palmerston (Department of Education and Science 1969). South Australia had not made any provision for formal post–primary school, adult or technical education for the white population during its time in control of the Northern Territory. Vocational education and training was solely a philanthropic tool used by the missionaries motivated by concerns for the welfare of Aborigines during colonial rule and the early years of Federation.

Figure 4. Finke River Mission, September 1905.
Source: Creator Unknown, PH0763/0003, Smith Collection, Northern Territory Library.

Towards the end of South Australian control, a number of other religious groups became active in their philanthropically inspired desire to both spread their systems of faith-based belief and to improve the living circumstances of the Aboriginal residents of the Northern Territory. For example, the apostolic administrator of the Catholic Church in Darwin, Francis Gsell, persuaded the South Australian Government to grant him 10,000 acres for an Aboriginal Mission on Bathurst Island in 1910 (Donovan 1983). In 1908, the Anglican Church had also negotiated the establishment of a mission on the Roper River in the southwestern Gulf of Carpentaria region of the Territory.

Figure 5. Tiwi people on Bathurst Island, January 1941, with Bishop Gsell.
Source: Creator B. Clarke, PH0094/0002, Duncan Jenkins Collection,
Northern Territory Library.

As with Central Australia, the issues facing the Anglican missionary endeavour in the tropical north also reflected the political tensions between violent conquest and the application of British middle-class philanthropy's reliance upon education and training. In addition, eugenic views of race featured prominently in decisions about how to improve the lot of Aboriginal Territorians and moderate the impact of their dealings with the European settlers' voracious appetites for their traditional country and consequent destruction of centuries' old lifestyles. The following account of the first 10 years of the operations of the Roper River Mission describes how vocational education and training was being used as a form of social control over a problematic group of people. It also portrays the environment and use of vocational education and training when South Australia shed its northern responsibilities and the Commonwealth took control of the Northern Territory. Vocational education and training was not for the relative handful of white citizens who had the vote, but was reserved as a significant mechanism of social control and economic improvement on the frontier.

The Reverend RD Joynt (1918) furnished the following descriptions and opinions in *Ten years' work at the Roper River mission station, Northern Territory, Australia, August 1908 to August 1918: A short history of the Roper River Mission written by the Rev. R. D. Joynt, pioneer missionary to the Roper Aborigines*:

> They are the original owners of this fair land of Australia, and in the north, and where the white man has not overrun the country, they are able to live the lives their forefathers did (p. 2).

> The conditions under which the Aborigine used to live are now changing, and will soon be eliminated altogether. Civilisation is creeping up northwards, and the white man is penetrating the hunting grounds of the black. It is sad to think that, wherever the white man goes, the black man loses his privileges, and works for the white man, thus losing his cunning, which means he is not so at home in the bush as heretofore (p. 4).

> The Australian Aborigine is in many ways an asset to the country. There is much more in the black than we whites credit him with. All he needs is the opportunity to develop and a patient teacher to instruct him. The girls can learn to cook, sew, wash and iron splendidly. With training, the boys have done almost every kind of manual labour. They are, on the whole, if treated kindly, faithful friends and valuable workers (pp. 4–5).

> Everything is against the Aboriginal population increasing. Customs, change of food, communistic life in place of the nomadic life, clothing in exchange for nakedness. Their days are numbered. They are a strong race, fine and active, and when working, develop wonderfully. They are a lovable race. Many have sweet natures, make good and faithful servants, but by many they are treated worse than animals, and sometimes even referred to as 'black animals,' and terms even worse (pp. 5–6).

> There are many deeds of shame and cruelty that could be recorded against the white man. In years gone by the natives have been shot down like game, and hundreds killed in a spirit of revenge. I have met men that boast of shooting the poor, unprotected black, 'just for fun.' These deeds of shame happened in the early days, but even during the last ten years some deeds have been perpetrated that make a man that has any feeling utterly disgusted (p. 6).

> The Roper River Mission stands for the protecting and uplifting of the black race in Northern Australia, and the methods used to bring about that result are twofold — (1) The Gospel of Work. (2) The Gospel of Love. Our work is of an industrial nature. Gardening, building, stock work, school, sewing, laundry, and raffia, cooking, house work, cleanliness, all taught under the influence of Christianity: the ideal, of course, being Christ-likeness (p. 7).

Reverend Joynt closes the report on his decade of missionary work with an appeal to both church members and the general public for assistance to continue and further the work of the Roper River Mission. In describing the ultimate goal of converting Aboriginal people to Christianity, he also adds the consideration of race:

> A White Australia. Yes, Most Decidiedly [sic].
> 'Though your sins be as scarlet, they shall be as white as snow'.
> The best kind of a 'WHITE AUSTRALIA'.
> Who will help us to make it white?

For reasons unspecified by the British Colonial Office, the transfer of control over the Northern Territory of Australia was not made a permanent arrangement in spite of strenuous representations for its incorporation into the colony of South Australia in the 1860s. When the cost of administering this troublesome and non-productive region began to outgrow the state's financial capacity, the South Australian Premier argued that 'the only way to ensure successful development was either by a chartered company with the free use of coloured labour or by the Commonwealth' (Heatley 1979, p. 25). Given the country's overriding concern with racial matters and maintaining the White Australia policy, the immigration of large numbers of 'coloured' labourers ceased to be a practicable policy option for the colonisation of the Northern Territory. The newly formed Commonwealth Government provided the only socially and politically viable solution to the problems of the North.

In addition to the problems caused by South Australia's settlement strategy that allowed land speculators to hold onto the very best parcels of land while neither paying rates nor developing the plots, a new force emerged. According to Cross (2011, p. 337) encroaching pastoralists represented a 'new breed of colonist':

> They were courageous, rough and enterprising, and not always straight in their dealings. Their story is worth telling because it is symbolic of wholly different, rough form of colonisation, marked by strenuous individual toil and loss of government control.

The South Australian dream of establishing instruments of civilisation, like the school, the chapel and the rule of law at the very edges of colonisation, was brought to an end in the late nineteenth century by the actions of these pastoralists and their cattle (Cross 2011). The unruly nature of the Territory, and the consequent need to establish government control, is a recurring theme in the history of this jurisdiction. Even though the South Australian attempt to replicate the dense settlement patterns that had been used to establish that colony had failed, the dream of improving and making the Northern Territory into a viable economic entity was not diminished and remains central to the events described in the remainder of this story.

The negotiations associated with Federation provided South Australia the opportunity to remove the financial millstone that had replaced the envisaged financial bonanza that was touted in 1863. After five years of negotiations, South Australia passed the *Northern Territory Surrender Act* in 1907 and after further negotiations concluded in 1910, the Australian Parliament enacted both the *Northern Territory Acceptance Act* and the *Northern Territory (Administration) Act* providing for the government of the Territory by an Administrator appointed by the Governor-General (The Parliament of the Commonwealth of Australia 1974, p. 83).

During this first period of the European history of the Northern Territory, vocational education and training was not a mainstream socioeconomic concern at the cultural boundaries where isolation, survival, matters of race and control of land dominated daily life. However, training Aboriginal people for what is perceived to be useful work was firmly in the toolkit of the missionaries and their philanthropic task of social improvement. The political change in the constitutional status of the Northern Territory, from being part of a state with its constitutional protections to an administered colonial jurisdiction, introduces the next era.

4

Early Commonwealth control, 1911–46

The transfer of responsibility for the Northern Territory from the South Australian Government was made possible when the Commonwealth agreed to allocate £6,170,548 to retire accumulated debt and to purchase various infrastructure assets (Heatley 1979, p. 27). In addition, the Commonwealth agreed to construct a north–south railway through the Territory to link Adelaide and Darwin, but refused to set a time frame for the completion of this transport link. This particular issue had contributed to the lengthy negotiations surrounding the handover and would not be resolved until nearly a century later with the Federal Government only partially meeting this undertaking.

When the Commonwealth Government assumed responsibility on 1 January 1911, the Territory's non-Aboriginal population was 3,271 (2,673 males and 598 females) and the Indigenous population was estimated at 50,000 (National Archives of Australia 2014a). As it turns out, the number of Europeans remained at about this level until World War Two. The handover also resulted in these Europeans losing their ability to vote in South Australian elections as well as for the House of Representatives and the Senate. By 1922, this lack of representation was partially addressed with the passage of the *Northern Territory Representation Act* that provided for a single member from the Territory in the House of Representatives without voting powers (The Parliament of the Commonwealth of Australia 1974, p. 83). Full voting rights would not be granted to the member from the Northern Territory until 1968 and the jurisdiction was given two Senators in 1974 as a result of the *Senate (Representation of Territories) Act* (The Parliament of the Commonwealth of Australia 1974, pp. 84–85).

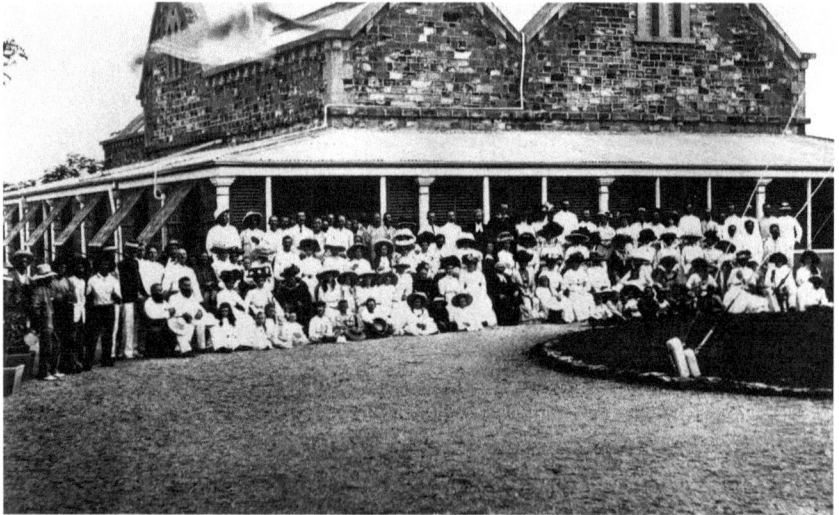

Figure 6. Transfer Ceremony, 2 January 1911.
Source: Creator Paul Foelsche, PH0747/0060, Foelsche Collection, Northern Territory Library.

In keeping with Australia's propensity for state-led social experimentation, the Northern Territory provided the Commonwealth with a place to make and implement public policy that did not require complex negotiations with the states nor did the programs have electoral consequences given that Territorians could not vote. In *The history and problems of the Northern Territory Australia* (Price 1930), a bleak future is predicted for the region due to banning of 'coloured labour' as a result of the White Australia policy.

> The story of the Northern Territory presents both national and world problems, because it deals with a part of *the greatest biological experiment in history*, the attempt to keep a whole continent white. It also represents the first effort of the Europeans in a southern continent to develop by white labour their own tropical zone (Price 1930, p. 56, emphasis in original).

This early period of Commonwealth direction did not see a significant change in the role assigned to vocational education and training. The European population was deemed to be too small and widespread to merit the provision of post–primary school education or formal adult training. For example, the first high school was established in Darwin in 1921 but closed in 1925 due to a lack of students—secondary education would not be reintroduced until 1948 (National Archives of Australia 2014a), which was the same year that apprenticeships were regulated in the Northern Territory. Heatley's (1979, pp. 136–137) account of the governance of the Territory reports that the Commonwealth maintained the essential features of the South Australian *The Northern Territory Aborigines Act 1910*, which allowed for the setting up and control of hunting and living reservations and the regulation of Aboriginal labour. Between the two world wars, extensive Aboriginal reserves were established in the Northern Territory:

> into which missionary groups moved to set up centres for religious, charitable and training purposes – the basic view that part-Aboriginals should be separated from Aboriginals and trained to be useful citizens remained unchanged (Heatley 1979, p. 137).

The policy settings regarding the application of vocational education and training were still firmly guided by its mid-nineteenth century philanthropic motivations when the Commonwealth assumed responsibility for governing the Northern Territory in the second decade of the twentieth century. In describing the general results of the interaction between English-speaking people and Aborigines in Australia, Price (1949, p. 124) reports that 'the British philanthropic revolution did create some improvements'. These included the appointment of Protectors of Aborigines, improved justice, establishment of reservations and modest levels of expenditure on health, religion and education. 'Missionary enterprise was to be the basis of this new endeavour' (Price 1949, p. 124). The main usage of vocational training was as a mechanism to prepare Aboriginal people for their transition into the dominant culture by acquiring the skills that would be necessary to lead to productive employment in the face of the predicted demise of their own culture (Joynt 1918).

Two events in this initial phase of Commonwealth governance demonstrate the transition from physical violence to more philanthropically inspired methods of social control in the Northern Territory. The last recorded official punitive expedition against Aborigines accused of murdering a European occurred in Central Australia in 1928 (National Archives of Australia 2014a). The death of a dingo trapper resulted in what became known as the Coniston Massacre.

Over a period of several months, the shooting deaths of dozens of Aboriginal men, women and children took place at a variety of locations to the northwest of Alice Springs. In a sign of changing social values, only four years later in 1932—following the killing of five Japanese fishermen at Caledon Bay, two European settlers on a nearby island and the spearing death of the policeman who had been sent to investigate—the response was quite different (National Archives of Australia 2014a). Although there were demands from the white residents of Darwin for a punitive expedition to be sent into Arnhem Land, a party from the Church Missionary Society went to the area and negotiated the surrender of those Aborigines believed to be responsible for the deaths. All were tried and sentenced to prison terms with one condemned to death for his part in the crime. However, this result was appealed and overturned by the High Court of Australia leading to his release from jail in 1934. The Caledon Bay episode illustrates a change in the tactics that would be used by future governments in the management of society in the Northern Territory. Brutal summary justice, aimed at punishing and terrorising segments of the population, had been replaced by the trappings of the British legal system with its notions of democratic citizenship, civil rights, humanity, fairness and an expectation of obtaining a job. Of course, these are also the same characteristics that describe the middle-class philanthropy that accompanied the settlers when they came to South Australia 100 years earlier.

While this transition in methods of directing the conduct of the population was occurring, the activities of the religious missionaries steadily expanded with the explicit approval and minimal support (usually through the provision of land) from the Australian Government. The *Northern Territory Aborigines Act 1910* allowed for the setting up and control of reserves and the regulation of Aboriginal labour and, between the world wars, extensive portions of the Northern Territory were designated as Aboriginal reserves. The Catholic Church established a mission to the southwest of Darwin at Port Keats (now Wadeye) in 1935. After becoming the Bishop of Darwin, Father Francis Gsell established another Catholic mission at Arltunga to the northeast of Alice Springs in 1942 (later moved to Santa Teresa further south) and had also set up a settlement for part-Aboriginals at Garden Point on the Tiwi Islands in 1940 (Donovan 1983).

Figure 7. Catholic Mission School at Arltunga, January 1947.
Source: Creator Richard Duckworth. PH0542/0033, Richard Duckworth Collection, Northern Territory Library.

In addition to the Roper River Mission Station mentioned previously, the Anglican Church Missionary Society opened another outpost on Groote Eylandt off the east coast of the Territory in 1921. Elsewhere in the northeast of the Northern Territory, 'the Methodist Church established missions along the coast of Arnhem Land on Goulbourn Island in 1916, on Milingimbi in 1923, at Yirrkala in 1935 and Elcho Island in 1942' (Baker 2012, p. 2). In a demonstration of the importance of employment to the missionaries' goals, it is reported that 'Indigenous workers on Methodist missions in Arnhem Land were not only vital to mission development and survival, over time, they became an increasingly skilled, competent and reliable workforce' (Baker 2012, p. 1). These newly established missions continued to use the now traditional approaches that positioned vocational education and training as an important element of the efforts to 'improve' the living standards of Aboriginal people and prepare them for a productive working life in the mainstream economy that was bearing down upon the traditional tribal lifestyles. 'Indigenous participation in the economy of these missions led to an increased skills base amongst the majority of workers' (Baker 2012, p. 1).

For a variety of reasons including the absence of voting rights, two world wars and the Great Depression, the day-to-day governance of the Northern Territory by nine Commonwealth-appointed Administrators in this time period did not provide residents with the same social and economic arrangements as experienced by other Australians.

> In particular, Territorians were unable to exert sufficient political pressure on appropriate Governments and their instrumentalities to ensure the completion of educational infrastructure comparable with the Australian Capital Territory and the other States (Urvett 1982, p. 1).

In his 1930 analysis of the problems presented by the experiences of developing the Northern Territory as a successful contemporary economy, Price (1930, p. 58) argues against public, non-market investment in the jurisdiction as a partial result of the prohibition on the importation of foreign 'coloured labour'. Up to that date he reports that only the private sector efforts in the cattle, mining and pearl-shell industries have turned a profit.

> Australia should learn from the Territory the greater safety of private as opposed to public enterprise, and the costly failures which State Socialism and Paternalism if misdirected, may bring in their train (Price 1930, p. 58, emphasis in original).

The Commonwealth's reluctance to invest in the Northern Territory during this early era of control was reflecting the national political and economic realities of the times. According to Butlin et al. (1982, pp. 29–37), the states were still the main spenders and funders of capital development and the Federal Government was forced to limit rather than expand expenditure. 'Public policy was now accommodated to the interests of three distinct groups: farm, manufacturing and labour (largely urban labour) interests' (Butlin, Barnard & Pincus 1982, p. 29). The various states' attempts to increase the farm populations and open up rural areas to development through assisted immigration ended up in the situation where 'many of these public efforts were disastrous failures' (1982, p. 30). As prescribed by Price above, the Commonwealth had little appetite to risk adding to the mounting number of failed development ventures funded out of the public purse. In fact, in 1933 a proposal for the Territory to be administered by a chartered company re-emerged after having been rejected in the initial handover discussions between South Australia and the Commonwealth (National Archives of Australia 2014a). Similarly, this revised proposal did not proceed even though the

Federal Government showed little interest in the social and economic development of the Northern Territory in the face of economic recessions following World War One and the Great Depression of the 1930s.

Public business undertakings aimed at improving capital infrastructure ensured that 'the interests of urban and especially metropolitan activities were the primary beneficiaries' most clearly demonstrated by the shift in resources to the building of highways and away from railways (Butlin, Barnard & Pincus 1982, p. 33). Although South Australia had extracted an undertaking from the Commonwealth to build a transcontinental railway in order to further develop the Northern Territory, this was only partially attended to by the end of this early period of Commonwealth control. In 1929, the southern railway from Oodnadatta to Alice Springs was completed providing a link to the emerging national railway system and a northern portion was completed from Darwin to Birdum about 500 kilometres away from the capital (National Archives of Australia 2014a) leaving a gap of some 1,000 kilometres. This marked the end of Commonwealth investment in the promised railway until the line was finally completed in 2004 having been funded by the South Australian, Northern Territory and Australian governments' joint contributions.

Figure 8. Train (Commonwealth line) with new engines, Northern South Australia, January 1920.
Source: Creator Unknown, PH0386/0050, Bill Littlejohn Collection, Northern Territory Library.

Nevertheless, the Commonwealth was still willing to experiment with different forms of governance in its 'social laboratory' and electorally insignificant Northern Territory. In 1922, Commonwealth legislation (*The Northern Territory Representation Act*) provided for the election of a single member from the Territory to sit in the House of Representatives, but this member did not have any voting rights (The Parliament of the Commonwealth of Australia 1974, p. 83). From 1927–31, the Northern Territory was divided into separate administrative areas each controlled by a Government Resident assisted by an Advisory Council. Central Australia was administered from Alice Springs while Northern Australia's governance structure resided in Darwin. Due to the high costs of this arrangement, the Northern Territory was reconstituted as a single jurisdiction in 1931 when the Commonwealth repealed the original legislation (The Parliament of the Commonwealth of Australia 1974, p. 84). In 1936, the second step towards the reinstatement of political representation was taken when the member for the Northern Territory in the House of Representatives was given 'the right to vote on matters relating to Ordinances of the Territory' (The Parliament of the Commonwealth of Australia 1974, p. 84).

The governance of the Northern Territory during this era was characterised by Heatley (1979, p. 82) as a situation where 'both policy-making and administration have been largely in the hands of [federal] ministers and the senior public servants' who were located initially in Melbourne and then Canberra. The mundane daily implementation of policy was left to the Administrator (with several exceptions to do with structural changes to the bureaucracy and military rule during World War Two). The behaviour of the ministers and administrators unwittingly provided a model of ministerial decision-making and direction that would be continued following self-government. While there is no record of government-funded vocational training for non-Indigenous Territorians from this period, the Administrator was willing to make detailed interventions into education resourcing. In a memo dated 25 March 1941, from the Administrator to the Director of Native Affairs, concerns about the proposed distribution of tools and machines to Aboriginal settlements are expressed:

> I am not in favour of this. Under all the circumstances, I consider that when the half-caste school at Alice Springs is closed, the woodwork equipment should be forwarded intact to the Alice Springs school, where it would be utilised (National Archives of Australia 1961a).

The Director wrote back to the Administrator the following day agreeing to implement the decision and citing a similar precedent had been set in Darwin when the Bagot Reserve Aboriginal School had been closed and the equipment was transferred to the Darwin school.

The relationship between the European residents of the Northern Territory and the Federal Government's representative, the Administrator, got off to a poor start and never really recovered. The first Administrator, John Gilruth, clashed strongly with elements of the Territory population, particularly the trade unions, which eventually resulted in Gilruth's retirement and the subsequent forcible removal of his successor (Heatley 1990, p. 7). The federal ministers and senior public servants became very wary of the 'wild men of Darwin' (Heatley 1990, p. 10) and felt they could not be trusted with significant decision-making power or control of financial resources. Heatley (1990, p. 7) summarises this pre–World War Two period of Commonwealth control thusly: 'the brave new world of political and economic advance had not eventuated and the soaring hopes of 1911 had been replaced by truculence, disenchantment and even despair'. This antipathy towards the Commonwealth was ruthlessly exploited for decades to create an identity of a 'true Territorian' who is a victim of distant, uncaring governance that would usher in the next era following the war.

While the Northern Territory did not have any formal system of vocational education and training in this first period of Commonwealth control, it does not mean that the government had no interest in adult education more generally. Tannock (1975) has described how the Commonwealth Government's first major moves into education and training policy came about in an exercise of the emergency powers it had acquired in the name of national security to prosecute World War Two when it set up the Walker Committee in 1943. This interdepartmental committee was established to review Commonwealth responsibilities in the field of education and 'to recommend administrative machinery which might be established to facilitate the future development of Commonwealth education policy' (Tannock 1975, p. 4). The chair of the committee believed that 'the political future and unity of the country depends very largely on the use we make of general education, especially for adults' (Tannock 1975, p. 11). In addition, in support of the war effort the Commonwealth had affected a virtual takeover of the state-based technical education systems through the Technical Training Scheme and the programs offered to armed forces personnel through the Army Education Service (Tannock 1976).

Towards the end of World War Two, the Federal Government became more active in the provision of social services generally and the use of vocational education and training more specifically. In order to avoid a repetition of the economic depression and high levels of unemployment that had followed the end of World War One, a Commonwealth Reconstruction Training Scheme was introduced in 1944 to provide educational and vocational training to the returned service personnel from World War Two. Substantial federal public funding was provided to the various state training systems and individuals to gain the skills that would allow these ex-service personnel to re-establish themselves in suitable civilian occupations. Training was available in one of three categories—professional, vocational or rural—and by the end of the scheme in mid-1951 over 300,000 people had been trained 'making it one of the most significant strategies for social change in Australia' (National Archives of Australia 2014b).

Because the actual delivery of this training was undertaken by the State Training Authorities, the Northern Territory's lack of training facilities and capability meant that this major scheme bypassed the jurisdiction. While some characterise the lack of vocational training in the Northern Territory as purposeful neglect on the part of the Federal Government, it more accurately can be portrayed as an inability and incapacity on the part of the Commonwealth. Quite simply, with the exception of the emergency conditions associated with World War Two, the Commonwealth did not have either the desire or the infrastructure to provide training to the Territory's civilian population. After considering the findings of a review it had commissioned, the Australian Prime Minister rejected the recommendations made in the 1944 Duncan Report into adult education that proposed a national system and the provision of Commonwealth funding. Whitelock (1973, p. v) reports, 'Chifley himself, Duncan tells me, remarked that he did not wish "to buy into a fight with the States" on the issue of Federal control of an educational system as recommended in the Report'.

Writing towards the end of this early period of Commonwealth control of the Northern Territory, Price (1949, p. 142) describes the terrible living conditions and exploitation of Aboriginal people and declares that up until the end of World War Two, the 'Federal record was darker and meaner than that of any state'. Aboriginal residents were not alone in this level of neglect. During the first 35 years of Commonwealth management there was no local provision for secondary education, apprenticeship training, adult education or university study for the small European population in the Northern Territory either:

> It is most noticeable that the Commonwealth Government did practically nothing for Aborigines until the 1940s and educational schemes did not start until the 1950s. The welfare of Aborigines up to that time had devolved upon the Christian missions (Hart 1970, p. 82).

In 1937, the report of the Northern Territory Investigations Committee that had been established by the Federal Government recommended a 25-year northern development plan to counteract '75 years of mismanagement and incompetence by both South Australia and the Commonwealth' and made particular reference to the blanket application of national planning that made little sense in this remote jurisdiction (Anon. 1937, p. 1).

Vocational education and training remained an apparatus to be used by the various missionaries to 'improve' the lot of Aboriginal Territorians. This commonsensical and philanthropically inspired use of training, and its associated funding, obscured what the future would hold for the incorporation of vocational education and training into public policy responses to problems associated with managing the entire population. The opportunity for the Commonwealth Government to take charge of training and use it as a device to monitor and direct the population was brought about as a consequence of the Japanese bombing Darwin and several other northern towns in 1942–43. This external threat to national security catalysed Australia's efforts to finally 'develop' the north following the end of World War Two, if only to protect from a possible future land invasion (Slim 1954).

5

The post–World War Two
period to 1978

As a result of the bombing of Australia's north by the Imperial Japanese Navy, a new political motivation to develop and populate the region replaced the three decades of neglect that had been the hallmark of the Commonwealth's early administration of the Northern Territory. With most of Darwin's pre-war population of 2,000 evacuated to the south, military government was introduced for the duration of the war. The civil administration of the portion of the Territory not under martial law was conducted from Alice Springs until the end of the war. In the final years of World War Two, the Commonwealth took renewed measures to build a sustainable economy and increase the European population of the north with the establishment of an Interdepartmental Committee on the Development of Darwin and the Northern Territory in 1944 and the creation of the North Australia Development Committee in 1945 (National Archives of Australia 2014a). The advancement of Northern Australia has re-emerged as a major public agenda item with the election of the Coalition Government in 2013. This serves to demonstrate the longevity of some ideas, particularly the desire to develop the north being rediscovered by a new generation of politicians.

With the return to civilian control and governance still provided by the Administrator—who was responsible for the implementation of ministerial decisions made in Canberra—the final three decades of Commonwealth management of Territory affairs demonstrate a glacially paced evolution of constitutional development leading to the local exercise of state-type functions as described in the Australian Constitution. The first section of this chapter describes the implementation of legal structures and processes, before turning to the use of vocational education and training in the social and economic improvement of this still problematic territory.

The Commonwealth continued with experiments in political structures and processes in response to demands from Territorians for a greater say in the governance of the jurisdiction; a deep distrust of the intentions of Territorians on the part of Commonwealth bureaucrats and politicians; and an Administrator's office that had grown comfortable with applying a British colonial style of management to the Northern Territory. A partial return to the rule of parliamentary democracy, eliminated with the handover from South Australian governance to the Commonwealth, was made possible by the creation of the Legislative Council in 1947.

This council consisted of six elected members representing vast geographical divisions of the Territory and seven official members who were mostly drawn from the senior public servants based in Darwin. The council was presided over by the Administrator—it had the power to make ordinances for 'the peace, order and good government' of the Territory subject to assent by the Administrator or the pleasure of the Governor-General, both being highly responsive to the policies and pragmatics of the Commonwealth Government of the day. This Legislative Council met for the first time in 1948. Heatley (1979) reports that the parliamentary processes of the Legislative Council were characterised by an absence of party politics, having been replaced by continual bickering between the elected members seeking greater influence, and official members that were reluctant to release their grip on public finances and staff:

> Once on the Council, the chances of re-election depended upon the success of its members in promoting or defending the interests of their electorates, in supporting the Territory's constitutional, social and economic progress and in attacking the bureaucracy's handling of Territory affairs (Heatley 1979, p. 55).

In 1958, the member for the Northern Territory in the House of Representatives was allowed to vote on any proposed law or matter relating solely to the Territory. In the following year, the official members of the Legislative Council lost their hold on the majority of positions when the composition was altered to eight elected members, six official members and three non-official members appointed by the Governor-General. In 1968, the Administrator was replaced as President of the Legislative Council by an elected member. The non-official seats were redesignated in

1968 making the composition of the Legislative Council 11 elected and six official members. At the national level, the member for the Northern Territory in the House of Representatives was granted full voting rights that same year.

Figure 9. The first Legislative Council, 16 February 1948.

Seated, left to right: JN Nelson (Stuart), JG McGlashan (Chief Medical Officer), WS Flynn (Acting Deputy Crown Solicitor) AR Driver (President), M Luke (Darwin) RW Coxon (Director of Mines), FC Hopkins (Darwin); standing, left to right: A Turner (Acting Clerk), RS Leydin (Government Secretary), LC Lucas (Director of Works), VH Webster (Tennant Creek), FH Moy (Director of Native Affairs), RC Ward (Alice Springs), HC Barclay (Director of Lands), W Fulton (Batchelor), DRM Thompson (Clerk).

Source: Creator Unknown. PH0120/0060, N Gleeson Collection, Northern Territory Library.

Finally, in 1974, a fully elected Legislative Assembly of 19 members was established. In addition, federal legislation was passed to give Territorians two Senators in the 1975 Australian Government elections. The overall result was a return to state-type parliamentary government and a voice in both the House of Representatives and the Senate that had been in place (albeit via South Australia) prior to the handover in 1911. The constitutional development of the Northern Territory during this latter period of Commonwealth control climaxed in the introduction of limited powers to a Northern Territory Executive (similar to a government ministry) from 1974–78. It was this Territory Executive that negotiated and planned the transition to self-government.

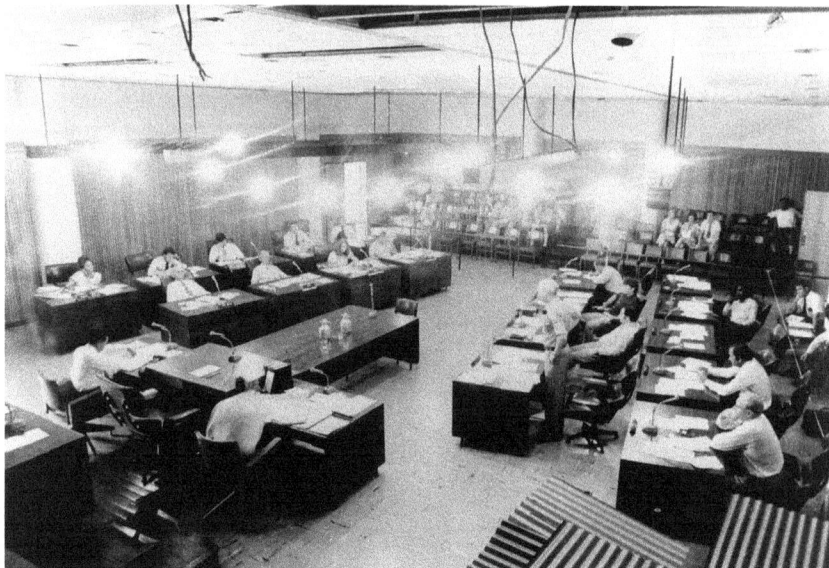

Figure 10. First Legislative Assembly sitting, 19 March 1975, in the cyclone-damaged chamber. Corrugated iron sheets in right foreground were used to channel rainwater away from members' desks.

Source: Creator Unknown. PH0120/0040, N Gleeson Collection, Northern Territory Library.

Post-war, the Commonwealth Government retained its newly found war-time enthusiasm for the use of formal training to support individual skills acquisition that would lead to employment, generating consumption of goods and an overall improvement to the national economy. The Commonwealth's position was clearly laid out in Prime Minister Curtin's 1945 *White Paper on Full Employment* (Coombs 1994). At the national level, public policy at the end of World War Two positioned vocational education and training as a vital component of Australia's social and economic well-being, a stance that has not substantially altered since, regardless of which political party has been in office. However, the Commonwealth's activity in social welfare areas that had been reserved to the states was challenged by constitutional experts even though both the state and federal governments were supportive. The bipartisan consent for Federal Government funding of social welfare benefits was reaffirmed and explicitly formalised in 1946 when the Australian Constitution was amended through the torturous national referendum process. In response to a ruling by the High Court calling into question the Australian Government's ability to fund certain programs, this amendment removed any doubt by allowing the Australian Parliament:

> to make laws for the provision of maternity allowances, widow's pensions, child endowment, unemployment, sickness and hospital benefits, medical and dental services, benefits to students and family allowances (Commonwealth of Australia 1946, p. 587).

Unlike the Reconstruction Training Scheme, this amendment to the constitution substantially increased the Commonwealth's reach into the socioeconomic lives of citizens and would have major impacts in the Northern Territory. During the parliamentary debates on this alteration to the Commonwealth's responsibilities, the 'benefits to students' phrase was singled out for attention. The Federal Manpower Minister Barnard spoke in favour of inclusion because Australia had subscribed to the 1944 International Labour Organization recommendations and 'the assurance of equality of educational and vocational opportunities' served as a major rationale for the amendment to the constitution (Commonwealth of Australia 1946, p. 992). In reflecting upon the history of Commonwealth support that allowed 'basic-wage-earning families' access to higher education in Western Australia, the Member for Fremantle Mr Beazley pointed out that 'benefits to students have been used as a means of social transformation and has democratised the universities' (Commonwealth of Australia 1946, p. 1025); to which the Member for the Northern Territory, Mr Blain, queried 'is the University of Western Australia as full of "commos" as those in Melbourne and Sydney'?

At the resumption of the debate four days later, Mr Blain (Commonwealth of Australia 1946, pp. 1170–1171) supported the provision of a free university education as long as matriculation was used to 'cull' entrants to ensure that education was not wasted upon those without 'the necessary talent to continue them to the end'—those without this talent should 'learn a trade at the age of 15 years and later have taken their places in the community'. Mr Blain was concerned that if education is given to too many people:

> we shall have a community of democratic idealists and misguided intellectuals who will be a menace to the country. The true unionist, the craftsman, is the salt of the earth while the democratic idealists poison the minds of people when they turn to pseudo-sciences such as economics (Commonwealth of Australia 1946, p. 1171).

Of the 44 proposed amendments to the Australian Constitution that have gone to referendum, the 1946 Social Services Amendment is one of only eight to have met the requirements for change, including support from both houses of the national parliament, an absolute majority of voters nationally as well as a majority of votes in the majority of states. The peculiar Australian attachment to colonial socialism has surfaced yet again, this time with support from across the political spectrum to promote government involvement in areas that had previously been the domain of philanthropic activity. Familiar arguments were used to justify this incursion—those to do with social and economic improvement, equality, humanity and the promotion of democracy and the related rights of citizens. The provision of 'benefits to students' who undertake education and training programs allowed the Commonwealth Government to behave like the British philanthropists of the previous century by devising schemes to promote access to these services in the name of equity.

The Commonwealth Government's interest in education and training did not take long to find its way into Northern Territory political calculations with the post-war return of civilian administration along with the resumption of popularly elected representation in a local legislative body. The inaugural piece of legislation passed in the first session of the newly formed Legislative Council was the *Apprentice Bill 1948*—partly because this ordinance was considered to be 'non-controversial' (Northern Territory of Australia 1948, p. 88). 'The purpose of the bill is to set up machinery whereby apprentices may be trained in a proper and regularised manner' (Northern Territory of Australia 1948, p. 92). This 'entirely new venture' for the Northern Territory would address the general scarcity of trained tradesmen and 'also help to keep lads within the Territory because they will not be forced to go to the Southern States to qualify for trades they wish to follow' (Northern Territory of Australia 1948, p. 90). The legislation provided for a four-person Apprentices Board to oversee the use of South Australian correspondence lessons augmented by visits from the supervisor of technical correspondence. Northern Territory Administration workshops and machinery were used for training due to the absence of dedicated vocational education and training facilities while the Board also employed staff to monitor employment conditions of the apprentices. The Director of Works and official member, Mr Lucas, enthused, 'I agree that this is one of the best things that can happen in the Territory' (Northern Territory of Australia 1948, p. 91). The fledgling Northern Territory politicians, with the wholehearted support of the Commonwealth bureaucrats and trade unions, believed that bringing vocational education and training under the control of a government body was a very high priority and important contributor to social and economic development. Although the local politicians wanted to have control over vocational training, they did not want to be responsible for the actual delivery. They followed a precedent that had been set by the missionaries' philanthropic use of training— they outsourced it. This contracting out of the delivery of training by the Northern Territory Government is still in force today.

A few years later, the 'common sense' logic of training for employment would also take over the space that had been occupied by the missionaries undertaking their philanthropic activities in the Aboriginal communities. The Legislative Council enacted the *Welfare Ordinance 1953* (Northern Territory of Australia 1960) that, following the Administrator's assent, created the Welfare Branch and gave its director a range of powers over those declared to be wards of the state. These responsibilities included the promotion of:

> their social, economic and political advancement for the purpose of assisting them and their descendants to take their rightful place as members of the community of the Commonwealth (Northern Territory of Australia 1960, p. 2309).

This was to be achieved through a variety of educational, medical, housing and social interventions into their lives including:

> to arrange for their vocational training and to obtain suitable employment for them in industrial and other enterprises and for this purpose to establish and maintain a liaison with appropriate organisations (Northern Territory of Australia 1960, p. 2310).

While in theory any person in the Northern Territory could be made a ward, Aboriginal Territorians were the target of the legislation. Following a detailed census of the entire Indigenous population of the Northern Territory that was completed in 1956, all but six full-blood Aborigines were included in the so-called 'stud book' that ran to 272 pages listing each ward's district, European name, tribal or personal name, group, tribe, sex, year of birth and subdistrict. This register of wards was abandoned in 1964 and Aboriginal people were progressively brought into mainstream social welfare programs.

As a result of the *Welfare Ordinance*, the Commonwealth Government developed a new interest in the work of the missions and began establishing its own settlements throughout the Northern Territory following World War Two. This heralded the beginning of more direct government provision of public funding to the missions to replace the private philanthropy that had sustained their work for almost 70 years. The missionaries that would come to work in the new settlements, such as the Baptists at Yuendumu, Hooker Creek (Lajamanu) and Warrabri (Ali Curung), would be more focused upon spreading the Christian faith within Indigenous culture and less concerned with the provision of vocational training (Jordan 1999). From 1952, according to Baker (2012), Commonwealth funding for the Methodist Missions in Arnhem Land was channelled through the recently established Welfare Branch of the Northern Territory Administration 'with the new emphasis on the Aborigine as an individual and with increased demands for welfare and training', leading to the Church seeking even greater levels of government monies. Along with the public funds came the inevitable demands for more government bureaucratic control over the use of the resources.

The *Ward's Employment Ordinance* of 1953 provided more protection for Aboriginal workers (as wards of the Territory) and an Employment Advisory Board was also established. The ordinance permitted wards to be apprenticed and included provisions allowing for part of the ward's wage to be placed into a trust account administered by the Director of the Welfare Branch. 'Provisions were set down for training, employment and assistance to wards. The director decided the suitability of wards for training and the type of training they would receive' (Baker 2012). For a brief period, the missions argued for and won an exemption from the Ward's Employment Ordinance on the grounds that they were not employers but providers of welfare and training. However, this exception was revoked in 1963 giving those Aborigines living on the missions the same opportunities and scope for training as those living in other parts of the Territory:

> From 1951 until the introduction of the government funded Training Wages Scheme in 1969, The Church Synod set rates of pay. A portion of the wage subsidy received by the missions paid for the missionaries and the rest of the subsidy money was used to finance more mission employees and to pay Indigenous workers (Baker 2012, p. 142).

The gradual increase of government-directed funding and the implementation of national industrial award wages and conditions through the 1960s spelled the effective end of the missionaries being the sole providers of philanthropically inspired vocational education and training to Indigenous Territorians. In a description of the intended outcomes of vocational instruction in this period (Working party on vocational training for Aboriginals in the Northern Territory 1973, p. 2), it is noted that 'settlements and missions in the Northern Territory were regarded primarily as training centres to promote social change amongst Aboriginals'. The Aborigines were being instructed on the need to work to get money to buy food and other things rather than a traditional lifestyle: 'this is the primary and complex lesson for the Aboriginal to learn' (Working party on vocational training for Aboriginals in the Northern Territory 1973, p. 2). In addition to the work on missions and settlements, a Central Training Establishment operated in Darwin from 1959 and a small-scale vocational training centre operated at Batchelor in the late 1960s using the facilities taken over from the Australian Atomic Energy Commission that had become idle due to the cessation of uranium mining at nearby Rum Jungle.

Figure 11. Mission Aboriginals [sic] working in a carpentry shop, May 1968.

Source: Creator Unknown. PH0139/1599, Northern Territory Department of Lands Collection, Northern Territory Library.

The transition of training Northern Territory Aborigines from private philanthropic provision to government responsibility provides a clear example of the Commonwealth's willingness to use the jurisdiction as a social laboratory. The lack of training capacity on the part of the Federal Government and its purposeful decision to leave adult and vocational training to the states has already been described. However, that did not stop the Commonwealth from effectively taking over training from the missionaries in the pursuit of population control and socioeconomic development. Training became an essential pillar of the Commonwealth's policies for the assimilation of Indigenous people into mainstream society.

Assimilation was built upon the rather simplistic belief that in order to survive and prosper 'the Aborigines must live and work and think as white Australians do so that they can take their place in social, economic and political equality with the rest of the Australian community' based upon social rather than racial principles (Minister for Territories 1958, p. 1). The *Assimilation of Our Aborigines* is a small booklet that describes the new national policy and proposes that 'education programmes should aim at preparing Aborigines for suitable employment according to local circumstances' (Minister for Territories 1958, p. 2). In describing the work of the Commonwealth and its replacement of missionary philanthropy, the Minister for Territories (1958, p. 3) proudly recounts that in 1949 there was only one government Aboriginal school in the Territory with 20 pupils and that by 1958 this had grown to 1,850 pupils enrolled in 27 schools. Hart (1970, p. 197) provides a rather more prosaic rationale for the Northern Territory Administration Welfare Branch's takeover of the education of full-blood Aboriginals being due to the refusal of the South Australian Department of Education to enrol Aboriginal students into the Territory schools it was engaged to operate on behalf of the Commonwealth Office of Education. South Australia furnished staff and curricula for schools, apprenticeship training and adult education in the Northern Territory under contract to the Commonwealth from 1 January 1945 until 1972 (National Archives of Australia 2014a; Urvett 1982).

'The training of Aboriginals for suitable employment and establishing them in industries is a major aspect of assimilation' (Minister for Territories 1958, p. 4). The Northern Territory Ward's Employment Ordinance provided for the full educational needs of Aboriginals up to and beyond university level and, in addition, provided for up to £1,000 for individuals to establish economic enterprises of various kinds. The take up and success rates of these two measures are not described. Two years later, the rationale for the policy of assimilation is further elaborated in *The Skills of Our Aborigines*:

> The philosophical basis of Aboriginal society is rather too fragile to withstand the stresses of social change; there are no suitable Aboriginal institutions that can easily be used as a basis for community growth (Acting Minister for Territories 1960, p. 19).

'The Commonwealth Government and the various State Governments, with the help of Christian Missions, are now guiding and helping Australian Aborigines towards their proper place in the world' (Acting Minister for Territories 1960, p. 21) and this was being done in the Northern Territory through the provision of vocational and other training to both children and adults who were deemed to be able to benefit from it. Hart (1970, Appendix E) recounts the 'Philosophy of Aboriginal Education' that had been adopted by the Welfare Branch of the Northern Territory Administration: 'in deciding upon an educational programme which will meet the needs of the Aboriginal population we need a basic philosophy; the Government's policy is that of assimilation'. In describing the theoretical basis for programs of assimilation, Elsey (1986, p. 89) relates it to 'an eugenic ideology' where 'the social strata that exist are simply outcomes of different endowed abilities'. This interpretation is based upon ideas of individualism, *laissez faire* and residual welfare where the impoverished are seen as a burden to society. The official policy of assimilation remained in place in the Northern Territory until 1973, when all schooling and adult education was brought under the control of the Commonwealth Department of Education Northern Territory Division. In particular, vocational education and training for Aborigines became 'mainstreamed' at this time and was to be guided by principles of self-management aligned with a community development approach to training (Strike 1981, p. 26).

The assumption of complete responsibility for vocational education and training by the Commonwealth in the 1970s marks the end of the missionaries' exclusive philanthropic use of training for the envisaged project of improvement aimed at Aboriginal people in the Northern Territory. Although the Independent Schools Association and Nungalinya College still provide some training for Indigenous Territorians, they are funded on the same basis as all other providers and are subject to government procurement processes and quality arrangements.

Vocational education and training as a tool of social control and population conduct had become completely dominated by the state by the mid-1970s due to its superior funding capacity and will to train people.

Having described the transition of vocational education and training from its roots in British middle-class philanthropy and its initial use as a technique to change Aboriginal society, it is now time to examine how training would be positioned as an important consideration in the post-war development of the Northern Territory and for those residents who were not subject to the *Welfare Ordinance*. As described previously, prior to and including World War Two, vocational training was not formally supplied to Northern Territory residents for two major reasons: the population was too small, and a more general incapacity on the part of the Commonwealth to intervene in and deliver services that were constitutionally reserved to the states at the time of Federation. However, following World War Two, the Commonwealth became more active in workplace skills formation as a result of the war time experience of training through the Army Education Service (Whitelock 1974); the report of the Walker committee, which found adult education to be an important national economic concern (Tannock 1976); Prime Minister Curtin's *White Paper on Full Employment* (Coombs 1994); and the Social Services Amendment to the Constitution. The following will concentrate upon adult education and apprenticeships—the two areas that would eventually be combined and recognised as Technical and Further Education (TAFE) in 1974 and then be rebadged as 'vocational education and training' in 1992.

The very first attempts by the Commonwealth Government for the provision of adult education in the Northern Territory were planned to commence in 1951 with two mobile vans, one in Central Australia and one in the Top End, fitted out with the modern technologies such as film projectors, sound systems and musical recordings to supplement their small mobile libraries. Berzins and Loveday (1999, p. 2) report that the Territory's Administrator in 1950, AR Driver, said that 'adult education was not yet absolutely necessary' and that the Assistant Supervisor of Education (NT Schools), LC Dodd, 'doubted whether adult education should be undertaken in the Territory'. The original plan for the use of the mobile vans was dropped altogether in 1951 in response to the Administrator's views.

In the meantime, Administrator Driver had approved the introduction of evening classes in Alice Springs in April 1950. These lessons would allow students to reach the South Australian intermediate level of secondary schooling. In the following year, Darwin was given approval by Driver for supervised apprenticeship study to support the correspondence courses from South Australia as well as other courses in typing, shorthand, French and subjects leading to public service employment (Berzins & Loveday 1999, p. 2). In 1949 the Apprenticeships Board commenced formally regulating apprentices and by 1953 there were 33 apprentices under indenture in the entire Territory (Wilson & Estbergs 1984, p. 43). By 1954, all of the educational provision for Darwin's 9,000 residents was delivered through the Darwin Higher Primary School, which incorporated the Adult Education Centre operating under the direction of its part-time registrar who was also the school's headmaster (Giese 1990, p. 1).

Because of the contractual links to South Australia for the provision of educational services, the Northern Territory was included in the rather aggressive extension of adult education through the Education Department schools located in so-called country areas, that is, places outside the Adelaide metropolitan region. According to Alexander's (1959, p. 24) history of adult education, the South Australian Premier was reluctant 'to embark on any very costly and sweeping reorganisation of existing adult education services' in 1956–57 and this set the scene for open competition over the provision of post-school education between the University of Adelaide and the Education Department. It seems likely that the contestation between institutions over the control of vocational education and training that will be so highly evident in the remainder of this story can trace its roots back to this demarcation dispute between the university and the government department. Certainly, the South Australian Education Department was determinedly positioning itself in the field by changing the names of its country technical high schools to 'adult education centres' to facilitate 'a very considerable expansion of services' under the supervision of the Superintendent of Technical Education (Alexander 1959, pp. 24–25).

Figure 12. Alice Springs High School from Anzac Hill, October 1958. This was the site of the Adult Education Centre and it became the first home of the Alice Springs Community College in 1974.

Source: Creator Geoff and Lois Helyar, PH0092/0121, Geoff and Lois Helyar Collection, Northern Territory Library.

As a result of this contest, fully fledged adult education centres were established in Alice Springs and Darwin in January of 1957 with part-time registrars in charge and casual staff providing the instruction (Economic and Statistical Branch 1961). In 1958 the Administrator, JC Archer, recommended the creation of the position of principal for the Darwin Adult Education Centre and this position was filled from January 1959 by Harold Garner who oversaw a 'spectacular growth in enrolments' (Berzins & Loveday 1999, pp. 4–5). In 1957, the number of enrolments in Darwin stood at 482 students in 16 classes while Alice Springs had 129 people studying in 11 different areas (National Archives of Australia 1961c). The number of students studying at the Alice Springs Adult Education Centre increased to almost 1,000 by 1972 (Urvett 1982, p. 14). In the Top End, the Darwin Adult Education Centre had 993 students in 1961 and this would continue on an upwards trajectory to reach 5,974 in the Centre's final year of operations in 1973 (Berzins & Loveday 1999, p. 6). Between 1963 and 1966, additional adult education centres were opened in Katherine, Tennant Creek and Batchelor (Urvett 1982, p. 14). Due to the increased workload experienced by the principal, the Alice Springs Adult Education Centre was removed from Garner's responsibility and returned to the control of the South Australian Adult Education authorities in 1969. This allowed Garner to concentrate upon operations in the Top End.

The Apprenticeship Board had the legally enforceable power to declare trades as a result of the 1948 ordinance, which made it illegal to work in a declared trade except as an apprentice or journeyman. Twenty-two trades had been declared by 1953 but the reality was that the Territory had less than three dozen apprentices in only eight different trades that year. In 1958–59 there were 79 apprentices in 10 trades with 15 of them being employed in Alice Springs (Berzins & Loveday 1999, p. 11). With the 1967 appointment of three full-time trades teaching staff to the Darwin Adult Education Centre to conduct apprentice training in the automotive, electrical and carpentry and joinery trades, the total Territory numbers grew to almost 300 in 1973 (Berzins & Loveday 1999, pp. 11–12).

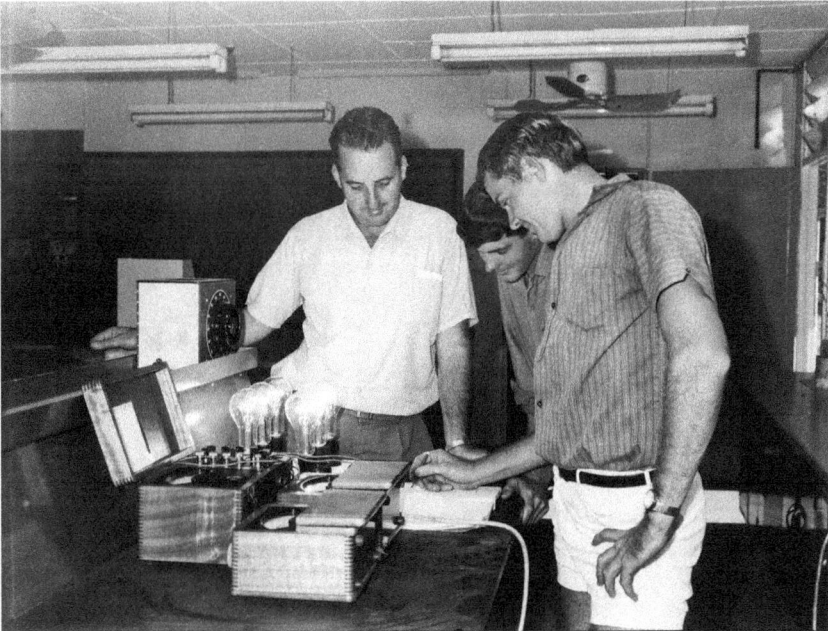

Figure 13. Electrical experiments at Darwin High School adult training classes, 30 June 1967.

Source: Creator Unknown. PH0139/1418, Northern Territory Department of Lands Collection, Northern Territory Library.

In 1960, as a result of changes made the previous year, the elected members of the Legislative Council had finally broken the political dominance exerted through the absolute majority that had been held by the public service–based official members. The Legislative Council was composed of eight elected members, six official members and three non-official members who were appointed by the Governor-General. The Commonwealth Government was not yet ready to hand over its control over Territory affairs to the elected representatives of the people, however. The national political scene was dominated by the policies of the Liberal Party and Australia's longest-serving Prime Minister, Sir Robert Menzies. The era was characterised by rapid population growth due to both immigration and the post-war 'baby boom' and a focus upon industrial development in the southern capital cities:

> The post-war growth of Australian secondary industry into technically more demanding fields; the technical transformation of primary industries requiring complex machinery and biological and chemical knowledge; and the changing character of service industries, especially public administration and community and business services with informational and interpretative functions—all demanded a more highly skilled workforce (Butlin, Barnard & Pincus 1982, p. 205).

While the Northern Territory was not sharing in the industrial development experienced in other parts of the nation, its population was rapidly increasing nevertheless. There were about 3,300 non-Indigenous residents in the Territory in 1911 at the time of the handover to the Commonwealth—this had grown to almost 26,000 in 1960 and, by including Aboriginal residents in the official census for the first time in 1961, would leap to 44,481 the following year (Australian Bureau of Statistics 2011). In keeping with the increased national interest in improving Australia's human capital that would contribute to economic and social growth, the Commonwealth established the Education Enquiry Committee in 1960 to investigate and recommend upon the future education and training needs in the Northern Territory. Three public servants comprised the membership of this committee: Mr R Marsh (Assistant Administrator of the Northern Territory), Mr J Pratt (Deputy Director of the Commonwealth Office of Education) and Mr C Griggs (Deputy Director of Education in South Australia).

The Education Enquiry Committee was very busy throughout the year and by October 1960 had conducted consultations in the major population centres of the Northern Territory. Up until this time, some 78 persons had appeared to give evidence to the committee, nine written submissions had been received and several others were expected in the near future (National Archives of Australia 1961c, folio 165). One of these latter submissions came from the senior psychologist for the South Australian Education Department, Mr LS Piddington, in November 1960. While Piddington's proposals canvassed a wide range of educational matters, he singled out vocational training for very specific roles:

> A large number of those children will require various forms of technical education as they will be going into skilled and highly skilled trades. To this end, therefore, the secondary schools plans for the Northern Territory should be along the lines somewhat similar to the Whyalla Technical High School [in regional South Australia] where a variety of courses are [sic] available. Special consideration must be given to slow learning children and the part Aboriginal children, as well as dull whites, who are not going to work beyond the semi-skilled level, and for a number who are going to work only at the unskilled level (National Archives of Australia 1961c, folio 193).

> If assimilation [of Aboriginals] is the policy then an important step is to apply the principle of goodwill and this should involve a major adult education drive with the white and part Aboriginal population [to overcome prejudice] (National Archives of Australia 1961c, folio 192).

Piddington's comments clearly demonstrate the migration of vocational education and training that was taking place in the public policy arena. Training was moving from a philanthropic tool used by the missionaries solely for Aboriginal 'improvement' to a set of actions that could be used by government to better manage the whole population. The new conception for government deployment of training was less focused upon race and more interested in those problematic groups who were deemed to be disadvantaged, slow, dull and low- or unskilled. This transition had commenced with the Apprenticeships Board being established in 1948 and continued to build momentum. For example, another submission to the committee on education from the Northern Territory Administration's Director of Agriculture, WM Curteis, proposed the necessity of establishing 'an agricultural college in the Northern Territory' to assist in 'the development of the Territory' and 'afford Asiatic students facilities for training that at present are not available to them' (National Archives of Australia 1961c, folio 174).

In presenting his evidence to this committee on education, the principal of the Adult Education Centre, Harold Garner, reported that 14 different courses were offered in Darwin in 1959 and that 'the present system of providing [apprenticeship] courses by correspondence together with supervised periods once a week is not entirely successful and only few apprentices complete theoretical studies' (National Archives of Australia 1961c, folios 106–107). As described previously, this situation would not be addressed until 1967 when three full-time technical teachers were appointed to Darwin by the South Australian Education Department.

Figure 14. Darwin Primary School in January 1957, it later became Darwin Higher Primary and then Darwin High School. This building in Woods Street became the Adult Education Centre under principal Harold Garner.
Source: Creator Unknown. PH0320/0009, WC Laidlaw Collection, Northern Territory Library.

The Committee on Education's report contained 121 recommendations, of which the most significant were that the Territory sever its links with South Australia's Education Department over an 8 to 10-year period and assume responsibility for education matters through the establishment of an Education Branch to take over responsibility for general education, adult education, vocational training and preschools (National Archives of Australia 2014a). The major organisational response to the Education

Enquiry Committee's work came about in 1961 when the Commonwealth Government Minister approved the establishment of a Northern Territory Education Board 'to advise the Administrator on matters of education policy and planning and coordination of the operations of the Education Branch and the Welfare Branch' (National Archives of Australia 1961b, folio 6). This board held its first meeting on 24 November 1961 and its members included the Assistant Administrator Economic and Social Affairs, the Director of Welfare, the Superintendent of Education and the Superintendent Special Schools. The history of vocational education and training in the Northern Territory is littered with the establishment of committees and their eventual demise.

In common with many other areas of governance in the Northern Territory, the elected members of the Legislative Council felt that the public service was not always working in the best interests of the electorates and established its own Select Committee on the Educational Needs of the Northern Territory, which issued its final report in 1962. Despite finding that the topic was very complex and there was insufficient time available and not enough resources for the Select Committee to make a detailed investigation, the report was 'able to distinguish quite clearly three problems':

a. the problems associated with the administration and staffing of schools through the medium of the Education Department of South Australia;

b. the problem of the integration of the separate administration of the European population and the Aboriginal population; and

c. the difficulties arising from the fact that post–primary education in the Territory is incomplete (The Legislative Council for the Northern Territory 1962, p. 7).

The first problem could be addressed by taking over local control of schooling from the far-distant South Australian Department of Education, as had been recommended by the Education Enquiry Committee the year before. The Select Committee also recommended that the resolution of the matter of separate schooling for European and Aboriginal residents be accomplished by 'one control for both types of schools with a view to ultimate integration' (The Legislative Council for the Northern Territory 1962, p. 6).

In describing the post–primary education and training situation, the Select Committee noted that some higher education tutorial classes in English, accounting, economics and public administration were on offer at the Darwin Adult Education Centre in conjunction with the University of Queensland. The small number of apprentices and their difficulties with correspondence theory lessons was also reiterated with the observation that:

> the establishment of the new Technical High School may open the way to the provision of some advanced technical training above the secondary level, but at present the demand is not sufficient to call for any measures beyond those mentioned (The Legislative Council for the Northern Territory 1962, p. 7).

Following on from these two major examinations of the provision of education and training, the Northern Territory Administration commissioned a detailed review of Indigenous schooling by BH Watts and JD Gallacher in 1963–64. The *Report on an investigation into curriculum and teaching methods used in Aboriginal schools in the Northern Territory to the Honourable CE Barnes, MP, Minister of State for Territories March 1964* made several direct references to vocational education and training and the role it would play in the assimilation of Aboriginal people into mainstream Australian society:

> The settlements and missions now provide training in a wide range of vocational skills, gradually increasing in scope as more facilities and staff become available. All staff on settlements have, as one of their many responsibilities, the training of Aborigines in special fields related to their own technical skills (Northern Territory Archives Service 1964, p. 17).

> Adult education classes were introduced on most missions and settlements in the early 1950s because of the official view that adult education was of vital importance to the assimilation program. In 1964 there are over 40 instructors employed (Northern Territory Archives Service 1964, p. 53).

> Aboriginal adolescents need to develop pre-vocational skills and work attitudes, vocational interests and ambitions. In due course, they must also acquire vocational skills in their chosen field (Northern Territory Archives Service 1964, p. 211).

The report of this investigation, more commonly known as the Watts-Gallacher Report, had a major influence on the contents of the Aboriginal school curriculum and how it would be taught. Equally importantly, it also established a way of thinking about the purposes of education and training that would spread far beyond remote primary school classrooms and influence the development of specialised Indigenous training institutions. For example, in 1968, a teaching assistant course for aspiring Aboriginal teachers was established at Kormilda College, the Darwin-based boarding school for remote Aboriginal secondary school–aged students. In March 1972, as part of a purposeful desire to rationalise Aboriginal adult education in the Darwin region, the teaching assistant course and several others were moved to the Batchelor Vocational Training Centre in the former Atomic Energy Commission buildings (Uibo 1993, p. 9). After further consolidation, the Batchelor College opened in 1974. In Central Australia, the Uniting Church opened the Institute for Aboriginal Development under the guidance of the Reverend Jim Downing in 1969 and handed over control of this training organisation to an Aboriginal controlled board of management two years later. Nungalinya College was also established in Darwin in 1974 and continues to operate as a combined churches training college for Indigenous Australians.

There was also activity in the non-Indigenous post-school space at the same time. In 1968, the Commonwealth Government commissioned Max Bone, the Director of Technical Education in South Australia, to report on post–secondary education in the Northern Territory with a clear term of reference that excluded the possibility of a university being established (Giese 1990, p. 2). His major recommendation was for the establishment of a community college in Darwin—a 'unique' type of institution that was relatively unknown in Australia at the time (Urvett 1982, pp. 39–40). It was envisaged that this dual-sector college would deliver vocational and advanced education courses and would increase in scope and complexity as the population of the Northern Territory increased. The Commonwealth Minister for Education and Science accepted the key recommendation and established a planning committee to undertake detailed scoping and public consultation for the community college. This group supplied two reports to the minister in 1970 (Darwin Community College Planning Committee 1970a, 1970b). The contents of these reports guided the development of a greenfields site in Darwin's northern suburbs at Brinkin, and the Darwin Community College commenced operation on 5 March 1974 (Urvett 1982, p. 39) having incorporated the operations of the Darwin Adult Education Centre. In August of that year, the Darwin Community College also gained managerial responsibility for the Alice Springs Adult Education Centre, which was rebadged as the Alice Springs Community College (Giese 1990, p. 6).

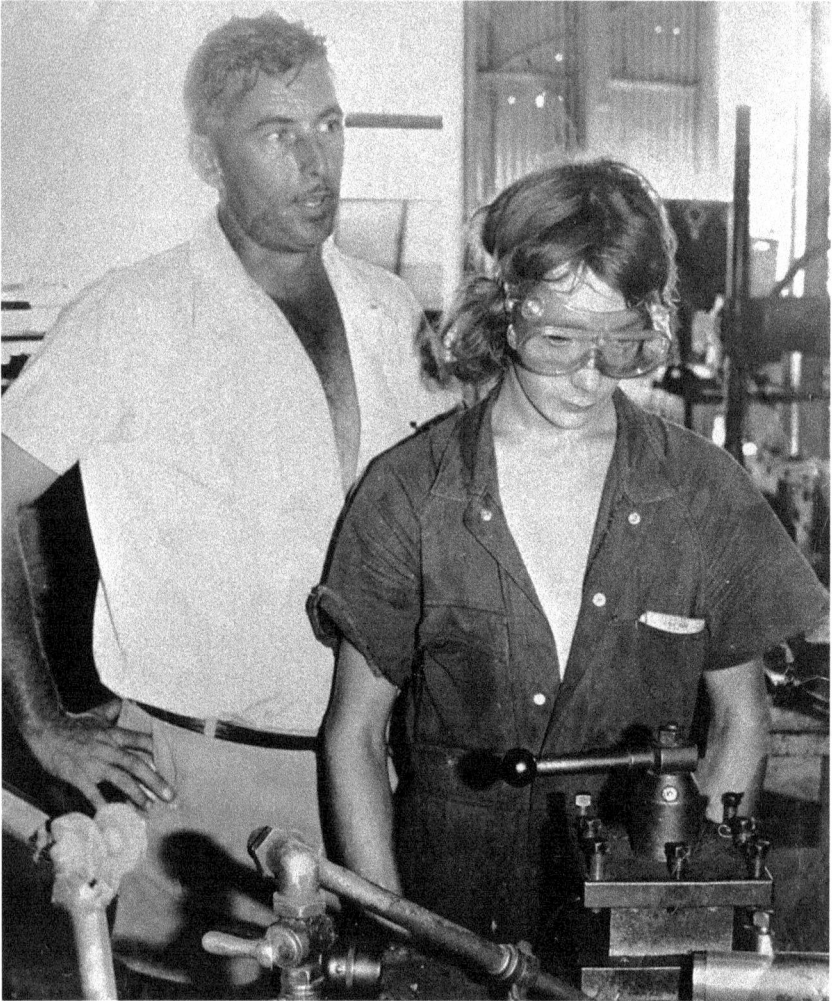

Figure 15. Apprentice training in the former World War Two railway workshops in Katherine, February 1974. David Handley, first-year apprentice and Robert Scott, trades foreman.
Source: Creator Unknown. PH0663/0275, Henry and Gwen Scott Collection, Northern Territory Library.

Heatley (1990, p. 40) argues that in the early 1970s, the federal Labor Government's commitment to the Northern Territory was focused upon the social rather than the economic. This period saw the first Labor government at the national level since 1949, and they brought a new social agenda to Australia generally and, due to the Commonwealth's continued control, had unfettered capacity to introduce change into the Northern Territory. This was certainly evident in matters to do with education and training. In addition to establishing major post–secondary school institutions described previously, the Commonwealth brought to fruition the decade-long recommendations for the removal of South Australian provision of education and training in the Northern Territory and bringing general and Aboriginal schools under the control of a single agency. The transition commenced in 1971 with a phased five-year withdrawal; this gained momentum in 1973 with the establishment the Commonwealth Department of Education Northern Territory Division, which took over the management of all general and welfare schools as well as the activities of the adult educators in remote communities (Urvett, Heatley & Alcorta 1980, p. 13). The new 'unified' school system commenced operations on 13 February 1973 (Department of Education Northern Territory Division 1974) and ended the contractual relationship with South Australia for the operation of schools and adult education that had commenced towards the end of the Second World War. Operational support for the Apprenticeships Board was also incorporated into the new department although the board still had its own legal identity and membership. The number of registered apprentices had grown to 360 in 38 declared vocations by June 1973 (Department of Education Northern Territory Division 1974, p. 40). It was also foreshadowed that the Darwin Community College would take over 'responsibility of technical training of apprentices in the Territory' when it became operational in 1974 (Department of Education Northern Territory Division 1974, p. 40).

The Labor Party's views on the role and place of vocational education were captured in a series of essays written by leading members several years after the Whitlam Government left office. In the introduction to the series, Evans and Reeves (1980) reject setting up a dichotomy between 'efficient economic management' versus 'radical social change' because a strong economy is required to finance social policy objectives. They believe this to be a long-standing feature of Labor policy dating back to World War Two expressed through programs that encouraged full employment; greater fiscal power centralised with the Commonwealth; large scale migration; and major expansions in health, education, industrialisation and social security (Evans & Reeves 1980, p. 1). Labor Party policy would continue to 'give special emphasis to the relation between education and employment by encouraging technical training, retraining programs and recurrent education' (Evans & Reeves 1980, p. 78). In his contribution, Bennett (1982, p. 162) notes that the Australian Labor Party lacked interest in education in the first half of the twentieth century with the significant exception of technical education, which was seen to be more appropriate for the working class. He also argues that education systems are the ultimate normalising institutions and deeply reinforce and entrench class divisions. However, the counter view that Australia would be a more just and equitable place if there were 'more equal opportunities to obtain an education' became the centrepiece of Labor policy (Dawkins & Costello 1983). In particular, Dawkins and Costello (1983, p. 70) saw a very specific role for vocational education and training to increase post–compulsory school aged retention and skill levels in order 'to seize economic opportunities' that would allow Australia to become its own economic master.

It is this pattern of thinking that envisaged the economic and social development of the Northern Territory as being integrally linked to the increased provision of vocational education and training through Labor's bipartisan support for the community college concept; the unification of the separate school systems; and an increase in apprenticeship numbers in the Northern Territory during the Labor years 1972–75. The anticipated social improvement would be supported by economic development that, in turn, would require a more highly skilled workforce and higher rates of labour force participation. One of the major policy shifts that accompanied Labor's use of the Northern Territory as a 'social laboratory' (Heatley 1990, p. 29) was the replacement of the Aboriginal assimilation policy of the 1950s and its related integration policy of the 1960s with one of self-determination and self-management (Uibo 1993, pp. 13–14). The policy of self-management is part of a complex web of economic ideas that presupposed that individuals will make rational choices that are personally beneficial. Such thinking underpins human capital theory (for example, see Becker 1993) and supports policies that are predicated upon the belief that equal opportunity will arise from equal access to education and training.

The reverse side of this policy regime is that individuals can also be deemed to be personally responsible for making bad or incorrect choices that limit their social and economic opportunities in society while ignoring such factors as racism or even the possibility that people will frequently make economically irrational choices in the face of social pressures. Strike (1981, pp. 26–28), an adult educator working at Bamyili in the Top End, believes that the introduction of the policy of self-management was premised upon Aboriginal people 'establishing their own goals and making choices as to their lifestyle, recognising the rights and obligations that flow from them'. The adult educator function in the remote settlements and missions would be based upon 'the philosophy, one of developing the individual in relationship to *their* needs, in a time/space relationship appropriate to them, relating to their community development is an appropriate role' (Strike 1981, p. 75, emphasis in original).

The final four-year phase of Commonwealth control of the Northern Territory and the transition to self-government commenced in earnest in 1974. This year would also be significant in the history of vocational education and training in the jurisdiction due to both man-made and natural events. The Northern Territory Legislative Council passed the *Darwin Community College Ordinance*, which received the Administrator's assent in July 1973. The importance of ministerial control and relationships between the various government agencies were crucial and contested from the very establishment of the Territory's largest training organisation. This legislation gave the College the power to provide:

> for Darwin and such other parts of the Northern Territory as the College considers necessary or desirable education and training in such fields of science, technology, the arts, administration, commerce and other fields of knowledge or the application of knowledge as the Council, with the Approval of the Minister, determines or as the Minister requires. It was, as people came to appreciate later on, a very broad empowerment, giving the College ample room for experimentation and development.
>
> The broad charter of the College embroiled it later on in arguments about the coordination of post–secondary education in the Northern Territory and its own autonomy. Technical, trade and further education was under the control of the special projects branch of the Northern Territory Education Division, but the College, in respect of all its work, was directly responsible through its Council to the [Commonwealth] Minister (Berzins & Loveday 1999, p. 31).

The Darwin Community College was officially opened on 10 March 1974 by HRH Prince Philip, Duke of Edinburgh, deputising for the Queen, even though many of the facilities were yet to be completed and handed over to the council (Berzins & Loveday 1999, p. 32). In common with the rest of Darwin, the operations of the College came to a screeching halt on Christmas Eve 1974.

Figure 16. Opening ceremony of the Darwin Community College
by HRH Prince Philip; Prime Minister Gough Whitlam is on the right.
Source: Creator Unknown. PH 0703/0428. Tschirner Collection. Northern Territory Library.

Cyclone Tracy swept into Darwin overnight and by Christmas morning almost 70 per cent of the small tropical city's buildings were destroyed and 71 people were killed. In a repetition of events following the bombing of Darwin during World War Two, much of the population was evacuated south, reducing the number of residents from about 47,000 to just over 10,000 in less than one week. Although the population's progressive return to Darwin (and many former residents did not desire to do so) commenced by late January 1975, entry to the city was strictly controlled by a permit system that was monitored by police checkpoints at both the airport and on the Stuart Highway near Noonamah for the next six months. As the Northern Territory was still a Commonwealth responsibility, the relief effort was directed by Major-General Alan Stretton and the rebuilding of Darwin was undertaken by the Darwin Reconstruction Commission. While the initial relief effort was well-received, the bureaucratic processes of the Reconstruction Commission further fuelled the demands for greater autonomy in the conduct of Northern Territory affairs. The post-Tracy actions taken by Commonwealth technical experts reinforced the absence of genuine local contributions to the planning and execution of the Territory's future. While not being ungrateful for the Commonwealth and national response to the resurrection of Darwin, the members of the first fully elected Legislative Assembly, put into office on 19 October 1974, some two months before the cyclone, were left in no doubt as to their inferior position and which level of government was making the most important decisions.

By May 1975, the city's population had increased to about 30,000 residents and the decision made in early January 1975 to reopen the Darwin Community College, commencing with a limited number of trade courses, seemed well-founded. By mid-January, it was determined that by redeploying staff and moving some offerings to Alice Springs, making temporary repairs to the Casuarina campus, and using other available facilities around Darwin, the College could offer technical, trade and recreational courses, library services, tutorials for Queensland external university-level courses and classes for humanities, matriculation and public service entrance examinations (Berzins & Loveday 1999, p. 48). As Darwin was rebuilt, the Darwin Community College was also repaired and expanded its offerings in line with the original vision of a multi-campus, multi-level institution and as the provider of technical education in those trades with sufficient numbers of apprentices. The Technical and Further Education Commission report for the triennium 1977–79 (1976, p. 226) shows that the Northern Territory had some 4,138 enrolments in the post-school technical courses in 1975, with adult education having over half of these students, followed by art and design with 995 enrolments and closely followed by personal services on 819. The report also rather blandly describes, 'In the Northern Territory the administration of TAFE [Technical and Further Education] is shared by the Commonwealth Department of Education and the Darwin Community College' (Technical and Further Education Commission 1976, p. 38).

The other significant influence upon vocational education and training that occurred in 1974 was the release of *TAFE in Australia: Report on needs in Technical and Further Education (Kangan Report)*

(Australian Committee on Technical and Further Education 1974). This report identifies Technical and Further Education (TAFE) as an equal, but different, mainstream educational sector allowing for the Commonwealth to provide funding to the various state training systems to improve both the quantity and quality of students who study what would come to be known as vocational education and training (Australian Committee on Technical and Further Education 1974, p. 1). The Kangan Report, named after the chair of the Commonwealth-appointed committee and Australia's leading expert on personnel management, reflected the national Labor Party platform of 1971, which defined equity as 'equality of opportunity' (Goozee 2013, p. 140). Numerous descriptions of how TAFE contributes to modern society are listed in the Kangan Report's summary of conclusions and recommendations. These are used to justify the provision of Federal Government funds to support an area that has been constitutionally reserved to the states:

(2) The main purpose of education is the betterment and development of individual people and their contributions to the good of the community. Technical and further education should be planned accordingly.

(3) The emphasis in technical college type institutions should be primarily on the needs of the individual for vocationally oriented education and the manpower needs of industry should be seen as the context for courses.

(5) There should be unrestricted access to assessments of knowledge and skills for the purpose of gaining formal qualifications, irrespective of where or how the individual prepared himself. Entry requirements should be progressively eased.

(10) Opportunities for recurrent education should help individuals who wish to repair inadequacies in their initial formal education or add to their knowledge and skills in order to change the direction of their vocational interests.

(24) Access to further education by many persons who reside outside large metropolitan areas would be facilitated by the development of community type colleges which would help adults overcome deficiencies in their primary and secondary schooling and offer courses up to diploma level, where necessary, in addition to the range and level of courses customarily available from technical colleges (Australian Committee on Technical and Further Education 1974, pp. xxiii–xxvi).

In terms of national policy, the Kangan Report also positions vocational education and training as a tool of government that can be used to alter the conduct of individuals and allow them to gain the necessary skills to be gainfully employed in productive economic ways. The original philanthropically inspired benefits of training directed at the individual that had guided the missionaries' activities in the Northern Territory Aboriginal population have been updated and translated into more contemporary terms, but serve a similar role. Vocational education and training becomes an unquestionable good that is applicable to everyone at any stage of their life in order to give them the skills to meet the economic and industrial needs of the economy. It is such a good thing that it also justifies the expenditure of public monies in a manner approved by government ministers without regards to the once-important separation of powers that reserved education as a state function at the time of Federation in 1901. The release of the Kangan Report in April, the election of the first fully representative Legislative Assembly in October, the destruction of Darwin in December, when combined with an activist Commonwealth Government that ran the Territory through ministerial fiat, made 1974 a pivotal year in the evolution of greater local control and demonstrated to political aspirants the possibilities of exercising ministerial power in Australia's least populous jurisdiction. Jaensch (1981, p. 87) believes that despite warranted criticism, censure and condemnation of political representation in national and state politics elsewhere, 'the Northern Territory, as a new polity, has the opportunity to produce something better'. In keeping with this theme of fresh starts, the first Chief Minister of the Northern Territory, Paul Everingham (1981, p. 2), proposed that in spite of the small and remote population, the decisions taken by the Northern Territory politicians:

> are no less important than those of other states. In fact, many are more important, since in the Legislative Assembly, as in many facets of Territory life, we are laying the groundwork. We are setting precedents where other Australian governments are only modifying them. There is a refreshing quality to starting anew all things. I like the Territory as it is but for me development is a tool – not an end in itself. We need it to create jobs to expand the population to a level of, say, half a million to provide a reasonable home market and support the level of social infrastructure most of us would like.

With the demise of the Whitlam Labor Government at the national level in 1975 and the election of the Fraser Coalition Government, the politics of self-government moved into the realm of the possible. Darwin was well on the way to recovery and the other population centres of the Northern Territory were also in a substantial growth phase. The fully elected Legislative Assembly negotiated with the Commonwealth for the establishment a so-called Territory Executive under the leadership of Goff Letts. Executive members acted in a manner that was similar to a more traditional Cabinet and each would-be 'minister' was responsible for the transfer of state-type governance functions from the Commonwealth to the Northern Territory. Nevertheless, Heatley (1990, p. 56) reports that 'the real work of negotiation took place between federal ministers, senior public servants and Letts and Grant Tambling, who had become Deputy Leader'. The first tranche of functions to be transferred on 1 January 1977 included the staff of the Administrator and Legislative Assembly as well as the police, fire and prisons branches. Some 20 statutory boards and authorities to do with areas such as professional registration, tourism, museums, ports, parole and housing were also negotiated to be in this initial handover. Also included were public service functions to do with legislation, local government, libraries, emergency services, correctional services, water supply, electricity and sewerage and motor vehicle registration.

The protracted negotiations conducted by the Letts Executive for the handover of the remainder of state-type functions to the Northern Territory produced a timetable that would see the final tranche leave the Commonwealth on 1 July 1979 (Heatley 1990, p. 68). The Apprentices Board would come over in January 1978 and in the last group would be education services and the Darwin Community College. While there would be much debate and a reordering of particular agencies, this timeline was met. The process was complicated by the requirement to hold an election for the Legislative Assembly in 1977 that served as a type of referendum on self-government. In the end, the Country Liberal Party was returned with a healthy majority, although Letts lost his seat. Heatley (1990, p. 77) attributes this loss due to Letts' inability to service his large rural seat, a very hard-working opponent and the leader's 'sometimes imperious and patronising leadership and his volatile and often abrasive temperament'. In his place, Paul Everingham became the Majority Leader in the second Legislative Assembly and he concluded the transfer of powers that had commenced in 1974.

Figure 17. Goff Letts, former Chief Secretary of the Northern Territory.
Source: Creator Unknown, PH0416/0069, ABC TV Collection, Northern Territory Library.

The Apprenticeships Board was not included in the first group because of its attachment to the Northern Territory Division of the Commonwealth Education Department, while the Darwin Community College, although established by Northern Territory Ordinance, remained responsible to the Commonwealth minister because the 'education function' (and most other major agencies) remained with the Federal Government. By June 1976, the Apprentices Board reported that 830 apprentices were registered across the Territory and 'there was considerable public debate about the operations of the Board and it was suggested in some quarters that the Board should be served by a department other than the Department of Education' (Department of Education Northern Territory Division 1977, p. 44). It was also reported that six of the eight members of the Apprentices Board represented private enterprise.

This rather banal bureaucratic account masked a frequently heated and much larger debate over which level of government would control education and training as the Territory moved towards self-government. Quite simply, the Commonwealth Department of Education public servants did not believe that the Northern Territory possessed adequate local resources or expertise and that the peculiar problems of the Territory required the Commonwealth to retain responsibility for this nationally important function (Heatley 1990, p. 115). This position was further reinforced with the previously mentioned release of the Kangan Report into Technical and Further Education and the impending federal funding and policy direction that would follow Kangan recommendations in the area of training. In the Northern Territory Education Division's 1974 submission to the Joint Parliamentary Committee on the constitutional development of the Northern Territory, a firm line was drawn in the sand:

> The Department's view is that whatever form of self-government the Northern Territory may attain, responsibility for education services in the Northern Territory should continue to be a function of the Australian Minister for Education (Northern Territory Archives Service 1974–1987).

To further stress the importance of the Commonwealth's contribution, the submission also noted that the Education Division's resources were used to provide secretariat function as well as the chairman of the Apprenticeships Board; the Darwin Community College (having taken over the Adult Education Centres) would remain a semi-autonomous provider of post-school education and training into the foreseeable future in both Darwin and Alice Springs; and that this unique community college would need to rely upon the department for a considerable time into the future. Both the teachers' union and the government school parent body supported the strongly held position that the Commonwealth should retain control and that a statutory authority, distanced from Northern Territory Cabinet responsibility, would be 'the ideal organisational form for educational administration in the Territory' (Heatley 1990, p. 115).

Although proposals for Commonwealth retention and an education commission had the support of major interest groups, the idea was never politically feasible in the spirit of self-government negotiations. The Northern Territory politicians had experienced the influence and control that emanates from remote ministerial offices and faceless bureaucracies for the past 65 years and they were not going to bypass the opportunity to assume direct management of state-type responsibilities. In reflecting upon the proposals for health and education commissions to be established in the Northern Territory in conjunction with self-government, the Territory's first Chief Minister, Paul Everingham, leaves no doubt as to his views:

> I wasn't going to become Chief Minister and hand over whatever control I might have [to commissions]. It doesn't matter whom you put on those statutory bodies. They can be your best friends but they soon turn into crazy megalomaniacs and empire-builders. The most logical, sensible or rational businessmen, when put on a statutory authority, seem to become putty in the hands of the bureaucrats who work for it and start running along its boundary fence like a dog (quoted in Heatley 1990, p. 89).

Based upon the experiences of Commonwealth colonial rule, two things were made clear by the majority party members of the Legislative Assembly as the Northern Territory assumed its new constitutional status:

- ministers and Cabinet would be in charge, making the key decisions; and
- public servants were unelected and must be responsive to their ministers.

The anti-self-rule positions that had been taken by the various vested interests in the robust discussions over the relocation of responsibility for education and training gave rise to quite strained relationships between the Northern Territory Government, the successor organisations to the Darwin Community College and the various government agencies with responsibility for training that occasionally reappears even today. However, disharmony in the education and training field was not a sole product of self-government discussions. With the annexure of the Apprentices Board into the newly established Northern Territory Education Division in 1974 and the creation of a unified education agency, arguments with the Darwin Community College and its Territory-wide training mandate soon erupted over the coordination of post-school education and training. Unsurprisingly, each organisation sought domination over vocational education and training and proposed different administrative arrangements to give effect to their preferred position. The Commonwealth minister was strongly lobbied by all parties making their claims on the basis that they could best provide that Holy Grail of public service functions—coordination.

Figure 18. Elizabeth Andrew, February 1974.
Source: Creator Unknown, PH0120/0056, N. Gleeson Collection,
Northern Territory Library.

In response, Minister Carrick established a three-member Northern
Territory Technical and Further Education Advisory Council in late
1976. They would advise the minister on 'all matters relating to post–

compulsory education in the Northern Territory. One member is to be a nominee from the Legislative Assembly' (Northern Territory Archives Service 1971–2003). The member for Sanderson, Elizabeth Andrew, proposed Marshall Perron as the Legislative Assembly nominee on 2 March 1977 after he had been endorsed in a Cabinet meeting 17 February. In speaking to the nomination as former Executive member with responsibility for education, she noted that 'the need for this committee has become very obvious since the last election. Ministers of the Federal Government in many portfolios suddenly bounded on a great urge to vocationally train everyone' (Andrew 1977, p. 34). Perron, in accepting the Assembly's endorsement, notes that of the council's terms of reference, 'I believe that decision-making at the local level is the most important of all areas' (Andrew 1977, p. 37).

Vocational education and training was high on the agenda of the Northern Territory Government-in-waiting. The discussions endorsing Perron's appointment to the Technical and Further Education Council took place in only the third meeting of Cabinet. In his Cabinet Submission, Perron informed his colleagues that the Legislative Assembly nominee would join the Director of Education, Jim Eedle, and the Principal of the Darwin Community College, Joe Flint, on the Council. This group was to rationalise, coordinate, promote and plan improvements in all aspects of further education in the Northern Territory in response to 'a confusing range of departments and agencies involved in further education that included the Department of Education, the Darwin Community College, Department of Aboriginal Affairs, Employment and Industrial Relations and the Apprentices Board' (Northern Territory Archives Service 1971–2003). Perron summarised his views on the impending work of the Council as follows:

> My impression from the first meeting is that the Council will involve a lot of work, some travel and the wisdom of Solomon to ensure co-operation from a hundred people who see the Council as a threat to their empire (Northern Territory Archives Service 1971–2003).

The setting up of the Technical and Further Education Council for the Northern Territory would only be the first move in a never-ending struggle for the control of vocational education and training policy, finance and programs that continues to this day. It must have brought some sense of poignant satisfaction to Minister Carrick's office that the creation of the Council met the spirit of impending self-government by forcing those who fought the battles over TAFE domination in the Territory to present him with potential solutions rather than the problems. Whether intended or not, the composition of the Council effectively positioned the future Minister for Education, and eventual Chief Minister, as the arbitrator between the heads of the two institutions who vigorously squabbled over the future direction of training at every opportunity. While it may not have seemed obvious at the time, the precedent of ministerial discretion and decision-making in vocational education and training was built into the very genetics of Northern Territory governance. There is little evidence that this Council made a significant impact on the overall coordination of training and certainly one of the early actions of the newly formed Northern Territory Government in mid-1978 was to disband this group.

In the same Cabinet Meeting held in February 1977, Perron also initiated the process to transfer responsibility for the Apprentices Board when the second suite of state-type functions was scheduled to take place on 1 January 1978 (Northern Territory Archives Service 1977–2003a). He ensured that his colleagues knew of Senator Carrick's support for the move. Perron also proposed that 'the composition of the Board leaves much to be desired and I would suggest a complete review at the time we accept responsibility' (Northern Territory Archives Service 1977–2003a). Cabinet's 14th decision approved in principle: the transfer of the Apprentices Board to the existing Department of Transport and Industry as soon as possible; the conduct of an inclusive consultation with all those who could provide useful and constructive advice on a review of the existing Ordinance; and, if possible, joint timing of the introduction of a new Ordinance with the transfer of the Board.

This decision is notable for a variety of reasons. It separates vocational training from the general education function and introduces yet another government agency into the already crowded space—a department whose focus in unashamedly economic. The first Northern Territory Government use of the review process in vocational education and training would eventually be replicated by most ministers over the following years. The transfer also demonstrated to senior public servants that Cabinet and ministers will be deciding on which functions will be undertaken by each department. But this decision is much more than rearranging the bureaucracy. The rather innocuous reference to six of the eight members of the Apprentices Board representing private enterprise that was made in the Northern Territory Education Division's Annual Report for 1976 was referring to a much larger political debate.

The Apprentices Board did not agree with the position taken by senior public servants of the Education Department that the Northern Territory was incapable of taking responsibility for education. These representatives of private industry were much more closely aligned with the political aspirations of Cabinet in the pursuit of self-government regardless of Perron's concerns about the composition of the Board. When it became apparent that the education function would not be handed over until the very end of the transfer process, the decision was made to place as many allies and supporters into every function that was now under Northern Territory control as a matter of priority. This initial divorce of training and education would be only the first of many institutional reorganisations that would come to characterise the vocational education and training sector and its usefulness to ministers in the making of public policy. Regardless of the vigorous debates and political manoeuvres, by mid-1977, the number of apprentices had grown to 869 employed in 51 declared trades. In addition, the Northern Territory Executive had asserted its authority because 'as from 1 January 1978, the responsibility of the Apprenticeship Board was transferred to the Northern Territory Public Service' (Department of Education Northern Territory Division 1978, pp. 36–38).

With Everingham's elevation to the position of Majority Leader of the Northern Territory Executive as a result of the 1977 election, a concerted effort was made to accelerate the handover of functions from the Commonwealth. Everingham argued that the politics of implementing new policies and inserting a more responsive administration into the Territory required enough time to take effect before the next election was due to be held in 1980 (Heatley 1990, p. 88). While this advocacy for increasing the pace of transfer had success in some areas such as land administration, education and health were specifically singled out by Prime Minister Fraser as areas that should stick to the July 1979 date set out in the original transfer program to 'ensure a smooth transition and obviate administrative difficulties and untidiness which could occur otherwise' (quoted in Heatley 1990, p. 88):

> Neither Everingham nor Jim Robertson, as the Executive Member (and later Minister) concerned primarily with education, readily accepted that reasoning. To them the delay was unnecessary and possibly politically disadvantageous. Moreover, it appeared to afford the Commonwealth considerable leverage over the fashioning of the new system, a matter for which the Territory ministers saw as their sole prerogative.

Both Everingham and Robertson later admitted that their handling of the transfer was flawed, particularly in their tolerance of complex consultative mechanisms and in their willingness to brook unwarranted compromise. Both factors, they believed, effectively eroded their control over policy-making (Heatley 1990, p. 116).

The high level of frustration in the Northern Territory Executive was clearly evident in a memorandum from Robertson to Everingham dated 19 May 1978 (Northern Territory Archives Service 1977–1979):

The people clearly expect us to govern in this at the same level as if I had executive responsibility in the area. As I have previously indicated to you, my main difficulty is going to be maintaining my present level of enthusiasm for the education side of my portfolio for another full year under these circumstances — when the satisfaction of demands, and their cause, remains absolutely beyond my control and when the abuse is being taken on behalf of someone else.

In looking back upon the general relationship between the Northern Territory and the Commonwealth, the Territory's third Chief Minister, Steve Hatton, recounts how 'the Commonwealth Public Service still wanted the NT to be their social agenda playground and was opposed to anything that would further erode their power over the NT' (Martin & Dewar 2012, p. 50). Nevertheless, with the advent of self-government on 1 July 1978, Northern Territory ministers had already commenced exercising political, financial and organisational control over a wide range of areas in their desire to transform the jurisdiction from a colonial backwater to a modern and economically viable society in Australia's centre and north. Although the new Cabinet was clearly frustrated at not yet having operational control over education and training, Robertson negotiated the eventual transfer as both a member of the Northern Territory Executive and eventual Minister for Education from September 1977 until November 1982. He would be the first of 26 different ministers that have had either full or partial responsibility for vocational education and training in the Northern Territory since self-government. Only one, Labor's Syd Stirling from 2001 to 2006, would serve as long in the portfolio as did Robertson.

Figure 19. Jim Robertson, Member of the Legislative Assembly, February 1974.

Source: Creator Unknown, PH0120/0050, N Gleeson Collection, Northern Territory Library.

Even though the highly visible self-interested pressure groups (principally the teachers' federation, government school parent groups and the Darwin Community College) had delayed the transfer of education and training to the new government, they had only postponed the inevitable. Their tactics only served to make the politicians even more determined to exert their authority over the sector and to seriously discount any submissions made from those groups. On the other hand, with the electoral demise of Letts as the first majority leader, the ministers were already acutely aware of the unique power of electors. The miniscule electorates and the intensely personal interaction with a population that expects governments to do things reinforced the importance of ministerial decision-making.

In the characteristically pugnacious and forthright style that marked his leadership of the Executive and Government, Paul Everingham's determination to exert ministerial authority is exemplified in the following extract from a letter dated 21 March 1978 when he wrote to a senior member of the Country Liberal Party's organisational wing, Graeme Lewis. Several Country Liberal Party members of the Legislative Assembly had been speaking out against a number of land developers who were putting poorly serviced parcels into the marketplace in order to make a short-term profit without due consideration of the longer-term consequences for those who purchased the blocks and for town planning principles. Lewis had made strong representations to both Marshall Perron, member for Stuart Park, and Everingham following comments in the Assembly that had upset the developers and surveyors and, consequently, their support for the party. The Majority Leader responded to Lewis in a manner that left no doubt as to how his government would work when he wrote:

> I want it to be made perfectly clear that I will not ever under any circumstances, buckle under to threats or any attempts to intimidate me or other Members of the Parliamentary Wing. Once a person tries this on me, so far as I am concerned, he loses any chance of my sympathetic consideration. I told you this on the day in question and I repeat it now (Northern Territory Archives Service 1977–1979).

The politically inspired desire for Northern Territory ministerial accountability and the eventual federal handover of responsibility for vocational education and training provide the backdrop and set the scene for the next era. The enthusiastic fresh ministers would finally have access to all of the contributing factors that would enable them to act as wealthy philanthropists. They had both a desire and a publicly validated mandate to improve the social and economic conditions experienced by Territorians as well as access to the financial means that would allow many agendas to be set locally. In common with the original Australian states, vocational education and training is important to ministers because it is one of the few policy areas that remain under provincial control.

6

TAFE in the era of self-government, 1978–92

The various education and training lobby groups proceeded on the basis that no detail about the transfer of responsibility was too small to be contested and, as a result, Minister Robertson was bombarded with letters, submissions and personal communications demanding one thing or another. In terms of macro-policy matters, three major areas of contention required resolution before the handover could take place: the type of bureaucratic structure required to operate an education system; determining who would employ education and training staff; and the role of the Darwin Community College.

Through its continuing opposition to the transfer of the education and training functions to the new government, the Northern Territory Education Division only served to reinforce the generally negative views about the public service held by the members of the Legislative Assembly. Deep distrust emanated from the previous actions of the official members of the Legislative Council and their perceived role in building and maintaining their own empires and careers while ignoring the aspirations of Territorians. Weller and Sanders (1982, pp. 11–13) report that 'the ministers were determined that whatever happened they would not become captives of the public service. The public service was an organisation to be tamed, to be the servant, not master'. They go on to describe that, due to their deep suspicion of the public service, the early Northern Territory ministry was more decisive in changing the operations and accountability of public servants than any of the counterparts in the other states. 'Like it or not, a minister has been given a licence not accorded to a public servant regardless of experience and expertise, a mandate to govern' (Chief Minister Everingham cited in Weller & Sanders 1982, p. 15). The transition from reporting to a large, distant bureaucracy based in Canberra to being immediately responsive to a local minister with frequently populist political imperatives was not easy for the public servants either—one senior public servant is reported to have described the new Territory ministers as the 'last of the cattle barons' (Weller & Sanders 1982, p. 42).

Figure 20. Ministers of the new Northern Territory Government, 1 July 1978, swearing-in ceremony.

Left to right: Jim Robertson, Marshall Perron, Paul Everingham, Roger Steele, Ian Tuxworth and Administrator John England.

Source: Creator Unknown. PH0093/0188, Northern Territory Government Photographer Collection, Northern Territory Library.

In order for the Northern Territory to make progress on matters to do with education and training, Cabinet came to rely upon a mere handful of trusted senior public servants hand-picked to give effect to ministerial decisions. Unlike current ministers that have the entire education bureaucracy at their service, to address the large policy matters Robertson had to work with an actively resistant Northern Territory Education Division of the Commonwealth Department of Education, the Darwin Community College Council with its extensive legislated powers not yet subject to his intervention, and antagonistic groups of teachers and parents. While not fully resolved until many years later, all teachers and public service positions in the Education Department would eventually come under the general employment conditions of the Northern Territory Office of the Commissioner of Public Employment—that is, under the direct control of Cabinet. However, the other two matters have remained topics of discussion, contestation, change and tinkering. The organisational arrangements used by government to manage vocational education and training and the place and powers accorded to the Darwin Community College's various predecessor institutions remain interrelated and subject to intense ministerial interest and intervention.

Since those who opposed the transfer of education and training to the Northern Territory could not stop the process, advocating for an arms' length commission was the next best remedy to the perceived problems of a nationally important function falling into the hands of an 'ill-prepared and inexperienced' government. Heatley (1990, p. 116) believes that the establishment of a commission or statutory authority for education and training had never been a viable option for the Territory Executive's consideration prior to self-government. This view is supported by the contents of a letter written on 3 March 1978 by Ken Jones, the Commonwealth Education Department's Secretary, to the Northern Territory Director-General of the Department of Chief Secretary and member of the trustworthy senior inner circle, Martyn Finger, in which the view was provided that:

> the most appropriate system for the Northern Territory would be a single administration under ministerial control covering policy formulation at all levels of education. It would probably be necessary to amend the Darwin Community College Ordinance to specify that responsibility for broader policy development in the tertiary area is vested in the minister and not in the Darwin Community College Council (Northern Territory Archives Service 1977–1979).

In preparation for the legislative program that would provide the mechanisms for the Northern Territory Government to assume responsibility for education and training on 1 July 1979, Robertson established an Education Advisory Group on 11 May 1978. This group's membership consisted of representatives of the major pressure groups and had highly restricted terms of reference to guide their task of consulting with Territorians and making recommendations to the minister on the preferred structure of educational administration post-handover.

The Education Advisory Group held public consultations and received written submissions. The contributions were almost exclusively from the same lobby groups that had dominated the discussions for the past two years. In a further demonstration of fine political instinct that characterises successful Northern Territory politicians, one analysis reports that:

> given the late establishment of the Education Advisory Group and the extremely short period within which it had to operate, it appears that general community input into matters relating to the transfer of education was not a matter of high priority with the Northern Territory Government (Urvett, Heatley & Alcorta 1980, p. 55).

Guided by the terms of reference, the Education Advisory Group's recommendations included a department of education with a TAFE branch answering to a fully responsible minister through a permanent department head while the Darwin Community College was recommended to be a separate body corporate that would follow Northern Territory Government policy and direction (Education Advisory Group 1978, p. 1). They also proposed that the vexed matter of TAFE coordination be achieved through an Education Advisory Council that would provide advice to the minister on all levels of education. This Council would incorporate the existing Further Education Council as a specialist advisory body on vocational education and training (Education Advisory Group 1978, p. 13) because all post-school education and training was to be part of the coordinated system of education envisaged for the Northern Territory by the new government. Robertson tabled this group's report in the November 1978 sittings of the Legislative Assembly, and Cabinet commenced consideration of the recommendations during their meeting held on 22 December 1978 (Northern Territory Archives Service 1977–2003b).

The Cabinet notes supporting the proposed legislation contained provision to give the minister power to appoint or approve the appointment of staff to the Darwin Community College (Section 11b) and to transfer the employment responsibilities from the Darwin Community College Council to the minister (Northern Territory Archives Service 1977–2003b). Additionally, 'the powers of the Darwin Community College to assess the needs for education and training courses throughout the Territory, and to make provision to meet those needs, should be curtailed'. Finally, it was proposed that the new Director-General of Education should enforce the legislative requirements in all areas of post-school education except for the daily operations of the community college. Robertson went on to inform his Cabinet colleagues 'that the major concern of the Darwin Community College would appear to be a belief that the autonomy of the college is under threat', but dismisses the issue as speculation guided by self-interest (Northern Territory Archives Service 1977–2003b).

Figure 21. Darwin Community College looking towards Alawa, April 1979.
Source: Creator Unknown. PH0095/0217. Northern Territory Government Photographer Collection, Northern Territory Library.

Berzins and Loveday (1999, p. 54) recount that 'the Darwin Community College was greatly alarmed by the prospect of subordination to the Department of Education and protested strongly in November'. In the December Cabinet meeting, Robertson tabled a letter from the Chairman of the Darwin Community College Staff Association, Alan Powell. These 10 single-spaced pages vigorously attacked the Education Advisory Group recommendations by rejecting an Education Department TAFE branch and the concept of a single Education Advisory Council to advise the minister, instead arguing for a separate Post-Compulsory Advisory Council (Northern Territory Archives Service 1977–2003b).

After deliberating, Cabinet endorsed a repeal of the *Darwin Community College Act 1973* and replaced it with one that 'curtailed' the college's powers over vocational education and training provision. This made the terms and conditions for Darwin Community College staffing subject to the approval of the Administrator; renamed the position that would head the Department of Education to 'Secretary'; and agreed to form a Post-School Advisory Council to advise the minister as a separate body from the Education Advisory Council, whose focus would now be on schooling up to year 12 (Northern Territory Archives Service 1977–2003b). The federal minister's Further and Technical Advisory Council was disbanded and replaced by the Post-School Advisory Council, which was appointed by Minister Robertson on 12 November 1979 and held its first meeting in February 1980 (Northern Territory Archives Service 1980–1982b).

Dealing with the Darwin Community College was only one of many changes in the vocational education and training landscape following the functional transfer to the new Northern Territory Government on 1 July 1979. From September 1974, the former South Australian-operated Adult Education Centre, operating out of the old Alice Springs High School buildings at Anzac Oval, had been redesignated as the Alice Springs Community College. While it was operationally a part of the Darwin Community College, there was a local advisory council. During the period 1975–79, complaints about remote control, previously aimed at Canberra, appeared at the Northern Territory level with Alice Springs residents being quite critical of the management of the college being based in Darwin, some 1,500 kilometres away. In April 1979, the college decided to take up an offer from the Education Department for independent management of day-to-day operations and the newly named Community College of Central Australia was transferred from the Darwin Community College to the Northern Territory Government on 1 July 1979 (Berzins & Loveday 1999, p. 56).

This separation was also undertaken because of 'the Minister for Education's [Robertson] desire to decentralise decision-making and encourage community participation' (Northern Territory Archives Service 1984–1991a). It is more than mere coincidence that Robertson's electorate of Gillen covered a large portion of urban Alice Springs—this was a clear example of a local member responding to a major issue in his constituency. A ceaseless debate about how much higher education should or could be offered in Alice Springs by the local institution accompanied the Community College of Central Australia being placed under the control of the Northern Territory Education Department's Director of TAFE, Geoff Chard. In advising Minister Robertson on how to respond to aspirations held by some locals for the new college to become more than a TAFE college along the lines of the Darwin Community College, Chard recommended that it 'would be prudent for both practical and political reasons to nip these visions in the bud' (quoted in Berzins & Loveday 1999, p. 56). Expectations were managed and the Darwin Community College remained the sole provider of advanced and higher education throughout the Northern Territory.

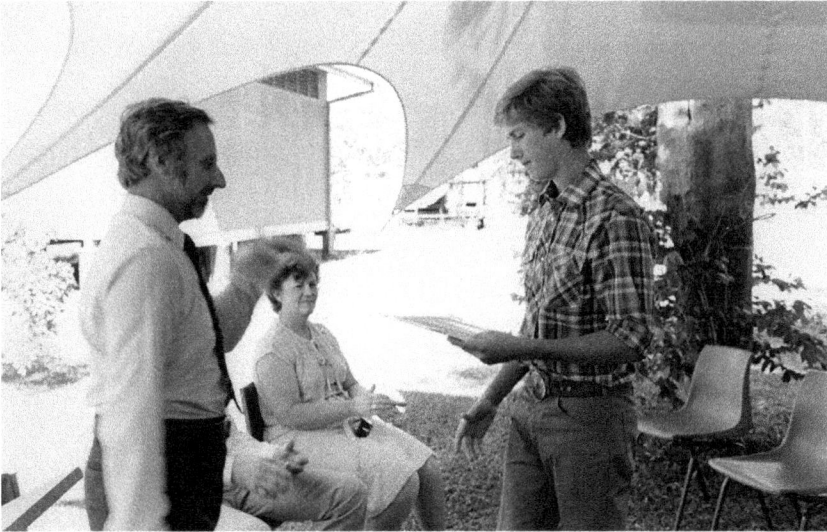

Figure 22. Geoff Chard (Left).
Source: Creator Unknown, PH0703/0063, Tschirner Collection, Northern Territory Library.

In other electorates around the territory, the various activities being undertaken at the Batchelor Vocational Training Centre, including the Aboriginal Teacher Education Course, were to come under the auspices of a revamped organisation—the Batchelor College of TAFE in 1979 (Uibo 1993, p. 29). After an extended period of intense lobbying by both the community and local members of the Legislative Assembly (Northern Territory Archives Service 1977–1979), Cabinet agreed to act upon the *Katherine Rural College Planning Committee Report* (Katherine Rural College Planning Committee 1976) and establish what would commence as the Katherine Rural Education Centre in 1979 as well. On another front, the 25 May 1979 Cabinet meeting decided to finally act upon recommendations from the 1960s reports on education to establish a technical high school in Darwin. However, the Director of TAFE, Geoff Chard, responded that the matter could not be progressed 'primarily due to insufficient data' and Minister Robertson approved keeping 'the matter under review as suggested' (Northern Territory Archives Service 1981). Each of these moves were aimed at increasing access to training throughout the Northern Territory and demonstrating the hallmark behaviour associated with ministerial responsiveness to the perceived needs of local electorates. In spite of several bursts of enthusiasm in Cabinet over the years, the technical high school first mooted for Darwin in the 1960s has yet to materialise.

However, these actions to increase access to vocational training and create space for more local influence in the operations of the provider institutions was not just a set of random acts. On the contrary, they were part of a very carefully thought out strategy being guided by the Chief Minister, Paul Everingham. The matter of an education policy review by the Darwin Branch of the Country Liberal Party led by the former member for Fannie Bay, Grant Tambling, is canvassed by Everingham in a memo, dated 27 October 1978, to his Private Secretary, Bryce McNair:

> I am not anxious to rock the education boat before the 1980 election, nor am I keen to see either the Community College or the Department of Education exercising a dominant role in Northern Territory; and bearing in mind that if I do not put in something significant now Tambling will overpower this Party Committee that he is chairman of, and bring in some sort of report, creating a huge empire for the Community College (Northern Territory Archives Service 1977–1979).

Ministerial control of the education and training function was clearly at the forefront of the Chief Minister's thinking when constructing this memo, as were the electoral consequences of being perceived as too aggressive in asserting authority over the disparate groups with an interest in training. On the other hand, the option to not take action was never seriously considered by Cabinet. In line with the guiding theme of 'starting all things anew' in the Northern Territory, the freshly minted ministers had one last task to complete in vocational education and training before the end of the year. As a consequence of passing the *Industries Training Act 1979,* the Apprentices Board was replaced by the Industry Training Commission to ensure 'that a trained and skilled workforce is ready to meet the challenges of industry and government in the years ahead' (Northern Territory Industry Training Commission 1981, pp. 1–2). The annual report also notes that there were 1,007 apprentices indentured at this time and that

21 trades required that local students be sent interstate for off-the-job training. The Northern Territory Industries Training Commission (1981) consisted of 5 divisions:

- manpower planning;
- training and development;
- trade training;
- industries training; and
- administration.

Figure 23. Industry Training Commission, first meeting, 1 July 1980, Geoff Chard at far right.
Source: Creator Unknown PH0107/0194, Northern Territory Government Photographer, Northern Territory Library.

The year 1979 had been a very busy one for the inexperienced Northern Territory Government in asserting Cabinet control over vocational education and training. The powers and geographic reach of the Darwin Community College had been 'curtailed'. Meanwhile, the Department of Education had entered into the direct delivery of training with the establishment of the Katherine Rural Education Centre, Batchelor College of TAFE, the Community College of Central Australia, remote Aboriginal adult education and a migrant English program. The Apprentices Board had also been replaced by the Industry Training Commission and new ministerial advisory arrangements had been put in place with advent of the Post-School Advisory Council. The leaders of each of these new entities was acutely aware of the priorities of an interventionist government driven by a mandate for change after decades of distant colonial rule, social experimentation and a level of benign neglect. With an election due in 1980, Everingham's preference for 'not rocking the education boat' was achieved while ensuring that there was no doubt as to who was in charge.

The general election held on 7 June 1980 provided the residents of the Northern Territory a chance to express their views on the progress towards self-government. The election essentially maintained the status quo with the Country Liberal Party only losing one seat, Nhulunbuy, to the Australian Labor Party and the single independent, Dawn Lawrie, being re-elected. This allowed the government to claim yet a further mandate to negotiate the handover of a variety of other state-type functions, such as the employment of teachers and adult educators. The major responsibilities that were not handed over included the non-controversial area of industrial relations, while Aboriginal land rights, uranium mining and control of the two major national parks, Uluru and Kakadu, were highly contested and are still the source of severe irritation for successive Northern Territory governments.

Figure 24. Jim Eedle.
Source: Creator Unknown, PH0703/0014, Tschirner Collection, Northern Territory Library.

The period leading up to the 1980 election was also very significant for another reason—the financial year 1979–80 would serve as the baseline year to determine how much funding the Commonwealth would furnish to the Northern Territory to carry out the functions of a state. Heatley (1990, p. 123) points out that the Commonwealth erred on the side of generosity in the early years to ensure that self-government did not fail. The Northern Territory Government was also doing everything it could do to ensure that this base year funding could be maximised. In a memo from Minister Robertson dated 11 September 1978 to the head of the Department of Education, Jim Eedle, the eventual fate of Dhupuma College, an Aboriginal boarding college near Nhulunbuy in East Arnhem Land, was discussed. Robertson proposes:

> What I am saying is that if we can get the money in our base year, it is then available for other purposes in education if we were to subsequently close Dhupuma College. I would suggest you destroy this memorandum (Northern Territory Archives Service 1977–1979).

Figure 25. Dhupuma College, February 1975.
Source: Creator Unknown, PH0703/0506, Tschirner Collection, Northern Territory Library.

Dhupuma College had been opened by the Prime Minister, Gough Whitlam, in 1972 as the Northern Territory's second Indigenous boarding school. It used portions of an abandoned missile tracking station and featured a number of specialist vocational training facilities. Despite its symbolic importance as a sign of the Commonwealth's support for greater Aboriginal self-determination, by the time of self-government the college facilities had become quite dilapidated and the number of students attending was small. However, in keeping with his soon-to-be minister's wishes, Jim Eedle, issued a media release detailing his recommendation to the Federal Education Minister Carrick for Dhupuma to remain open in 1979. The college did continue operations, but was consequently closed in the following year after education responsibility had been transferred to the Northern Territory Government.

In 1980, the Northern Territory Government brought in a consultant to develop an education specification for the Community College of Central Australia to guide the three-year construction schedule of a new campus on land adjacent to the Sadadeen High School in the New Eastside residential development of Alice Springs. According to the author of the final report (Pattinson 1980, p. 2), the government wanted to have a college that would give effect to a TAFE-only institution, as recommended by Chard the previous year, and would promote access to training and education by facilitating 'self-realisation, self-understanding and self-development' by 'deliberately encouraging the social, cultural, aesthetic, economic health and development of the community'. In addition, the Community College would develop both 'link' and 'transitional-vocational type courses for students' of Alice Springs schools 'who had no wish in attempting matriculation' (Pattinson 1980, pp. 14–16).

Pattinson (1980, p. 5) also reported that 'to date the Community College of Central Australia has not made considerable inroads into Aboriginal education. There are no full-time Aboriginal students at the college and part-time Aboriginal enrolments have been estimated at less than 5 per cent'. In response to this miniscule number of Aboriginal students, Cabinet decided in December 1979 to purchase a property and basic set of buildings in the Priest Street light industrial area of Alice Springs to serve as a space for a more culturally inclusive training facility. In 1980, the Centre for Appropriate Technology opened in these premises and, over a number of years, developed into a completely independent organisation with its own Aboriginal-controlled board. The Centre for

Appropriate Technology has gone on to open branches interstate and has also expanded into the former CSIRO buildings adjacent to the Desert Knowledge Precinct to the south of Alice Springs.

A series of Northern Territory Government decisions that were made in 1979 and 1980 regarding how vocational education and training would be conducted laid the foundations for the separation of policy, funding and delivery functions that remains in place today. Compared to the other states, these decisions have served the government well in terms of public policy flexibility. The operationally messy teaching of students and apprentices was assigned to two organisations. The Darwin Community College's offerings, including the provision of advanced education, were concentrated around the capital city. This left the Department of Education with control over a disparate group of institutions and programs based in regional areas of the jurisdiction. After the organisational and bureaucratic restructuring of the previous year, 1980 saw the Northern Territory Cabinet make a series of high-level vocational education and training policy decisions intended to provide the missing components of the single education and training system envisaged by Everingham when he spoke at the teachers' federation conference several years earlier.

In the Cabinet meeting held on 26 March 1980, the ministers held preliminary discussions 'to consider the establishment of a University for the Northern Territory within a Territory system' (Northern Territory Archives Service 1980b). Their deliberations were directed by a joint submission prepared by the head of the Education Department, Jim Eedle, and the Principal of the Darwin Community College, Joe Flint. These sometime protagonists and strong advocates for their own institutions had recommended a multi-college/university model growing from the existing Darwin Community College. When Cabinet next considered the matter of a university in July 1980, it 'approved the introduction of a Bill for an Act to establish a Planning Authority for the University of the Northern Territory' (Northern Territory Archives Service 1980b). The future of vocational education and training was now firmly tied to the extension of advanced and higher education provision in the Northern Territory.

In another major policy area, the Cabinet meeting of 7 May 1980 endorsed 'an integrated approach for Aboriginal communities' based upon three background documents:

- *Development of Aboriginal rural towns;*
- *A five year community development process towards a fair social influence for Aboriginal people;* and
- *Aboriginal vocational training* (Northern Territory Archives Service 1980c).

With the formal adoption of the concept of community development and policies built upon local responsibility supported by adult educators, all Northern Territory government departments were encouraged to employ the process and work through local community councils. In particular:

> Cabinet noted that the community development process increases employment opportunities for Aboriginal people and their need for skills and that the Department of Education will need to respond to this. There will be many skills required by Aboriginal communities so that they can seize these new initiatives. Vocational training, if developed with communities, is the logical coordination point for the many educational requirements of these new responsibilities (Northern Territory Archives Service 1980c, p. 5).

In the Cabinet paper *Aboriginal vocational training* (Northern Territory Archives Service 1980c, p. 4), the new public management style for the provision of training was also set out and would be used to guide the work of adult educators based in Aboriginal communities:

> The policy direction is for the Department [of Education] to provide resources and skill training, manpower, technology, buildings and funds in a form that is determined by communities. Eventually all training would be contracted by communities. The Department would provide a consulting service on contract to communities to provide all educational training services in a form they require.

The development of the Centre for Appropriate Technology in Alice Springs was one of the first concrete actions taken by government to implement this policy of self-management and self-realisation. The prominence given to vocational education and training also reinforced its long-standing use as a philanthropic intervention aimed at improving the lives of a target population. While the mantra of community development in Aboriginal training would guide much operational activity for the next two decades, the reality was that the ministers were not willing or able to relinquish control of vocational education and training policy and finance.

Nevertheless, with training delivery now 'outsourced' to the Darwin Community College, semi-autonomous colleges/centres and local Aboriginal communities, the Northern Territory Government confirmed and strengthened the policy role of the Industries Training Commission. In the Cabinet meeting of 30 July 1980 (Northern Territory Archives Service 1980d), in-principle approval was given to the commission's four-year action plan that included objectives to:

- introduce competency-based training to the Northern Territory;
- research the tasks and skills in over 160 major Northern Territory occupations to set up appropriate training programs;
- establish the Industries Training Commission's role as 'the main training' agency in apprentice, occupational and industries training as well as manpower forecasting and planning;
- assist Northern Territory industry in the development of its most vital resources, those of manpower, with the ultimate aim of promoting industrial growth;
- research vocational education and training; and
- promote training to Northern Territory industry.

In approving the above plan, Cabinet decided that where a functional task is to be carried out by the Industries Training Commission, it will utilise the agency within the Technical and Further Education (TAFE) sector of the Northern Territory Government, that is, the Education Department.

In the same meeting, Cabinet agreed to withdraw a part of the overall submission dealing with the Industries Training Commission's desire to move into the delivery arena through the establishment of a skills training centre in the former powerhouse buildings in the inner Darwin suburb of Stuart Park. The proposed centre was to be under the control of the Commission and provide off-the-job apprentice training while serving as the employer of Northern Territory Government apprentices. Much of the financial modelling in support of the skills training centre was based upon using the Commonwealth Rebate for Apprentices in Full-time Training (CRAFT) and it was envisaged that the centre would expand to private employers over time.

In a demonstration of the pervasive influence of colonial socialism, business and industry maintained pressure on the Northern Territory Government to provide for a more skilled workforce even when they were not prepared to employ apprentices in the private sector. The Industries Training Commission returned to Cabinet with a revised submission for the skills training centre based upon a significantly reduced budget for 40 first-year apprentices and confirmation that 'Darwin Community College advise there is no capacity for this number of additional apprentices without building expansions' (Northern Territory Archives Service 1980e, p. 4). On 8 October 1980, Cabinet approved the establishment of the skills training centre as an exception to the general policy of pushing delivery of training away from policy functions. The new skills centre would have to use trainers drawn from existing employees of the Electricity Commission and Department of Transport and Works. The business case relied upon the realisation of $85,000 from CRAFT sources to support the Northern Territory Government's commitment of $257,000.

Figure 26. Training Centre, Stuart Park, September 1981.
Source: Creator Unknown, PH0107/0340, Northern Territory Government Photographer Collection, Northern Territory Library.

In September 1980, Minister Robertson responded to continued bureaucratic boundary skirmishes between the Industries Training Commission, the Darwin Community College and the Northern Territory Education Department by commissioning a review to be conducted by the Assistant Director-General (Technical) of the Western Australian Education Department to 'report on options relating to the future development of Technical and Further Education in the Northern Territory' (Northern Territory Archives Service 1981). In his report that was handed to the minister in December, Peter Forrest found that the existing system suffered from a 'lack of coordination' and the Northern Territory Government should develop 'a TAFE Authority based on the Industries Training Commission' (Northern Territory Archives Service 1981). Additionally, Forrest rejected the so-called Alaska-model of a multi-college university that had been endorsed by Cabinet in favour of keeping vocational education and training as a separate sector. In his covering letter to Robertson dated 2 December 1980, Forrest states 'the present situation in the Northern Territory concerning post-school education is undoubtedly troubled and complex' (Northern Territory Archives Service 1981).

In the end, Forrest's advice was not followed. The ability to use Commonwealth TAFE capital infrastructure funding would allow Darwin Community College programs to be reconsolidated at the Brinkin campus by closing down the converted Winnellie warehouse that had been used since Cyclone Tracy. In addition, there would a number of potential efficiency benefits, such as a shared library, from creating a single campus that could be more easily modified to cater for the planned university. Again, the importance of ministerial discretion in vocational education and training outweighed the independence of the sector. In fact, Cabinet had already decided in meeting number 100 on 16 April 1980 (Northern Territory Archives Service 1977–2003c) to fund a range of vocational training building projects by allocating nearly $6 million in the period 1981–83 to the Darwin Community College for design and documentation for a school of general studies and a school of business and management. Funds were also earmarked for the survey and design of stage one for the Community College of Central Australia at the Sadadeen site. The Northern Territory TAFE infrastructure priority list that had been submitted to the Commonwealth Tertiary Education Commission also included facilities for Batchelor College, the Katherine Rural Education Centre, a technical high school in Darwin and yet another group of buildings for both Darwin Community College and the Community College of Central Australia.

In other actions taken during 1980, Cabinet approved (decision number 1162) amending the *Industries Training Commission Act* to make provision for a member of the Commission to be appointed on the basis of residing outside of Darwin in order to represent regional interests (Northern

Territory Archives Service 1980a). The intended tertiary educational future for the Alice Springs region was also reaffirmed when Cabinet accepted a recommendation of the Post-School Advisory Council that:

> the Community College of Central Australia develop as an institution emphasising courses identified with the technical and further education (TAFE) sector rather than the advanced or university sectors of tertiary education, although there could be provision for marginal development through tutorials, library resources and associate diplomas (Northern Territory Archives Service 1980–1982b, pp. 20–22).

By the start of 1981, Syd Saville was in place as the Secretary of the Education Department, having replaced Jim Eedle who was appointed by Minister Robertson to head up the University Planning Authority. While government had not been able to act upon the Forrest Report's specific recommendations on the future of vocational education and training, the 'troubling complexity' of the sector still occupied both bureaucratic and political considerations. Following normal protocol, Saville had circulated a proposed Cabinet submission on the 'Administration of post-secondary education other than university' to relevant government departments. As one of those elite senior public servants who was trusted by Cabinet, the Coordinator-General of the Chief Minister's Department, Ray McHenry, wrote back to Saville on 18 February 1981 commenting upon the proposal to establish a new statutory authority to guide vocational education and training in the Northern Territory:

> Without questioning the fact that coordination may be necessary, this reads to me as an exercise in bureaucracy gone rampant. In my view the submission lacks any political sensitivity given the government has only recently established the Industries Training Commission as a statutory authority. Whilst it may not be my place to say so, I observe what I regard as a proliferation of agencies destructive to the long term interests of those needing post-secondary education in the Northern Territory (Northern Territory Archives Service 1981).

Figure 27. Ray McHenry.
Source: Creator Unknown. PH0416/0006, ABC TV Collection, Northern Territory Library.

On 17 March 1981, Robertson wrote to Saville directing him to convene a meeting of the heads of the major organisations bickering over the control of TAFE on the basis that 'I have long been concerned to the lack of coordination, and at times spirit of cooperation, in the area of post-school education' (Northern Territory Archives Service 1981). As a result of the ministerial direction, Saville convened a meeting on 31 March 1981 and attendees included Jim Eedle from the University

Planning Authority; Geoff Chard representing the TAFE Division of the Education Department; Nan Giese in her role as the Darwin Community College Council chair; Joe Flint as Principal of the Darwin Community College; Harold Garner from the Post-School Advisory Council; and Bob Woodward on behalf of the Industries Training Commission. Minister Robertson approved most of the contents of Saville's long written report and the list of numerous recommendations aimed at improving TAFE coordination, however, two items stand out in terms of improving public policy. The participants agreed that there:

> is a real need to distinguish between the coordination role and the operational role within the TAFE area. It was felt that any unit involved with policy and planning matters should not be also involved in the delivery of TAFE programs.

> The Secretary of the Education Department should provide you with coordinated advice on policy development and planning of TAFE in the Northern Territory (Northern Territory Archives Service 1981).

Additionally, to assist the Secretary in the provision of this policy advice, a TAFE Planning Committee was to be formed and chaired by the Education Department Director of TAFE and the membership would include the principals of the Darwin Community College; the Community College of Central Australia; Batchelor College; and the Katherine Rural Education Centre. Membership of this planning group would also include the Chair of the Industries Training Commission and the Education Department's spokesman on 'extra-mural programs', which were mostly delivered by the adult educators located in Aboriginal communities. An important task for this committee would be to make recommendations for future funding priorities. In addition, the Planning Committee would take over responsibility for the accreditation of TAFE awards from the Post-School Advisory Council (Northern Territory Archives Service 1982d, p. 12).

As the year progressed, it became apparent that neither the recommendations from the March meeting that had been accepted by the minister or the existence of the TAFE Planning Committee had resolved the turf wars over vocational education and training. By August 1981, in his report to Robertson on the result of a review into TAFE functions in the Education Department, Saville (Northern Territory Archives Service 1981) proposes 'the establishment of a powerful TAFE Policy and Planning Unit' that 'separates within the Education Department the operations of TAFE from the Policy Unit'. Saville goes on to make a claim for dominance of the vocational education and training space when he states, 'Finally, and most importantly, the TAFE reorganisation provides for the integration of TAFE activities in the Department'. In November 1981, Robertson endorsed the establishment of the TAFE Policy and Planning Unit in the Education Department (Northern Territory Archives Service 1981).

In June 1981, Director of TAFE Chard had commenced a demarcation dispute between his Education Department, the Department of Chief Minister and the Industries Training Commission. On the basis of the government's integrated community development approach, he was seeking control of all Aboriginal training as a discrete function that would result in 'industry training' being the only role left for the Commission (Northern Territory Archives Service 1980–1982a). Chard was making a claim for his staff, adult educators that were in most of the larger Aboriginal communities, to coordinate all education and training at the community level. This was justified on the grounds that the Education Department was the only agency with staff already on location and that community development and education were inextricably bound together (Loveday & Young 1984, p. 4). In a 1982 response to yet another dispute over coordination and control over vocational education and training, the Chief Minister established the Aboriginal Training and Employment Board of Management consisting of the Director of Aboriginal Liaison from his department; the Secretary of the Department of Education; and the chair of the Industries Training Commission (Loveday & Young 1984, p. 4). There is no evidence that this board achieved any major outcomes and the creation of the Vocational Training Commission later in the same year apparently removed the need for this high-level coordinating body that eventually dropped out of existence.

In yet another example of the high levels of disputation, on 25 September 1981, Saville (Northern Territory Archives Service 1981) wrote to Robertson complaining about the Industries Training Commission's propensity to 'dictate to educational institutions as is now the case' in regard to the educational planning for programs to be offered at the Katherine Rural Education Centre. Saville continued:

> I recommend that you direct Mr Woodward to confine the objective of his seminar to the assessment of present and future requirements of the Primary Production Industries for skilled and semi-skilled labour with a view to making this information available to my academic planners.

While Cabinet had been strongly lobbied by a variety of groups to establish the Katherine Rural Education Centre on the basis of the 1976 Commonwealth report, not all parties were in agreement as to the need, capacity and programs that might eventuate. In response to these mixed messages, Robertson sought the assistance of Trevor Sterling from Queensland's Ithaca College of TAFE to analyse the operations of the two-year-old rural college at Katherine. In response to the review, representatives of the Australian Institute of Agricultural Science wrote directly to Minister Robertson indicating the belief:

> that the continuation and expansion of the Katherine Rural Education Centre (KREC) is not the appropriate course of action at this stage of the Territory's development due to poor employment prospects, small student numbers, lack of new technologies, lack of practical experience and the high cost when compared to sending students to Queensland (Northern Territory Archives Service 1981).

In a briefing minute from the Education Department to the minister, Director of TAFE Chard provides Robertson with information to refute the major complaints from the Institute but also reinforces the philanthropic characteristics of vocational education and training: 'The major benefit, however, on which the Northern Territory Government places high emphasis would not be available, namely, social stability and cohesiveness through local education provision' (Northern Territory Archives Service 1981). In the end, further development of the rural college was endorsed by Cabinet in the meeting of 16 July 1981 when the government appointed two of the trustworthy senior public servants (Martyn Finger and Bryce Cameron) to the Advisory Council; approved the creation of four full-time positions including a farm manager; agreed to install demountable buildings for staff and students for accommodation; and continued investment in more infrastructure as resources became available to further develop the property situated some 16 kilometres to the north of Katherine.

Ministerial control and intentions regarding the future of the rural college were made clear to Saville in a memo dated 9 August 1981 from Robertson's ministerial officer, Matti Urvett: 'Would you please ensure that the appropriate action is taken to ensure that the Government's wishes in this matter are carried out' (Northern Territory Archives Service 1980–1982a).

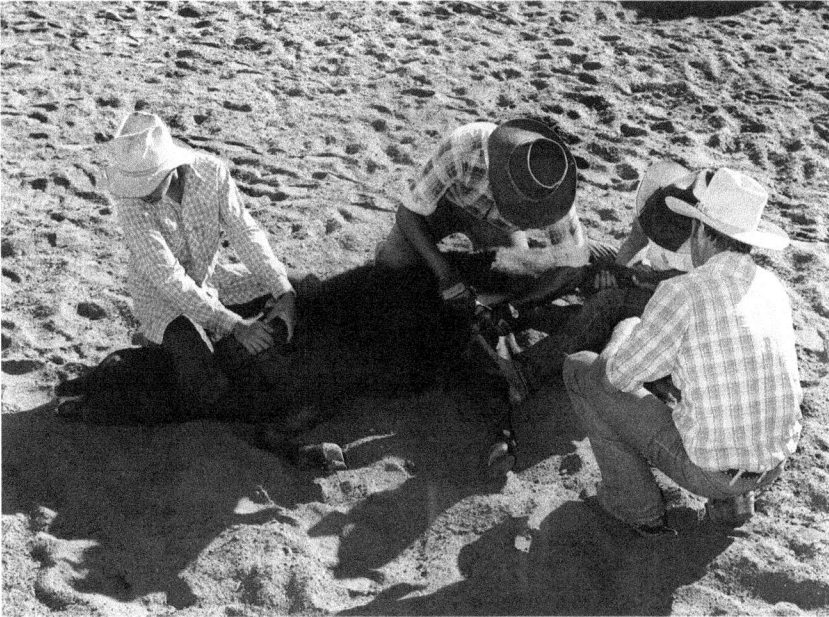

Figure 28. Training. Calf-tagging training for secondary school students.
Source: Creator Unknown. PH0703/0033. Tschirner Collection, Northern Territory Library.

In this same time period, similar skirmishes were also taking place in Robertson's Alice Springs electorate over the development of a training facility at Gillen House. The intended outcome was the production of a skilled tourism and hospitality workforce that would support business operators responding to the government's high economic priority accorded to the sector. The new government had made a massive investment of public funds to develop this industry in order to drive economic growth and had capitalised heavily in up-market Sheraton hotels in Alice Springs and Darwin in addition to the development of more hotels and a new Yulara township near Uluru. While some industry figures and the Darwin Community College had lobbied for the specialist training infrastructure to be built in Darwin, Cabinet decided to convert the former Baptist Hostel in Gillen on the basis that Alice Springs had a larger tourism market at the time. Local members of the Legislative Assembly were unmercifully lobbied by public servants, the Darwin Community College and tourism operators supporting either the Alice Springs or Darwin option. In his role as Director of TAFE, Chard wrote to Robertson seeking clarification about his intentions for the future operations of Gillen House in October of 1981:

At one stage it was on your mind that one of the accommodation blocks at Gillen House might be used by apprentices whilst on block release attending the Community College of Central Australia but you have since advised the Secretary that this is no longer your wish because you perceived problems associated with catering for the apprentices (Northern Territory Archives Service 1980–1982a).

In his reply, which approved the development of a plan to accommodate apprentices as well as provide tourism and hospitality training at Gillen House, Robertson replied, 'This was the result of your advice. I would still like to see full utilisation of the facility' (Northern Territory Archives Service 1980–1982a).

Figure 29. Restaurant interior, Gillen House, Alice Springs.
Source: Creator Unknown, PH0703/0204, Tschirner Collection, Northern Territory Library.

In a rather succinct summary of events that took place throughout 1981, Saville wrote to Robertson complaining yet again over the lack of clarity and separation of education and training functions. He proposes that after meetings between the belligerent bodies 'those matters where agreement cannot be reached will need to be brought before you for resolution and, in any case, some legislative change may prove necessary, subject to the Solicitor-General's assessment' (Northern Territory Archives Service 1980–1982a).

By the second half of 1982, the incessantly high levels of disputation over the command and operation of vocational education and training made ministerial intervention inevitable. The important decision-making role of the Minister for Education was reaffirmed in the effort to reduce the levels of conflict over vocational education and training. Geoff Chard had been appointed to chair the Industry Training Commission and was trying to go over Robertson's head by involving the Chief Minister in discussions to introduce a new statutory authority to manage TAFE in the Northern Territory. On 25 August 1982, Chard wrote to Robertson suggesting the urgent need for a meeting between the Chief Minister, the Education Minister, the Secretary of the Education Department, the Chair of the Industries Training Commission and the Public Service Commissioner, to discuss what would eventually become the Vocational Training Commission. Robertson's handwritten response in the margins of the memo states 'No meeting if I can help it' that was followed by an unsigned notation in another person's handwriting 'meeting cancelled' (Northern Territory Archives Service 1980–1982a).

Once he had considered the political and organisational implications, Robertson took a submission to Cabinet on 22 September 1982 where the ministers:

> approved the proposal to amend the Industries Training Act 1979 to create the Northern Territory Vocational Training Commission which combines the present functions of the Industries Training Commission and those concerned with TAFE policy formulation and planning (Northern Territory Archives Service 1982a).

The Vocational Training Commission would have 14 members comprised of:

- a public servant as the chair;
- another public servant as the deputy chair;
- three employer representatives;
- three employee representatives;
- the Secretary of the Education Department or nominee;
- a representative of the Darwin Community College;
- a representative of the Community College of Central Australia; and
- another three members appointed by the minister.

In describing the perceived shortcomings of the existing TAFE Planning Committee, Robertson's submission states that its 'membership is inappropriate as it comprises mainly operational people; industry and the community sectors are not adequately represented. Such representation ensures TAFE maintains its relevance to its consumers' (Northern Territory Archives Service 1982a, p. 2). It is also noted that the minister had taken administrative action to implement the proposed new structure to rationalise existing functions and this included setting up an Interim Further Education Committee to replace the TAFE Planning Committee, effective from 31 August 1982. Cabinet finally endorsed the draft amendments to the Act on 12 November 1982 (Northern Territory Archives Service 1982c). By this time, the former Director of TAFE in the Education Department and (briefly) Chair of the Industries Training Commission, Geoff Chard, had been installed as the Chair of the Vocational Training Commission.

Ministerial choice also featured in the determination of the new commission's membership. The government had decided that employer and employee organisations would submit lists of names to the minister who would then choose the member of the commission to represent those interests. The Northern Territory Teachers Federation's Di Foggo complained to Minister Robertson about the process and expressed her belief that her union should be able to make the choice. On 26 November 1982, Robertson responded, 'Surely common sense and common courtesy would dictate that such procedures are a matter for the minister concerned' (Northern Territory Archives Service 1980–1982a). The Teachers Federation eventually and unhappily provided three names to the minister for his consideration. In a related flexing of ministerial muscle, Chard wrote to Robertson on 29 November 1982 to confirm the minister's intention not to accept the Darwin Community College's nominee for the Interim Further Education Committee. 'In discussion with me you indicated your intention not to accept that nomination [of J Flint] and your preference for J Suitor' (Northern Territory Archives Service 1980–1982a).

Chard's unrelenting enthusiasm for battles over control emerged almost immediately in the form of his and Saville's inability to agree on which positions and budget lines would be shifted from the Education Department to the Vocational Training Commission. In a minute to the minister dated 24 November 1982, the Assistant Public Service Commissioner, PJ Bartholomew, supported Chard's broad claim on the basis that the new commission would:

- formulate policy and planning advice on the coordination of TAFE in the Northern Territory;
- handle the preparation of coordinated funding proposals on TAFE to the minister; and
- provide advice to the minister on TAFE funding and building needs (Northern Territory Archives Service 19801982a).

In preparation for the election that was due to be held in 1983, Chief Minister Everingham reshuffled the Cabinet on 1 December 1983. With this change the Member for Fannie Bay, Marshall Perron, assumed responsibility for the education portfolio including vocational education and training. Coinciding with the change of minister, Chard temporarily vacated his position of Chair of the newly created Vocational Training Commission. He describes:

> I spent the whole of 1983 as the Northern Territory (of Australia) Fellow of the Commonwealth Relations Trust at the University of London Institute of Education. I used the opportunity to study a selection of initiatives that have been, or are being taken in England and Wales directed towards preparing young people for employment, further education, or specialised training (Chard 1983, introduction).

Chard's (1983) report, *Enhancing the vocational preparation of youth in the Northern Territory*, set the scene for increased policy interest in the use of vocational education and training in schools and other programs aimed at early school leavers. For example, his commentary (Chard 1983, p. 135) describes the intended outcome of the Participation and Equity Program in addressing youth unemployment by encouraging 'young people to either complete secondary education or participate in other appropriate education or training'—otherwise known as 'earn or learn'. This report was also his swansong to vocational education and training. While Chard briefly returned to the Vocational Training Commission following his time in the United Kingdom, the combination of a different minister, new senior staff in the Education Department and an effective abandonment of the community development process for Aboriginal communities had reduced his influence in the sector. The abolition of the Vocational Training Commission in late 1984 removed not only Chard's formal position it disbanded the arm's-length statutory authority. This change also consolidated vocational education and training policy into the government departmental structure making it subject to even greater levels of ministerial decision-making.

From the end of 1982, an enthusiasm to use vocational training as a public policy response to problems in their portfolios had spread to other Cabinet members. In order to ameliorate a national contraction in the youth labour market and subsequent intense lobbying by local employers, Chief Minister Everingham took a submission to Cabinet that drew together the philanthropic capacity of vocational education and training, the popular desire for government action to solve problems, and the willingness of ministers to make decisions to improve social and economic outcomes for the Northern Territory. In writing his submission to improve 'the employment prospects of Territory school leavers', Everingham stated 'without Government intervention there is likely, therefore, to be a shortfall of around 500 jobs for current and recent Territory school leavers' (Northern Territory Archives Service 1982b). On 1 December 1982, coincidently Perron's first day as Minister for Education, Cabinet agreed to establish a committee of senior public servants to report back on a range of measures to address the projected unemployment problem. Specific remedies to be examined included:

- a system of preferential tendering for major government contracts that would specify numbers of apprentices that must be employed by the successful bidders;
- establishment of a pool of apprentices for private contractors undertaking government projects; and
- preference for local school leavers in entry-level recruitment to the Northern Territory Public Service.

In an October 1983 ministerial statement to the Legislative Assembly, Everingham described his government's planned interventions into the youth labour market, which not only included the original three activities but also added guaranteed employment after completion of higher level training in specific fields, competitive scholarships/cadetships and Northern Territory Public Service job reservation for school leavers (Northern Territory Archives Service 1983b).

The Minister for Housing, Nick Dondas, also envisaged vocational training as a useful response to concerns over a shortage of skilled labour that had been brought to his attention by the construction industry in Alice Springs. Dondas believed that his proposal for an apprenticeship scheme linked to building dwellings for the Housing Commission would align with the other government initiatives to increase school leaver employment prospects. In the Cabinet meeting of 1 March 1983, approval was given for an allocation of $320,000 to create a pool of 10 building trade apprentices and two supervisors to construct five houses each year over a four-year period. The project would be overseen by a Board of Management consisting of representatives from the Vocational Training Commission, the Housing Commission, the Master Builders Association (MBA) and the Community College of Central Australia. In his submission to Cabinet, Dondas proposed:

> It is anticipated that there will be a favourable reaction from the general public in Alice Springs to the news that a new Northern Territory Government initiative is to employ 10 of their school leavers (Northern Territory Archives Service 1983a, p. 6).

Both of these examples demonstrate the private sector's willingness to go to government and seek resolution of their economic and labour market problems. This approach can be aligned with the willingness of Cabinet to use vocational education and training as the vehicle to deliver public funds after a careful calculation of the economic, social and political impact on both the community's perceptions and their ministerial careers. Government intervention was required to address cases of labour market failure. The Chair of the Vocational Training Commission supported the need for the use of public funding by attributing blame for the labour and apprenticeship shortages when he reported that 'the Master Builders Association has agonised over the construction industry's poor training record in the Territory' (Chard 1983, p. 142).

The year 1983 proved to be a significant for several other reasons, including both Commonwealth and Northern Territory elections. Even though there was a massive vote to change the Federal Government with the return of the Labor Party to the treasury benches in March, Territorians again supported the Country Liberal Party's actions with little change to the membership of the Legislative Assembly. After five years, self-government had been firmly established for the Northern Territory and the new Commonwealth Government believed that the 'generous' financial support for the jurisdiction should be reduced and, of course, this was a direct threat to the philanthropic capacities of the local members of the Legislative Assembly. Despite vigorous protests from the Northern Territory Government, the federal Labor Government commenced a program to reduce financial support that some commentators linked to the re-emergence of a general lack of interest in Territory affairs that had been the hallmark of the Commonwealth approach in the 1970s (Heatley 1990, p. 154).

When the Northern Territory achieved self-government, it also became eligible to benefit from the financial and social impact of the Kangan Report on Technical and Further Education and the Commonwealth's generous response that had underpinned the redevelopment and growth of public training institutions right across the nation:

> The period 1975–1982 could be summarised as being one of growth for TAFE as the Kangan committee recommendations were implemented and the TAFE Council continued to support the need for ongoing capital and recurrent funding for TAFE. In many ways, it could be seen to be the 'golden age' for TAFE as it continued to grow, was held in high esteem by governments and finally acquired an identifiable role in the education spectrum. It was also a period of increased Commonwealth intervention in TAFE policies and programs as succeeding government inquiries saw TAFE as a vehicle for implementing change (Goozee 2001, p. 38).

While it would take a few years to build momentum, the Hawke/Keating governments would increasingly come to use the Commonwealth's funding for vocational education and training as a mechanism to both change the national economy and to harness the operations of the state-based TAFE systems to national policy. In order to keep federal TAFE funding flowing, in the face of less generous generic financial support than had accompanied the early days of self-government, the Northern Territory Government had to be very responsive to national economic restructuring, productivity improvements and social agendas. Unlike most of the other states, however, the Northern Territory was well-placed to respond to an activist federal government due to the early decisions not to establish a government-operated TAFE system in favour of new public management styles of contracting delivery to third parties. While the quantum of resources available to support the philanthropic behaviour of Northern Territory ministers was more tightly bound to national priorities, a continued interest in vocational education and training at the Commonwealth level provided an environment that was ripe with policy and program flexibility for the local political masters.

Even though the following TAFE historian's comment is based upon the situation in New South Wales, it also accurately reflects Northern Territory events from 1983 onwards:

> Public education and training was very much a tool of government. With any change of government (state or Commonwealth), came changes to the public sector in general and to technical and further education policies, in particular (Goozee 2013, p. 237).

In the Northern Territory during 1982–83, the bureaucratic and institutional struggles over the control of vocational education and training continued unabated, resulting in Cabinet receiving a continuous barrage of advice about how to best coordinate the sector. The creation of the Vocational Training Commission had removed yet another function from the Post-School Advisory Council whose main activity had become the development of funding submissions to the Commonwealth for advanced education courses being delivered by the Darwin Community College and 'coordination across' the three sectors of education (Northern Territory Archives Service 1983c). Government policy was for the Vocational Training Commission to 'become the single accrediting authority for all technical and further education and training courses conducted in the Northern Territory' in order to remove the 'very considerable duplication of effort' that was being expended in assessing and meeting the training needs of the Northern Territory community (Robertson 1982, p. 2997).

Even though the Northern Territory Government was very active in asserting its dominance over the training sector, Cabinet had to be on constant guard against those people and organisations who would seek to bypass local control by going directly to the Commonwealth. The recommendations put forward by the Alice Springs–based Tangentyere Council (1984) in *Employment and training needs of Aboriginal town campers in Alice Springs* provide a perfect example of this type of challenge to Northern Territory Government authority. This report was prepared for the First Assistant Secretary of the Commonwealth Department of Employment and Industrial Relations, Michael Keating, and handed over during his visit to Central Australia. While acknowledging that the various government training organisations had a role to play in 'addressing the scandalous rate of unemployment in the Aboriginal population' (Tangentyere Council 1984, p. 2), 'the right kind of training will never be available unless an Aboriginal controlled organisation is at the centre of the development of training programs' and the Institute for Aboriginal Development was singled out for the role (Tangentyere Council 1984, p. 9). In its bid to deal directly with the Commonwealth and establish Aboriginal control and direction of training programs, the report also suggested that 'the simple solution would be [for the Commonwealth] to recognise Tangentyere as a training institution and fund it accordingly' (Tangentyere Council 1984, Appendix II, p. iii). While there is little evidence of how the Commonwealth reacted to these suggestions, it does demonstrate that certain groups were willing to challenge Northern Territory ministerial control of vocational education and training by using the rhetoric of community development.

Another federal election was held on 1 December 1984 at which the Hawke Labor Government was returned. The most immediate political impact in the Northern Territory was the resignation of the first Chief Minister, Paul Everingham. He stood for the single House of Representatives seat and won the election for the Country Liberal Party. The member for Barkly, Ian Tuxworth, became the Northern Territory's second Chief Minister and wasted no time in announcing sweeping changes to the post-school education landscape. On 20 December 1984, the Northern Territory Government made a surprise announcement concerning eight significant organisational changes with immediate effect:

- the Post-School Advisory Council was to be abolished;
- the Vocational Training Commission was to be abolished;
- the Darwin Community College Council was redesignated as the Northern Territory Council of Higher Education;
- the Darwin Community College was renamed the Darwin Institute of Technology;
- most functions of the University Planning Authority were given to the new Council of Higher Education;
- a TAFE Advisory Council, chaired by the Secretary of the Education Department, Geoff Spring, was created;
- the State Reference Library was transferred to the Education Department; and
- the Oral History programs were handed over to the Northern Territory Archives Service (Northern Territory Archives Service 1981–1988).

Those accreditation and other activities that had been carried out by the Post-School Advisory Council were given to the Higher Education Council while '[t]he powers and functions of the Vocational Training

Commission were delegated to the Department of Industry and Small Business on 20 December 1984' (Northern Territory Vocational Training Commission 1984).

In Mather's (1982, p. 11) *Report on accreditation policy and practice for TAFE courses in the Northern Territory*, the distinction was made between accreditation being used to meet industry needs for centralised quality control of training and so-called community needs that emphasised educational standards. The transfer of the Vocational Training Commission's powers to an economic agency gave some indication of the government's wish to see training more directly aligned with industry needs. However, the simultaneous establishment of a TAFE Advisory Council serviced by the Education Department ensured the community–industry distinction would become magnified. This duality served to keep alive the contested nature of vocational education and training policy and purpose. Crucially, it also legitimised the direct involvement of two ministers, one from the education portfolio and the other from an economic agency, with their own views on the philanthropic ambitions for the application of vocational education and training.

As with the government departments, 20 December was a drama-filled day for the newly anointed Darwin Institute of Technology and its renamed council. The Chief Minister pre-empted the Darwin Community College's search for a new principal that had commenced following the departure of Joe Flint, by directly appointing long-serving education bureaucrat Kevin Davis to the role (Berzins & Loveday 1999, p. 94).

Furthermore, Davis had specific instructions from the Northern Territory Government to ensure that the new institute did not overspend its budget and to make sure there would be no impediments to the creation of a university emerging from the Darwin Institute of Technology. In the late February 1985 sittings of the Legislative Assembly, the Leader of the Opposition, Bob Collins, sought to censure Tuxworth over Davis's appointment. In response, the Chief Minister gave a clear explanation of his understanding and intended use of ministerial powers and accountability for public funds:

> Any department or arm of this government that receives $18 million of taxpayers' money per annum is very much my interest and my responsibility and so is the appointment of its minister and its head (Tuxworth 1985, p. 96).

Tuxworth's reply was only a contemporary manifestation of the wealthy philanthropist's interest in using education and training to improve society that had been exhibited by Northern Territory Government ministers. In examining the ministerial correspondence from these first years of self-government, both the accessibility of the minister to constituents and the sheer volume of detailed decisions being made at that top level are stand-out features. In addition to the big-ticket items of government agency structures, capital expenditure and policy development, the Education Minister dealt with an extraordinary range of other matters. The wide scope of activities included approval for all interstate travel for public servants and student groups, responding to disgruntled unsuccessful tender applicants, calming upset parents, sympathising with unhappy employers of apprentices, approving equipment grants, listening to aggrieved teachers, approving early school leaver applications, adjudicating on the placement of special needs students, approving university researchers seeking access to public schools, and being lobbied by zealots wishing to pursue arcane issues and a significant number of highly motivated people and organisations promoting a diverse range of views as to what should be taught in Northern Territory educational institutions (Northern Territory Archives Service 1980–1982a).

The University Planning Authority Advisory Committee met at the University of Queensland on 11 and 12 December 1984, the week before their announcement on post-school education changes. In his role as Planning Vice-Chancellor, Jim Eedle, presented a set of proposed actions to establish a University College of the Northern Territory as a 'first step towards the eventual development of a free-standing Northern Territory University' (Northern Territory Archives Service 1981–1988). In August 1985, the newly appointed Minister for Education delivered *The establishment of a Northern Territory University – a statement issued by the Hon. Tom Harris, MLA* to the Legislative Assembly in which he indicated that 'for us, it is of the highest priority and essential to our constitutional, economic and social development' (Northern Territory Archives Service 1981–1988).

Figure 30. Tom Harris.
Source: Creator Unknown. PH0703/0202, Tschirner Collection, Northern Territory Library.

In spite of the Commonwealth's absolute lack of interest accompanied by a point-blank refusal to provide funding for the move into higher education, the *University College of the Northern Territory Act* was passed by the Legislative Assembly in late 1985. Closely aligned with University of Queensland coursework and assessment procedures, the University College officially opened in the premises of the Old Darwin Hospital on the edge of the Darwin central business district on 4 March 1987. The Warden of the University College, Jim Thompson, has also made reference to ministerial power, but in a way that reflects its use in other states rather than in the Northern Territory context. In discussing the difficulties in establishing a totally new institution in the face of open federal hostility and doubts about the sustainability of higher education in the Northern Territory, Thompson (1999, p. 118) states:

> I appreciated too the confidence of Tom Harris as Minister for Education, especially in consistently supporting me when some people, used to the patronage system endemic in the Territory, lobbied him to overturn my decisions.

In response to the surprise reorganisation of post-school arrangements late in the previous year, the Northern Territory Department of Education conducted a review of its operations (Northern Territory Department of Education 1985). As a result, a Division of TAFE was created in the agency that took over program and policy control of the various colleges and centres that delivered training across the Northern Territory as well as responsibility for the Aboriginal community–based adult educators. The TAFE Division had three branches: Library; Adult Education; and Training for remote and regional Aboriginal residents. There was also the TAFE Policy and Planning Branch in addition to an Executive Support Unit. This latter group provided support services to the newly formed TAFE Advisory Council whose functions included:

- providing advice to the Minister for Education;
- TAFE funding;
- course and award accreditation;
- conduct of training for industry at the rebadged Territory Training Centre in Stuart Park; and
- training of Aboriginals for employment (Northern Territory Department of Education 1985).

The Darwin Institute of Technology retained its relatively independent relationship as the largest provider of training and its Council was renamed yet again—this time as the Northern Territory Council of Advanced Education. The Department of Industry and Small Business had its responsibilities, including the administration of apprenticeships, clarified in 1985 through the passage of the *Industry and Employment Training Act*. The department also established a body to serve as a conduit from industry to the Minister for Industry and Small Business—the Industry and Employment Training Advisory Council, which formally came into existence on 30 April 1986. The minister appointed its membership in July of the same year (Industry and Employment Advisory Council 1986). This council also served another important bureaucratic purpose: it would provide the mechanism to keep in check the ever-growing ambitions of the Education Department's TAFE Advisory Council. In addition, five Industry Training Committees were also made operational in 1985. Reporting through the council, their task was to better identify the training required to meet the labour market needs of Territory industry and business.

At the national level during this period, the Commonwealth Government was also taking major steps to deploy vocational education and training as part of a response to high levels of youth unemployment and the ineffectiveness of both employment incentives and public job creation based upon wage subsidies. The *Report of the Committee of Inquiry into Labour Market Programs* (Kirby 1985) made several recommendations that generally called for a greater emphasis upon education and training for individuals to prepare them for a variety of labour market conditions. Possibly the longest lasting recommendation to be taken up by the Commonwealth Government was the creation of a new category of formal training. The Australian Traineeship System would combine broad-based vocational training with employment in a related occupation. In its submission to the inquiry, the Northern Territory Government offered support for the existing federally funded programs and wage subsidies for apprenticeships such as the Group One Year Apprenticeships and the Commonwealth Rebate for Full Time Training, which had been used to support the operations of the Skills Training Centre in Stuart Park. It was also noted that because 'population growth is expected to remain central to the process of economic development in the Northern Territory' and 'to the end of the decade, we can expect industry to require an increasingly skilled workforce' that increased federal funding would be welcomed (Northern Territory Government 1984, pp. 5–6).

The Northern Territory Government agencies impacted by the Kirby Report put in a large amount of effort to estimate the benefits, costs and consequences of implementing the new training system. In February 1985, departmental officer Dennis Sutton recommended to the Secretary of the Department of Industry and Small Business that the main findings of the Kirby Report should be accepted by the Northern Territory Government. Sutton cautioned that some political considerations would be required to explain the simultaneous existence of high rates of unemployment and the undersupply of skilled labour (Northern Territory Archives Service 1984–1991d). In a letter dated 14 March 1985, Bill Grimster, the Assistant Secretary of TAFE in the Northern Territory Education Department, also indicated his agency's support for the introduction of traineeships (Northern Territory Archives Service 1984–1991d). In response to a letter from Prime Minister Hawke that had been written on 11 March 1985, Chief Minister Tuxworth replied a month later endorsing 'the concept of a traineeship system' and offering facilitation in the Northern Territory through 'cooperative arrangements within my Government which are parallel to those you have in place' (Northern Territory Archives Service 1984–1991d). At a seminar about the proposed traineeship system on 30 April 1985, views were solicited of the peak Northern Territory organisations with an interest in the area. Participants gave qualified support, although a note of caution was sounded by the Education Department's Bill Grimster on the 550 traineeships that were projected for the Northern Territory, 'I doubt the capacity of NT industry to offer this many traineeships, at this stage' (Department of Industry and Small Business 1985).

In August 1985, the Federal Minister for Employment and Industrial Relations, Ralph Willis MP, officially announced a new Youth Traineeships System that would assist with the transition from school to work and 'ensure Australia has a better educated and more adaptable workforce' (Northern Territory Archives Service 1984–1991d). While there was ongoing discussion between Northern Territory and Commonwealth public servants over levels of funding and the elusive search for national consistency, traineeships were successfully introduced and accepted by local Territory businesses. Nationally, the number of students undertaking traineeships surpassed those in traditional apprenticeships in 2000, but with changes to government incentives and policies the number in each category had returned to parity in 2013 at about 206,000 (National Centre for Vocational Education Research 2013b).

The implementation of the Kirby Report is significant for another reason. In the future, Northern Territory Government ministers would be treated much more like their state counterparts by the Commonwealth Government. Because of its superior financial resources, the national parliament was becoming more constitutionally bold in demanding nationally consistent polices for vocational education and training that would be enforced by monetary carrots and sticks. Because of its small size, distance from the main population centres and a single vote in the

House of Representatives, Northern Territory ministers would be more frequently put in a position of having to respond to, instead of set, policy in the training arena. When interviewed about the power discrepancy, the former Minister for Education and Training and Chief Minister, Shane Stone, recounted that Northern Territory ministers had to be better prepared than all the other participants in national forums, received good background advice from its cadre of faithful senior public servants, and were not constrained by the potential conflict of interest of having a state-type TAFE system to consider at national policy level when they attended ministerial meetings convened by the Commonwealth.

Another reason why Northern Territory ministers were so well-placed is related to legislative changes rushed through the Legislative Assembly by the Tuxworth Government in a three-hour time span on 6 June 1985. As the then Public Service Commissioner Ken Pope describes, 'the Act effectively passes control of the administration of the Public Service and the statutory (prescribed) authorities into the hands of the minister' (Pope 1986, p. 6). In reflecting upon the Northern Territory ministers' desire for control over senior level public service appointments and the power to transfer public servants between agencies, Pope goes on to state:

> It can only be surmised that the Tuxworth Government has seen the independence of the [Public Service] Commissioner as a threat to the introduction of new management and staffing practices which the Government is anxious to implement. It is unfortunate, but true, that the Country Liberal Party which has been in office since the grant of self-government in the Northern Territory has a marked characteristic — it has an inherent dislike of public servants, which often appears to amount to an obsession. There is a belief, almost an instinct, held by many politicians that autocratic and dictatorial approaches to problems must yield the best solutions (Pope 1986, pp. 8–9).

Certainly Pope was witnessing yet another, even though extreme, exercise that positioned ministers of the Northern Territory Government as the ultimate authority, allowing them to act philanthropically when they wished to do so. It also formalised the introduction of new public management into government agencies. The so-called 'dislike' of public servants was only a current manifestation of a long-standing suspicion of public service–driven government that dates back to the behaviour of the official members of the Legislative Council and the general feeling of benign neglect exercised by the Commonwealth Government throughout its period of control. In addition, traditional bureaucratic and rule-bound governance conflicted with what Heatley (1998, p. 77) describes as the Country Liberal Party's 'populist and pragmatic approach to politics, its political adroitness and its capture of the dominant symbols and values of the Territory'.

Heatley (1998, pp. 102–109) believes that the Country Liberal Party moved further in the direction of poll-driven and populist electoralism than other Australian parties because of the 'newness of the polity and the party' and 'the particular political culture and voting behaviour of Territorians'. In other words, ministers wanted to be seen to be in charge of the activities of their portfolios because they wished to be responsive to their identification with the needs of the electorate. As we have shown, the voters expect their elected members to take action and it is the minister who is held accountable at the next election, not public servants. In his typically straightforward manner, former Chief Minister Shane Stone has reflected on the relative roles of public servants and politicians, 'to indirectly quote and paraphrase Paul Keating, you are either in government or in power' (Martin & Dewar 2012, p. 117).

The year 1986 saw the Northern Territory Cabinet approve further reorganisations of both advisory arrangements and in the institutions undertaking delivery of vocational education and training. The Secretary of the Department of Education, Geoff Spring, was put in charge of a new Northern Territory Tertiary Education Council. This group was to advise the minister on funding matters for the sector and handle the relationship with the Commonwealth Tertiary Education Council. The other members were the chairs of the Northern Territory Council of Advanced Education (Darwin Institute of Technology's former council), the TAFE Advisory Council and the University College Northern Territory Council (Berzins & Loveday 1999, p. 101).

The agency with responsibility for apprenticeship training and its advisory council, the Department of Industry and Small Business, were not represented on the Tertiary Education Council. This resulted in the responsible minister, Nick Dondas, having reduced influence over the future development of the dual-sector institutions that provided the off-the-job training component for the 1,300 apprentices that were in declared trades (Northern Territory of Australia 1987b).

Figure 31. Geoff Spring.
Source: Creator Unknown. PH0703/0027, Tschirner Collection, Northern Territory Library.

As it turns out, the Department of Industry and Small Business was only in existence for 16 months (December 1984 to April 1986) when it was replaced by a new agency, the Department of Business, Technology and Communications. This revamped department took over responsibility for apprenticeship training that had previously resided with the former Vocational Training Commission. This change also brought a new minister into the mix, Ray Hanrahan. On 27 August 1986, one of the first actions taken by the new departmental head of Business, Technology and Communications, Col Fuller, was to appoint Ian Cummin, the group manager of employee resources in the Northern Territory Electricity Commission, to undertake a review of the Northern

Territory apprenticeship system. In the introduction to his findings, Cummin (1986, p. 3) provided the 'populist and pragmatic' content to which the minister, in particular, and Cabinet, in general, could respond: 'The employer is the key participant in the apprenticeship system. It is the employer who voluntarily provides, at considerable cost, the means for the apprenticeship system to operate'. Cummin also picked up on the never-ending bureaucratic demarcation disputes by suggesting that Fuller's new agency wholly administer training, the need for better coordination and more streamlined government support for employers. He also continued with populism in his recommendations on the need for 'theoretical' trainers to be more in touch with industrial environments, the inadequacy of practical skills of apprentices; the low apprenticeship completion rate, and the need to not allow apprentices to participate in industrial action (Cummin 1986).

However, Cummin was only tapping into a much older set of concerns about the shortcomings of Northern Territory apprentices. The Department of Industry and Small Business had published a report on areas requiring improvement in the previous year. One of the recommendations contained in the overview stated:

> That the Secretary, NT Department of Education, be notified of the general dissatisfaction expressed by apprentice employers, regarding inadequate literacy and numeracy skills of school-leavers to cope with apprentice training (Recommendation 17, Sri-Pathimanathan 1985, p. xi).

These two reports were only the mid-1980s version of concerns that were expressed almost 10 years earlier in the period immediately prior to self-government. In his address at the Apprentices' Presentation Night in February 1977, the Executive Officer of the Master Builders Association, Barry Whyatt (1977), made sweeping criticisms of Northern Territory schools, the Education Department, the behaviour of apprentices and the inadequacy of Commonwealth funding. In particular, he advocated for the elimination of bureaucratic government procedures and a much more streamlined administration of training. In response to this type of criticism, the Northern Territory Division of the Commonwealth Education Department had appointed one of its most experienced educators in the Territory, Charles Beresford, to survey employer sentiments on their pre-employment requirements with a view to updating course content at the Darwin Community College and in years 11 and 12 at school. Employers expressed concern about low levels of generic employability skills, high rates of staff turnover, the 'poor' attitudes of young people in general and the inferior nature/standard of apprentices 'today'; less than 4 per cent of employers interviewed were happy with the Northern Territory education system (Beresford 1977).

In a demonstration of how certain simple concepts can be carried forward, the issues from two decades before remained alive and well into 1997. Yet another report was produced, *Apprenticeships at the crossroads,* which opened with a sense of crisis that demanded government action: 'apprenticeship numbers in the Northern Territory were lower in 1996 than they were in 1984' (Trade Training Working Group 1997, p. 1). The many now familiar problems addressed in this report are summarised by the following need for 'recognition that, practically, at least, the available vocational educational and training products are not meeting the needs of industry and the workforce' (Trade Training Working Group 1997, pp. 17–18).

Returning to 1986, the Northern Territory Open College of TAFE was brought into existence through the amalgamation of disparate government operational units. With its head office located in Darwin, the Open College had regional campuses in Alice Springs, Tennant Creek, Katherine, Palmerston and Nhulunbuy as well as numerous adult educators that were still based in remote Aboriginal communities. In addition, the Secondary Correspondence School, the Adult Migrant English Program and the Territory Training Centre (originally the Industry Skills Centre that had been set up by the Industry Training Commission in Stuart Park) operated as functional units in the organisational structure (Northern Territory Department of Education 1992, p. 33). In common with the other colleges that operated under the Education Department umbrella, the Northern Territory Open College had a large council (17 members) representing a wide range of stakeholders and with significant levels of independence and local decision-making in college internal matters.

The Department of Business, Technology and Communications used the Cummin Review to guide its responsibilities for employment, apprenticeships, manpower and labour market through the provision of 'factual, objective and timely policy advice and to carry out the Government's policies in a professional and efficient manner' and in the belief that the current apprenticeship training arrangements did not meet anyone's needs (Northern Territory of Australia 1988b, p. 2). This department was only in existence for 13 months before the next departmental structure was put in place under a new Chief Minister.

Figure 32. The Honourable Terry McCarthy.
Source: Creator Bert Wiedemann, PH0730/1367, Northern Territory Government Photographer Slide Collection, Northern Territory Library.

Following considerable leadership turmoil in the parliamentary wing of the Country Liberal Party, Tuxworth resigned from the office of Chief Minister on 16 May 1986 and was replaced by the member for Nightcliff,

Steve Hatton. In Hatton's second ministry, commencing 19 March 1987, the apprenticeship and employment functions were transferred to a new Department of Labour and Administrative Services with Terry McCarthy serving as the minister. Local Government would be added to the name of the department in February 1988. The secretary of this new agency was Syd Saville, the former head of the Department of Education, who had fought many battles with the two training commissions over the 'ownership' and coordination of vocational education and training policy and operations.

Throughout the almost five-year existence of the latest incarnation of the Apprenticeship Board, the inter-agency conflict that had been created by the original decision to separate apprenticeship functions from other educational operations that had been made during self-government negotiations would not diminish. Like Geoff Chard before him, Saville would find no problem with changing sides whilst still vigorously fighting for control of the agenda. As a result of the public sector management changes made by the Tuxworth Government, senior public servants clearly understood that the highest priority was to marshal as many resources as possible to put towards the task of meeting 'their' minister's views of how to best pursue the social and economic improvement of the Northern Territory.

In Central Australia, 1987 also saw the renaming of the Community College of Central Australia to the Alice Springs College of TAFE, which immediately was reduced to ASCOT. The local community college had been progressively redeveloped in response to Pattinson's (1980) educational specification and Cabinet approval of building design and construction on a site on the east side of the town, adjacent to the Sadadeen High School (Northern Territory Archives Service 1977–2003c). The change in name also served several much more symbolic purposes. The title 'community college' had not been taken up by the various state-based education systems and with the changes mooted for the advanced and higher education sectors that would lead to the unified national system of universities, the term was no longer viable in terms of the connotations it carried. In addition, the Northern Territory Government wanted to make sure that its bid to establish a university was not side-tracked by ambit claims or speculation about the offering of advanced or higher education in Alice Springs—the focus was to be firmly on Darwin. Inside the Northern Territory, steps were also being taken to change the structure of secondary schooling to include senior secondary colleges for year 11 and year 12 students. In Alice Springs, the designated senior campus would commence in 1987 at Sadadeen High School and a clear demonstration of the linkage to pre-employment training and a sense of shared facilities were used to help promote the concept to the local voters (High schools and secondary colleges working party 1985). The designation of the Alice Springs College of TAFE suited a number of political agendas that were being pursued by the Northern Territory Cabinet at that time.

In remote and regional Aboriginal communities, 1987 came with a new organisational structure for the delivery of post–primary school education including vocational education and training. Many of the larger remote schools were to be rebadged as Community Education Centres operating as part of the Northern Territory Open College's responsibilities. This move would also incorporate the work of the adult educators into the mainstream operations of the Department of Education (Northern Territory Open College 1987, p. 1). The integration of post-primary and adult education into the Community Education Centres would be trialled in eight larger communities in 1988 and eventually rolled out to 20 sites over the next couple of years. The 'innovative programs' on offer were to be 'strongly linked to training and employment outcomes' and were 'endorsed by the NT Minister for Education, Daryl Manzie' (Northern Territory Open College 1987, p. 1). The minister appears to have been a supporter of the Duke of Edinburgh's Award scheme because the Community Education Centres would incorporate the ethos of the award program's emphasis upon 'high personal commitment, community service and identification with the program' (Northern Territory Open College 1987, p. 14). The new organisational structures did not produce the intended outcomes and Arnott's (2003) retrospective analysis puts this down to two factors. The former adult educators had two bosses: the locally based principal of the Community Education Centre (a school teacher) and a senior person located in the head office of the Northern Territory Open College. Inevitably, school-based leaders and bureaucrats frequently had different agendas and priorities driven by dissimilar perceptions of what was important. He also attributes the gradual reduction in human and other resources allocated to adult education in remote areas to the more centralised and managerial elements of new public management (Arnott 2003, p. 52).

By the end of 1987, substantial changes had been made to the vocational education and training landscape in the Northern Territory. The two government departments with the most direct interest and responsibility oversaw a plethora of advisory bodies designed to ensure that every possible interest group was given an opportunity, albeit once removed, to have input to the ministers. These advisory councils served two important political functions in addition to their operational responsibilities. They provided a venue that allowed the minister to be represented as listening and responsive, but also protected the minister from being directly linked to potentially unpopular or damaging decisions. Of course, the minister always made the final decision and may or may not have followed any advice that came out of these bodies or the government agencies. Students wishing to undertake studies in the various streams of Technical and Further Education could attend the Darwin Institute of Technology, the Alice Springs College of TAFE, Batchelor College, the Northern Territory Open College or the Katherine Rural Education Centre. Higher education students were limited to correspondence courses from interstate universities or attending the University College of the Northern Territory in Darwin.

Two other events on the national scene took place in 1987 and these would guide the development of the training sector for the next quarter of a century. As mentioned previously, one reality of self-government was that Northern Territory Government ministers were placed in the position of being policy responders, rather than setters, when the Commonwealth Government made decisions. While the implementation of vocational education and training policies, such as the introduction of traineeships or provision of capital infrastructure, could be negotiated to suit the peculiarities of this remote jurisdiction, ministerial attention in the Northern Territory was frequently focused on how to get the best deal rather than on the substance of the policy direction. The first of the major policy shifts on the part of the Commonwealth, to which the Northern Territory would have to respond, was promulgated through the release of *Australia Reconstructed* (Department of Trade, Australian Council of Trade Unions (ACTU) & Trade Development Council (TDC) 1987).

This report had been commissioned by the then Federal Minister for Trade and Minister assisting the Prime Minister on Youth Affairs, John Dawkins, and reported on the findings of a joint mission that had extensively consulted in a number of European countries about how Australia might address the emerging global economy, improve human capital and ensure social and economic prosperity could be achieved in the country's medium- to long-term future. The complex and interrelated set of recommendations called for no less than a radical overhaul of labour markets and social welfare—both underpinned by a much more responsive training system and a commitment to lifelong learning to ensure that workforce participation became the primary obligation of Australian citizens. While there is little evidence to suggest that the report itself had a major impact upon any particular activity in the Northern Territory, the development of human capital as an input into economic and social development fit well with local ambitions. *Australia Reconstructed* placed major emphasis upon the pivotal role that would be played by trade unions in revamping the nation's economic future and labour force. As events unfolded, the place of unions became less central in the renovated Australia, but almost every other major policy element concerning vocational education and training is still clearly visible in the contemporary national training system.

A second national policy action arose out of *Australia Reconstructed*. In order to implement many of the major findings contained in the seminal report, the Hawke Labor Government undertook a major program of macroeconomic reform. To harness the activities for the improvement of Australia's human capital, Dawkins advocated for and won federal Cabinet support for the creation of a 'super-department' of Employment, Education and Training in 1987. This was the very first time that 'training' had appeared in the name of a Commonwealth department. In his characteristically no-nonsense style, the minister set out in *Skills for Australia* (Dawkins & Holding 1987) the beginnings of the reform agenda that was about to sweep over the state-operated TAFE systems. This document outlined a highly interventionist and activist policy agenda that would use the Commonwealth Government's superior financial power to set priorities in order to achieve national outcomes.

While *Australia Reconstructed* set out the rationale for what would happen in the training arena, *Skills for Australia* introduced the specific programs and actions that would be used by the Commonwealth Government to achieve its goals. The Northern Territory Government had no option but to respond favourably in this space to protect revenue streams and to progress the establishment of a full university in the face of Commonwealth opposition. Some of the specific impacts upon the Northern Territory that were contained in *Skills for Australia* implementation actions included the need to sign a submission-based resource agreement with the Commonwealth (instead of historically untied per capita funding), bringing the Northern Territory's own expenditure on TAFE into alignment with national priorities and a threat to redirect funding from the Northern Territory Government to industry or training institutions if Commonwealth objectives were not met. In advising Minister Manzie on how to best deal with Dawkins's interventions, the Secretary of the Education Department, Geoff Spring, articulated the reality of a Northern Territory minister's options, 'It is clear from the TAFE document that the NT will need quick reaction procedures to respond to these new requests for submissions' (Northern Territory Archives Service 1 June 1987–26 October 1987). Dawkins wrote to the new Minister for Education, Ray Hanrahan, on 18 January 1988 confirming that the Commonwealth would provide $7.17 million for TAFE in that year based upon the Northern Territory meeting negotiated targets in the areas leading to:

- increased TAFE workforce productivity to do with class sizes, wages and operating hours;
- budget restraint;
- implementation of the Australian Traineeship System;
- increased tourism and hospitality training;
- increased enrolments at the Katherine Rural College; and
- increased Aboriginal training (Northern Territory Archives Service 1 June 1987–26 October 1987).

Dawkins would continue to dominate the vocational education and training agenda for the next two years. His government's policies and priorities were further elaborated in three more papers: *Industry training in Australia: the need for change*; *A changing workforce*; and *Improving Australia's training system* (Dawkins 1988a, 1988b, 1989). With the consolidation of employment, training and education functions in the one agency, Dawkins was also able to drive his comprehensive agenda for labour force development over these two years. The Commonwealth's single entity and aligned policy positions continuously exposed the bureaucratic rivalries between the two Northern Territory Government agencies: the University College and the Darwin Institute of Technology. In yet another attempt to reduce the friction, Cabinet decided to conduct a review of the *Employment and Training Act* in late 1988. Seeking to take advantage of Saville's resignation from the Department of Labour, Administrative Services and Local Government, Spring constantly attempted to exert his department's domination of vocational education and training policy with the reinstated Minister for Education, Tom Harris (Northern Territory Archives Service 20 May 1988–28 November 1988). This eventually resulted in Minister Harris writing to Minister McCarthy requesting that the Department of Labour, Administrative Services and Local Government improve its performance and become better at communication and coordination between the two departments (Northern Territory Archives Service 2 November 1988–30 December 1988). There is no record of McCarthy's response.

In the vocational education and training sector, the period 1989 to 1991 was characterised by the continuation of the types of government behaviour that has been described in the preceding section. The Commonwealth Minister Dawkins was driving what became known as the National Training Reform Agenda while the two Northern Territory departments and ministers squabbled over control but somehow cobbled together responses to the national policy environment. In summarising the overall relationship in education and training between the states, territories and Commonwealth Government, Geoff Spring wrote to the Secretary of the Chief Minister's Department:

> The Commonwealth is quite blatantly using its financial power to bludgeon states into accepting these resource agreements or risk funding being given to other states and territories. It seems likely that this process will continue unless there is a concerted action by all states/territories to resist. The trend will continue if states compete against each other and the Commonwealth is able to play one off against the other (Northern Territory Archives Service 1985–1990).

By late 1990, the national reform agenda had become much more refined as a result of the *Training costs of award restructuring: Report of the Training Costs Review Committee* (Deveson 1990). In preparation for the first meeting of the newly established Vocational Education, Employment and Training Advisory Committee, Dawkins wrote on 18 October 1990 to the members and the ministers with responsibility for training in each state and territory, giving his initial reaction to the committee's findings. 'I regard the Deveson Report as a significant milestone on the path of reform along which we have been moving over the last three years' (Northern Territory Archives Service 1985–1990). As a result of the ministers' meeting held in Melbourne on 22 November 1990, the major policy parameters suggested in the Deveson Report were agreed and they have substantially underpinned vocational education and training policy ever since. These reforms to training were intended to complement a range of other changes to industrial awards, the introduction of enterprise bargaining at work unit levels and other labour market and social welfare initiatives designed to improve the participation and productivity of Australia's workforce that had been imported as a result of *Australia Reconstructed*.

Minister Dawkins also believed that the training workforce itself needed to improve the way it operated. 'TAFE must lose its monopoly position in respect of many aspects of training', Dawkins wrote to the ministers before the November meeting (Northern Territory Archives Service 1985–1990). He signalled the Commonwealth's intention to establish an 'open training market' that would be serviced by both public and private providers who met registration standards. In return, the Commonwealth would remove its ban on the state TAFE systems being able to charge student fees, expand the Austudy program of financial assistance to the disadvantaged and provide capital funding for more skill centres. Future Commonwealth TAFE funding would be tied to demonstrable efforts on the part of the states to improve the efficiency of their training systems and programs that gave priority to national goals in entry-level training (to address youth unemployment), literacy, numeracy and English as a second language.

All of this activity would have to conform to and use nationally consistent mechanisms for setting skill competencies, curriculum, accreditation, certification and articulation into other education sectors. In order to monitor the progress of these sweeping changes there would be efficiency and equity audits, a new national managerial information system and the publication of key performance indicators. Dawkins also noted that the private sector had a role to play and demanded a 'substantial sustained increase in training provided by industry' and this was backed up the threat of introducing a training guarantee levy on large enterprises (Northern Territory Archives Service 1985–1990). For the Federal Government, the envisaged relationship between the two governments resulting from the implementation of the Deveson Report recommendations saw that 'state and territory authorities would continue to exercise their statutory functions but within an agreed national framework and lateral reciprocal framework' (Northern Territory Archives Service 1985–1990). In other words, the Commonwealth would exercise policy control enforced by their 'financial bludgeon', while the states and territories would be responsible for delivery and reporting.

In what must have been a very busy meeting on 22 November 1990, the various state, territory and federal ministers also agreed to support further progress on the introduction of competency-based training, the future funding for group training schemes, national training excellence awards, and national processes for the recognition of skills acquired overseas (Northern Territory Archives Service 1985–1990).

The Northern Territory Government was well placed to respond to the National Training Reform Agenda partly because, unlike the states, it did not operate its own TAFE system (Zoellner 2013a). The delivery of training was being undertaken by arm's-length organisations whose governance was provided by relatively autonomous college or institute councils. In fact, throughout 1988 and 1989 a number of steps were taken by government that would allow the Northern Territory to act favourably to the centralisation of policy and reporting at the Commonwealth level in ways that would become operationalised through the yet to be delivered Deveson recommendations. During 1988, the final decisions were being taken by the Northern Territory Government on how to best go about establishing the Northern Territory University. As with the handover of the education function from the Commonwealth a decade earlier, noisy interest groups were active in their efforts to lobby Cabinet ministers for an outcome they thought would be most beneficial to their own well-being. One of the key matters revolved around the future position and control of the TAFE functions of the Darwin Institute of Technology. Options ranged from returning training to the Education Department to the establishment of a new and completely independent institution. In his capacity as Secretary of the Education Department, Geoff Spring chaired a Higher Education Planning Group that had its first meeting on 28 April 1988 where the controversial idea of creating the new university through a merger of the University College and the Darwin Institute of Technology was canvassed:

> In this option it was stressed that the role of TAFE must not be compromised by being placed in an autonomous higher education institution and that the Northern Territory Government must be able to give direction in response to training requirements. The proposed place of TAFE is recommended as a key part of the University of the Northern Territory but with recognition that the Northern Territory Government has a responsibility to decide on policy matters and to determine priorities for funding and facilities for education and training in the TAFE sector on the basis of the Northern Territory Government providing 85 per cent

of the funding as opposed to 15 per cent Commonwealth funding which is subject to a resource agreement (Higher Education Planning Group 1988, p. 12).

The final recommendation to Cabinet was to have an Institute of TAFE within the new university structure. Two now familiar themes were reinforced with this recommendation. Cabinet ministers will have ultimate authority over vocational education and training and there would be no return to the original broad range of powers of the Darwin Community College that had been 'curtailed' immediately following self-government. After considerable further discussion, the Northern Territory University came into being on 1 January 1989 through the amalgamation of the University College and the Darwin Institute of Technology. The Institute of TAFE was also established as part of the new institution's structure. In his report to the Education Department on the results of a request from the university to the Commonwealth for an establishment grant in line with other higher education start-ups, the now Deputy Vice-Chancellor of the Northern Territory University, Jim Thompson, cites a letter from the federal minister dated 10 January 1989:

> Mr Dawkins concludes: The Commonwealth considers that the NT Government should continue to carry the costs of those diseconomies which are a direct consequence of its decision on this matter (Northern Territory Archives Service 1985–1989).

Accompanying the various activities being taken to establish the nation's first truly dual-sector university, the Northern Territory Cabinet was making other changes to its own agencies and their responsibilities for vocational education and training. Syd Saville had been shifted into the position of Public Service Commissioner and from 19 March 1987 his office 'also gained the employment and training functions formerly undertaken by the Department of Business, Technology and Communications' (Northern Territory of Australia 1987a, pp. 1–2). The annual report for 1986–87 shows that there were 1,361 apprentices in training at 30 June 1986 in 51 declared trades.

By the following year, the operations of the Department of Labour and Administrative Services had also been annexed to the Office of the Public Service Commissioner. The agency was busy across a range of research and policy issues including providing representation on no less than 13 Territory and national advisory committees, promoting training for women, publishing a labour market report, supporting local employment activities and developing trade training guidelines. In addition, support was being given to the introduction of the Australian Traineeship System and there were seven Industry Training Committees providing input into training priorities and content in the areas of:

- Fishing
- Building and Construction
- Tourism
- Local Government
- Retail
- Automotive
- Road Transport (Northern Territory of Australia 1988a).

By mid-way through 1989, David Hawkes had been appointed to the position of Public Service Commissioner and also served as the secretary of the Department of Labour and Administrative Services as well as the Northern Territory Teaching Service Commissioner. All three of these roles insured that he would inevitably end up in conflict with the ambitious and hard-working Geoff Spring, who continued his persistent efforts to increase the range and reach of power and influence exercised by the Department of Education. In the *Annual Report 1988/89 of the Public Service Commissioner and the Department of Labour and Administrative Services* (Northern Territory of Australia 1989), the Employment and Training Division reported on a variety of activities and outputs that were being achieved by the three branches of Research and Development, Aboriginal Development and Training Development.

Highlights included having 541 participants in the public sector School Leavers Program; 15 occupations had been declared suitable for the formal employment of trainees as part of the new national system; there were eight industry training committees operating; and three Group Training Companies had been established to serve as the employer for apprentices who could be moved to different work situations/sites/companies in order to complete their apprenticeship. These group schemes were the Housing Industry Associates, Top End Group Training and Central Australia Group Training. Their activities were jointly supported by both Commonwealth and Northern Territory resources and could trace their origins back to the ideas of 'pools' of housing and construction apprentices that had been created in Darwin and Alice Springs soon after self-government. The latter two companies mentioned above combined about a decade later to form GTNT, which celebrated its 25th birthday in 2014. There were 116 trainees and 1,299 apprentices in training at 30 June 1989 (Northern Territory of Australia 1989, pp. 84–86). The growth area for formal training was in traineeships as apprentice numbers in training had flatlined in the second half of the 1980s given that there were 1,290 apprentices at the same date in 1985. It was also reported that due to 'the limited range of course [sic] available from tertiary institutions' some 200 Northern Territory apprentices were funded by the Northern Territory Government to attend interstate TAFE colleges for their off-the-job training components during 1988 (Northern Territory Archives Service 1984–1991g, folio 72).

The activism of the Commonwealth Government and the responsive position assumed by Northern Territory Government ministers created an imperative to get the best possible advice to Cabinet to minimise federally driven financial reductions to the vocational education and training system in the Northern Territory while retaining the maximum amount of ministerial discretion. Clearly the Northern Territory politicians believed that the costs of continual bickering between its agencies and statutory authorities over TAFE were worth the political benefit. Various interest groups, who continually sought ministerial intervention, were enabled to be legitimate contributors to policy decisions, and ministerial responsiveness to the local electorates could be exerted through several mechanisms. On 8 February 1989, Chief Minister Marshall Perron wrote to Education Minister Tom Harris and the Minister for Labour, Administrative Services and Local Government, Terry McCarthy. He instructed them to pull their respective department secretaries into line and stated that he had no intention of joining training with education due to the need for 'providing an independent link with industry through the labour portfolio' (Northern Territory Archives Service 1984–1991g). Perron goes on to instruct both ministers to reassess the roles of advisory councils to avoid duplication and to clarify 'grey areas'. Perron's refusal to combine the roles is yet another example of the influence exerted by the Country Liberal Party's generalised distrust of public servants and the electoral imperative of being able to calculate and apply the political responsiveness expected of the Northern Territory ministers. Having two distinct methods of interacting with the public and using public sector expertise protected the minister from 'group think' and ensured that a wide variety of options were being actively canvassed by senior public servants and ministerial advisors prior to the minister having to make a decision.

Minister Harris wrote back to the Chief Minister on 22 May 1989 to describe the actions that had been taken to follow his instructions to better manage tensions between the two government departments. These included better agenda coordination, combined meetings, joint committee membership where possible and that both ministers were awaiting the results of the review into the *Employment and Training Act* (Northern Territory Archives Service 1984–1991g). Regardless of the bureaucratic battles for control over policy and funding, Territory residents experienced significantly increased access to a more varied range of training services during this period. The widely scattered colleges, community education centres and institutes had developed a range of programs to meet the diverse needs of the Territory's multicultural and widespread population. These included the remotely based adult educators, Mobile Adult Learning Units, itinerant lecturers and residential short courses. In fact, in its review of the contribution of the vocational education and training sector to national microeconomic reform, the Industry Commission (1998, pp. 133–139) describes the Northern Territory as a pioneer in flexible alternative delivery strategies designed to improve access to training and the programs it had in place in 1989. During 1989–90, this focus upon access was also enhanced by Batchelor College planning for and opening its Alice Springs campus, using the former Ansett Motel accommodation in Gillen, to extend training to a larger number of Aboriginal Territorians.

The review into the provisions of the Act that governed many aspects of vocational education and training, anticipated by Harris's comments above, was done under the instructions of the Secretary of the Department of Chief Minister, Alan Morris, and was to be completed by June 1989 (Northern Territory Archives Service 1984–1991f). Due to the high levels of contestation between the public service departments, Kent Maddoch of Network Australia provided an external consultancy service to conduct the review for a fixed fee of just over $16,000. His major recommendation was that training policy and the coordination of TAFE should be managed by a single ministry (Northern Territory Archives Service 1984–1991f). The results of the review supplied Minister McCarthy with an action plan to go against the express wishes of the Chief Minister for joint responsibility. The battles for control raged in mid-1989. The high levels of antagonism were exemplified by Spring's memo to Harris giving his initial impression of proposed changes to the *Employment and Training Act* that would remove

TAFE from the Education Department. Spring advised his minister that '[i]t is a very poorly researched, biased and inaccurate report' (Northern Territory Archives Service 2 November 1988–30 December 1988).

On 21 July 1989, the Public Service Commissioner, David Hawkes, wrote to Minister McCarthy requesting that another consultant and prominent Territory identity, Sue Bradley, be brought in to chair a joint working party on the *Employment and Training Act* that would have membership from the Industry and Employment and TAFE Advisory Councils 'given the sensitive nature of the task' (Northern Territory Archives Service 1984–1991f, folio 110)—this was approved just three days later. The original consultant's suggestions had given rise to a sustained and strong reaction from a wide variety of industry groups with the vast majority writing to the various ministers expressing their strong objection to employment and training functions being handed over to the Department of Education. This review of the review would take many months to complete and apparently had little public profile. On 1 May 1990, Hawkes sent a memo to Minister McCarthy indicating that the Bradley deliberations had produced a 'near final' product that would give the Northern Territory Government a clear policy direction:

> The principal thrust of the Working Party's Report is to involve industry to a much larger extent in the identification of issues and the formulation of advice to Government. I think it is a direction which Government should support (Northern Territory Archives Service 1984–1991e, folio 432).

Minister McCarthy signed off on the proposal with a handwritten note: 'Please proceed as discussed'. The need to get business and industry interests in the Northern Territory more closely involved with the emerging national agenda was becoming a major issue for the local ministers. One of the key national reforms was to introduce a range of registered providers into a training marketplace. This was to expose TAFE institutes, including the Northern Territory University and other local college providers, to competition so as to make the system more responsive to economic and industrial needs in a rapidly restructured economy entering a sustained period of economic downturn. However, major industry groups did not necessarily agree with the mechanisms that would be used to ensure the quality of training provision in this new quasi-market. On 25 July 1990, the Executive Director of the Northern Territory Master Builders Association wrote a letter to Chief Minister

Perron headed 'Bureaucratic Empire Building'. Merv Elliott (Northern Territory Archives Service 1984–1991c) started by complaining that he had not received a reply from Education Minister Harris when he had written to him on the topic and then went on to attack the proposed registration of training providers:

> Regarding the exercise in empire building being undertaken by the Education Department in seeking registration of all non-Education Department training providers — I seek your immediate intervention to put a stop to this exercise in stupidity, as there is no way that the private sector will accept this exercise as a valid activity of Government.

There is no record of the Chief Minister's response, but as events unfolded, the creation of the Northern Territory Employment and Training Authority, which implemented the Bradley recommendations for greater industry control, ensured that this type of dissension and its threat to the flow of Commonwealth funding was ameliorated. In fact, by 1991, the Northern Territory was again recognised for leading the nation in the implementation of training reform by passing legislation, which introduced competency-based training into apprenticeships and traineeships while also allowing for the recognition of skills demonstrated on the job rather than a strictly time-served basis to more rapidly progress participants through the training process (Industry Commission 1998). Indeed, the change in Chief Minister that took place in 1988 when Marshall Perron replaced Steve Hatton only served to support the more rapid adoption of training reform into the jurisdiction based upon Perron's previous experience as the Minister for Education.

The general election held in October 1990 saw a return of the Perron Government and introduced a new and highly ambitious member for Port Darwin, Shane Stone, directly into the ministry. Towards the end of 1991, Stone became the Minister for Education and Training in order to remove the division of ministerial responsibility that had resulted in conflicting views on training policy being continually aired in Cabinet. It also allowed Stone to engage fully with Dawkins's ambitious and hard-driven national reform agenda. When interviewed about this period of time, Stone recalls that he and Dawkins, despite their differing political party affiliations, got on well at a personal level and shared much common philosophical ground on the role that should be played by vocational education and training in social and economic development. Characterised by sometimes 'robust' negotiating exchanges between himself and the federal minister, Stone believes that his support for national reform and the Territory's capacity to respond rapidly resulted in highly favourable financial and policy considerations from the Commonwealth.

Figure 33. Former Minister for Education and Training, Shane Stone.
Source: Photograph courtesy of Shane. L. Stone.

Several other bureaucratic reorganisations took place during the Bradley-led deliberations over changes to the *Employment and Training Act*. Along with the introduction of the new minister, the separate Department of Labour and Administrative Services was abolished in October 1990; the Employment and Training Division was also briefly transferred into the Education Department Post-School Education and Training Division for the six-month period leading up to the creation of the Northern Territory Employment and Training Authority on 1 January 1992 (Northern Territory of Australia 1992). Out in the community, apprentice numbers had fallen to 1,190 by 30 June 1991 and there were 156 trainees. Of this total group, 119 apprentices and trainees were employed by four group training companies.

By 1992, the introduction of the National Training System had reached somewhat of an impasse with the states and territories seeking higher levels of funding, which the Commonwealth agreed to provide in exchange for greater centralisation of policy and operational control. In a typically bold move, Prime Minister Keating's February 1992 economic statement, *One Nation*, proposed that the Commonwealth would agree to take full funding responsibility for vocational education and training from the states much as it had done in higher education. Goozee (2013, pp. 353–354) reports that the bilateral negotiations between the state, territory and federal governments broke down over broader concerns about Commonwealth–state funding agreements. Given that the Northern Territory had only relatively recently gained responsibility for vocational education and training as part of self-government processes, there was little enthusiasm for handing back a function. In addition, there were just too many bitter memories of the Commonwealth agreeing to one level of funding for a particular function and then several years later reducing the amount or even unilaterally dispensing with a previously negotiated agreement. The Northern Territory Government also realised that, in addition to the justice system, training was one of the very few public policy tools that maximised local policy control and financial discretion.

In late May 1992, Keating upped the stakes (Goozee 2013, pp. 353–55). If the states and territories refused to agree to the Commonwealth takeover of funding and control of TAFE, the Prime Minster threatened to establish his own vocational training system. However, a combination of constitutional reality and political pragmatism intervened and, following both a Premiers' Conference and a Youth Summit in the middle of the year, a compromise agreement was reached that allowed for both increased federal funding and retention of state and territory influence over training delivery. The settlement involved the creation of a tri-partite body of industry, state and Commonwealth representatives to direct the introduction of the national training system that would be jointly funded by both levels of government: new money from the Commonwealth combined with the states maintaining their current financial support for the sector to avoid cost shifting. Thus was born the Australian National Training Authority. This statutory authority would be established by Commonwealth legislation and be responsible to a Ministerial Council that consisted of the ministers with responsibility for training from state, territory and the federal governments.

The start of 1992, the creation of the Australian National Training Authority and the establishment of an industry-dominated Northern Territory Employment and Training Authority marks the end of this chapter. Ministers of the Northern Territory Government still retained control over vocational education and training and the ability to use it as a mechanism to give expression to their philanthropically inspired visions for the future. In an organisational sense, the demise of both the Department of Labour and Administrative Services and the TAFE Advisory Council (and related Department of Education responsibilities) marked the temporary end of using departmental structures as the 'foundations' that would give effect to ministerial directives. However, the contested nature of vocational education and training would not be altered, just the locus of disputation would change to arguments between various federal agencies as well as between the states/territories and the Commonwealth. In addition, major industrial and employer groups would seek to protect their interests through controlling the emerging training agenda. These contests would be played out in the Northern Territory microcosm driven by two opposing considerations: a bipartisan belief in the desirability of introducing market mechanisms into the sector to increase efficiency and responsiveness, juxtaposed with the necessary political goals of protecting against market failure and allowing for maximal ministerial judgement and choice.

In addition, the previous two decades had seen the birth and coming of age of Technical and Further Education. In the next period, TAFE would no longer be able to be used interchangeably with training to describe this non-school, non-university sector of education; it would be reserved to describe the large state-operated and publicly funded training systems. Vocational education and training operating inside a series of national standards would represent the future of the sector. The Northern Territory was again leading the way by returning to the use of an arm's-length statutory authority that resembled the two commissions of the late 1970s and early 1980s. This new body would implement and report upon the success of ministerial philanthropy designed to economically and socially improve and control this still-frontier jurisdiction using vocational education and training.

7

Vocational education and training in the era of self-government, 1992–2014

Since 1974, politics in the Northern Territory had been dominated by the implementation of self-government and moves to exert ministerial authority, while a series of parallel national events, initiated by the Kangan Review, had created a new Technical and Further Education (TAFE) sector that simultaneously grew and matured through what some refer to as its 'golden age' (Goozee 2001, p. 38). This rather nostalgic view reflects the impact of Commonwealth financial support upon chronically underfunded TAFE systems that allowed state and territory ministers to preside over the construction of new facilities and strong growth in student numbers in response to each jurisdiction's idiosyncratic priorities. Whitelock (1974, p. 269) described the pre-1974 situation as a 'confusion of institutional eccentricity', totally unsuited to meeting the skills required for a contemporary labour force challenged by a more globally competitive economic environment and rapidly changing technologies in virtually every area of employment.

As a result of the National Training Reform Agenda and the linkage of vocational education and training to national economic and industrial imperatives, these publicly funded state TAFE systems lost their monopoly on the provision of formally recognised training in the new National Training System. Vocational education and training, universally shortened to VET, would be both the product and the service offered by a range of registered public and private training providers guided by the Commonwealth Government's domination of public policy and centralised priority-setting. The ostensible centralisation of policy formulation was the price paid by the states and territories in exchange for national funding. The reality has been more akin to a giant shell game in which state and territory bureaucracies and ministers use an ingenious range of techniques to reinterpret national agreements and retain as much local influence as possible. For example, the inability to achieve national recognition of occupational licensing and registration in the traditional trades stands as a monument to the strength of jurisdictional self-interest.

The introduction of vocational education and training into the Northern Territory was a relatively easy task for Cabinet given that the jurisdiction did not own and operate its own TAFE system, already outsourced delivery to a range of providers, was responsive to national agendas and was well-acquainted with the developing principles of new public management. The Northern Territory's early buy-in to Dawkins's national training system was facilitated by the local quasi-market in training that accommodated the liberal pragmatism and advantages of market-driven behaviours; the idiosyncrasies of Antipodean colonial socialism guarding against market failure; and the perceived benefits of retaining overall control in the hands of highly responsive and politically astute ministers.

By 1992, the Country Liberal Party had occupied the majority position in the Legislative Assembly for 18 years and it would be another 9 years before the Labor Party could finally break that stranglehold on ministerial power. At the national level, the Australian National Training Authority was created by the agreement of the Commonwealth, states and territories to give effect to the National Training Reform Agenda. This arm's-length authority was the compromise when the states rebuffed the Keating Government's offer to assume responsibility for vocational education and training as the Commonwealth had previously done with universities (Goozee 2013, pp. 353–359). Predating the establishment of the Australian National Training Authority, the complementary Northern Territory Employment and Training Authority marked the start of the next major phase in the history of vocational education and training, even if it would be accomplished by returning to the commission-style organisations that had been abandoned a decade earlier.

The endless bureaucratic battles over the control over TAFE policy and funding that characterised the first years of self-government had caused successive Northern Territory Government ministers to use a variety of institutional structures to give effect to their wishes. Training policy making and implementation commenced with the long-standing Apprenticeship Board in 1948. This influence was diluted and shared with a relatively powerful Darwin Community College Council in 1974. With self-government, the Industries Training Commission was established in 1979 and the powers of the Darwin Community College were made subject to ministerial direction resulting in a further dilution of control and an increase in the number of interested parties. In 1982, the next major body to emerge was the Vocational Training Commission— it would last for just over two years. In 1984, TAFE policy matters would be split between the Education Department—which had a mandate to focus upon delivery but an insatiable desire to take total control—and an equally ambitious sequence of three different government departments and ministers—representing business and industry sectors—who retained responsibility for employment and apprentice/trainee functions.

The period 1984–91 also saw the TAFE portfolio split between two different ministers who had their own agendas and views regarding best use of the sector to advance the development of the Territory and their own political interests. In addition, there had been numerous advisory committees and external reviews each of which had contributed to ministerial decision-making. In total, there had been eight government departments or commissions involved, five large advisory bodies and five publicly funded major training organisations active in the TAFE arena since self-government. Additionally, a host of councils, committees, reviews and other representative bodies had been sanctioned by the Northern Territory Government during that first period of self-government—and these do not include the unions, employer associations, professional organisations, registration and licensing boards and political parties that had also been active in the training policy space as well. When looking back along the path that has led to the contemporary vocational education and training system, organisational and institutional litter dominates the view. The next 20 years, by comparison, would be relatively stable in terms of organisational structures. The Northern Territory Employment and Training Authority would remain in place from 1992–2001 to be followed by another 10-year period where responsibility for employment and training was subsumed into the broader Education Department. Progressively, however, both functions would again be separated from education and returned to an economic portfolio—the Department of Business.

When Shane Stone, Minister for the newly combined portfolio of Education and Training, rose to his feet in the Legislative Assembly on 26 February 1992 to give his ministerial statement, *A New Era in Vocational Education and Training*, the Northern Territory's relationship with the Commonwealth and other states was very different from that immediately following self-government. The generous financial support given by the Fraser Coalition Government had been substantially withdrawn by the Hawke/Keating Labor governments for both political reasons and the realities of a very weak economy teetering on the edge of long-term recession. For very many purposes the Territory was treated as a state; this included allowing the Chief Minister to participate in the Special Premiers' Meetings—the forerunner to the current Council of Australian Governments. In addition, the Commonwealth had embarked upon a massive program of macro and microeconomic reform that had positioned vocational education and training as a key policy and programmatic response as articulated in *Australia Reconstructed*. The drivers of the national debates and changes were well-understood by the government ministers of the newest and least populous jurisdiction: a desire to change society for the better guided by politicly astute and electorally confident ministers. This nation-wide approach to vocational education and training resonated well inside the Northern Territory Cabinet and with the electorate in general. Both the left and the right of politics shared a common view as to how governments would deploy vocational education and training to improve society by having a strong, market-driven economy supporting a larger population. This situation and accompanying rhetoric remains substantially unchanged today.

Stone's (1992) ministerial statement was both a philosophical and pragmatic justification for the shift from TAFE to vocational education and training. It would also establish many of the parameters that still characterise the sector some 20 years later. In the new policy environment, the Northern Territory Employment and Training Authority was charged with the task of 'creating a new era for training in the Northern Territory' in which the policy direction would be guided by employers, unions and community leaders and 'both private providers of training and publicly funded but independent TAFE colleges will be empowered to exercise increased local governance in meeting the needs of the communities they serve' (Stone 1992, p. 1). In addition, the new authority structure was also intended to resolve the battles for control of vocational education that had been relentlessly waged inside the Northern Territory Public Service as well as positioning the Territory to best take financial advantage of the Commonwealth's reform agenda.

Because of the Sue Bradley-led second review of the *Employment and Training Act*, Cabinet had decided to put a halt to the squabbling between senior public servants and their departments. When interviewed on the matter, Stone reported that he had been strongly lobbied by industry leaders to remove training from the government bureaucracy, 'otherwise, it would wither on the vine'. He accepted the advice that the time required to ensure that energy and resources spent on demarcation disputes between the agencies would be better utilised on front-line delivery. In addition, Stone did not share the former Chief Minister Everingham's disdain for statutory authorities. He found that if he made the right appointments, these volunteers enjoyed the chance to participate and 'were mindful of giving sensible advice to me'. The four advisory groups attached to the Northern Territory Employment and Training Authority were also considered by Stone to be important as 'they gave everyone a role and a chance to have their say'. In addition, he believed that better public policy is created when more people are involved. Although he did not specifically say so, having an organisational structure that facilitates this deep interaction with a wide range of interest groups also reflects the political necessity of Northern Territory ministers being seen to be listening to their constituents and acting upon their concerns.

In his capacity as the Commissioner for Public Employment, David Hawkes was a key participant in the creation of the Northern Territory Employment and Training Authority. This authority was built upon the former TAFE functions that had been progressively removed from the Education Department as well as those tasks undertaken by the Department of Labour and Administrative Services prior to its abolition. When asked in an interview about these changes some years later, he did not believe that it made much difference if government chose either a departmental structure or an authority to control training. Hawkes believed that the important thing was to have a formal body with a separate identity and clear role that was being carried out by talented staff using mechanisms to 'keep up with' what is going on in business and the economy. Otherwise, it is too easy for the responsible agency to become 'just another processing bureaucracy'.

As an experienced public servant, it is unsurprising that Hawkes could easily accept either structure as this position gave him the best possible chance of being responsive to a constant change in ministers, each with their own skills and preferred working styles. Hawkes also described the importance of training to governments as a public policy tool and their reluctance to cede control to other interests. Training is 'the only answer if people are not behaving as they ought to—you have to train them'. In addition, Hawkes stated in the interview that training is attractive to ministers because it is:

- easy to do;
- the answer sounds right;
- you can throw money at it; and
- government is seen to have done something.

The importance of training to achieving ministerial ambition was reiterated in Stone's statement to the Legislative Assembly, 'The Northern Territory Government maintains that vocational education and training must remain a state and territory responsibility' (Stone 1992, p. 2). However, he also demonstrated an accommodating attitude when he went on to say that 'the Northern Territory Government looks forward to working with the Commonwealth minister'. Stone then returned to familiar Territory dogma when he declared:

> This government believes that a more competitive training environment will emerge from a new structure for the provision of vocational education and training in the Northern Territory and from the Government's attitudes to federal cooperation. I am convinced that our procedures will become precedents for other States to follow. This Government is not about large bureaucracies and the centralisation of power whether this be in Commonwealth systems, union structures or a Territory-wide monopoly of public providers of training (Stone 1992, pp. 3–4).

In addition, Stone also presented the Northern Territory Government's view as to how 'equity' in vocational education and training should be defined and made operational. Many in the broader community believed that access to training was the path to greater equity. However, the new Minister for Education and Training proposed that equity would be defined as a 'right of choice' on the part of each individual as to how much and what kind of training would advance their access to employment markets and that this choice would increasingly need to be exercised throughout life as the nature of jobs changed (Stone 1992, p. 12). History has shown that implementing genuine individual student choice and a demand-driven training system remains an oft-stated intention, but a very elusive practice to implement. The risk of individual community members not choosing an 'appropriate' training pathway— not behaving as they ought to rationally do—poses a major threat to the exercise of ministerial philanthropy.

While it would take many months to complete the bureaucratic re-organisation, training policy and funding were once again under the control of a single minister in 1992. Over the next 10 years of its existence as a stand-alone body, the Northern Territory Employment and Training Authority would have to respond to the priorities and interests of each of the five ministerial successors to Stone. In this new arrangement both private and public providers of training were encouraged to operate in a quasi-market overseen by the authority that was directly responsible to the minister's office.

Minister Stone was committed to an inclusive Northern Territory Employment and Training Authority that was representative of the various groups with an interest in training. More importantly, he also had the skills to work with the numerous advisory groups and boards that characterised the new authority. The Northern Territory Employment and Training Authority consisted of a 15-person board that had a full-time chairperson. Don Watts was the inaugural chair and he was joined by:

- the Secretary of the Education Department or nominee;
- four direct ministerial appointments;
- one Commonwealth Department of Employment, Education and Training official; and
- eight persons appointed by the minister drawn from unions, business, industry and the regions (Northern Territory Employment and Training Authority 1993, p. 2).

In effect, the minister either directly appointed or heavily influenced the appointment of all but one member of the Northern Territory Employment and Training Authority's board.

In addition to the board, the new authority had four advisory councils, each convened by a member of the board, whose membership was drawn from those in the community with an interest in formal training. While not being direct ministerial appointments, the members were vetted by the minister's office before taking up their positions. These advisory councils included:

- Planning and Resource: 10 members;
- Aboriginal Programs, Employment and Training: 17 members;
- Employment and Training Needs Planning: seven members;
- Accreditation and Registration: eight members; and the
- Women's Reference Group: six members.

In addition to the over 60 persons on the board and advisory councils, there were also a dozen Industry Training Advisory Boards that represented the major business and industry groupings operating in the Northern Territory. These boards each had their own full-time staff and a series of directors whose role was to provide the advisory councils and Northern Territory Employment and Training Authority board with industry specific information on employment trends, skills in demand and the related training plans required to develop the Territory's labour market.

Minister Stone's preferred working style was to directly engage as many people as possible in the training policy and funding arenas to guard against unintended outcomes and to minimise criticism of his decisions. Equally importantly, these formal boards and councils provided a direct conduit to the minister that ensured he had access to virtually every issue or problem that was being discussed or considered in the training system. As a result, the minister's office could constantly be assessing potential political benefits or risks. In addition, this enormous advisory superstructure provided the means to enact the most important determinant of philanthropic behaviour—self-identification with the intended recipient. The broadly based authority structure allowed for a much greater level of direct contact between the minister and the electors in the community and bypassed the filtering that takes place when the main method of interaction is made through a government department populated with full-time technical experts and transactional bureaucrats.

During its first full year of operations in 1992, the Northern Territory Employment and Training Authority held nine board meetings that deliberated upon a wide range of training-related matters. According to *Annual Report 1992* (Northern Territory Employment and Training Authority 1993, p. 10), major items for consideration included:

- functions of Group Training Companies;
- declaration of apprenticeships/traineeships in specific vocations;
- capital planning for teaching facilities;
- Commonwealth proposals to take over vocational education and training;
- teaching TAFE courses in secondary schools;
- the proposed merger of Sadadeen Secondary College and the Alice Springs College of TAFE;
- a review of the Northern Territory Open College; and the
- establishment of the Australian National Training Authority.

At the end of November 1992, a new minister gained responsibility for vocational education and training. Fred Finch served as the Minister for Education and Training until June 1995 and, after a year in other portfolios, spent June 1996 to July 1997 as the minister responsible for training. Finch resigned from the ministry in July 1997 and left politics following the August general election.

Like his predecessor, Finch's preferred style of conducting his ministerial responsibilities found a comfortable place with the myriad advisory bodies and boards. Finch relied upon these bodies to provide him with information and direction from the 'real world' of industry and business rather than from career public servants. In addition, Finch no longer had to adjudicate over the running battles between the Education Department and everyone else responsible for some aspect of training because the Northern Territory had lost one of the major protagonists. In October 1992 the robust and highly assertive secretary of the Northern Territory Education Department, Geoff Spring, had moved on to become the Chief Executive of the Victorian Education Department. Spring had been hand-picked by the newly elected Premier of Victoria, Jeff Kennett, to close hundreds of schools and remove thousands of staff from that state's education sector in a move that provoked strong reactions from both the union movement and the community. This was not a task for the faint-hearted and Spring's proven pedigree as a highly valued strategist and unceasing responsiveness to his political masters' priorities had served him well in the Territory and made him a natural choice for his promotion into Victoria and greater national prominence.

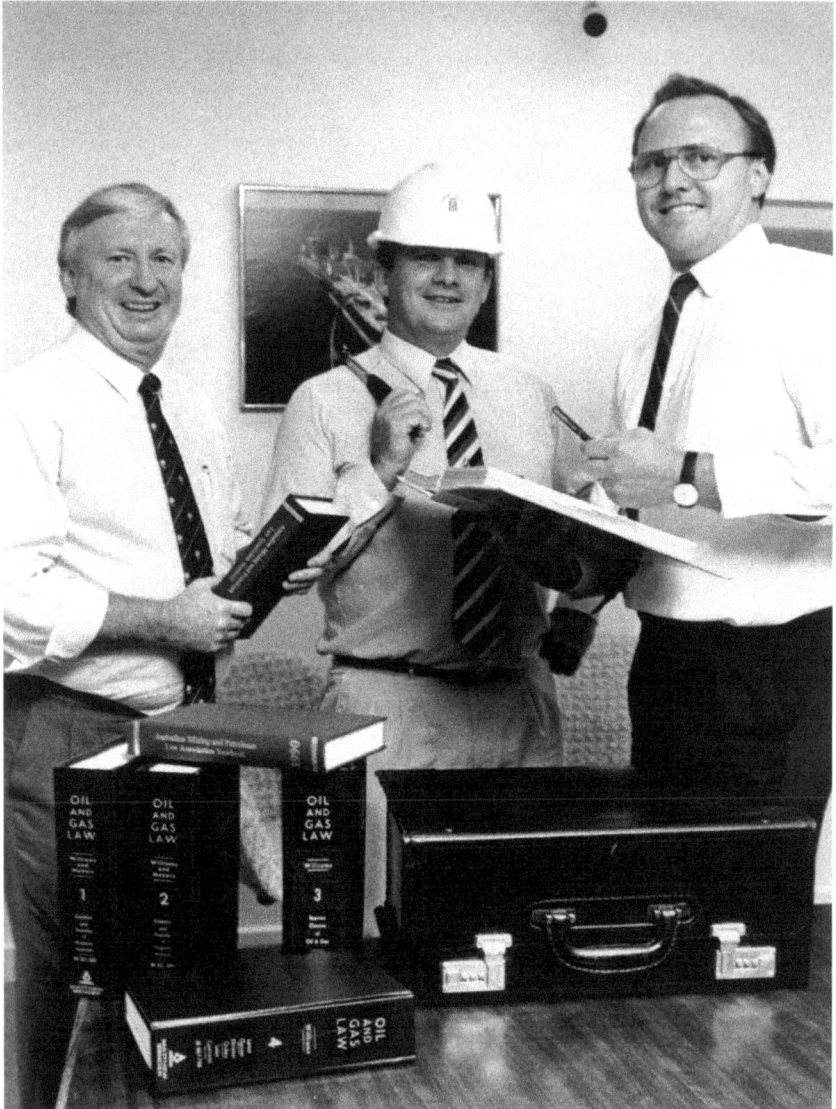

Figure 34. Ministers Fred Finch, Shane Stone and lecturer Kym Livesley celebrating the new course 'Introduction to Mining Law' at the Northern Territory University, April 1993.

Source: Creator Baz Ledwidge, Charles Darwin University Library.

Minister Finch oversaw the maturation of Northern Territory Employment and Training Authority as an organisation. Under the brief chairmanship of RA Cleary in 1993, 'the first profile of the training needs in the Territory' was produced as well as 'the beginnings of a demand driven delivery system and the emergence of a training market' (Northern Territory Employment and Training Authority 1994, p. i). The first Chief Executive Officer of the Northern Territory Employment and Training Authority was appointed in June 1993 when John Smyth, the former Principal of the Alice Springs College of TAFE, took up the position. During 1994, the Education Department transferred both the financial operations it had been conducting on behalf of the authority as well as the Post-School Division staff to the Northern Territory Employment and Training Authority. By the end of 1995, the authority had 'increased staff levels from 47 in 1994 to 67' and they operated in four divisions that included the Training Network NT, also known as the NT Open Learning Network, which provided basic training facilities in more than a dozen remote locations for the use of both public and private registered training organisations (Northern Territory Employment and Training Authority 1996, p. 26).

Andrew Bruyn, the manager of Darwin's first commercial television station, became chair of the Northern Territory Employment and Training Authority board during this time and would stay in that role until it was disbanded by the new Labor Government in 2001. The extensive advisory council structure remained in place under Finch. There were 98 declared vocations which required apprenticeships or traineeships to be formally registered and the 11 Industry Training Advisory Boards had each developed industry training plans to guide the use of public funds for training. From July 1995 to June 1996, Steve Hatton was the Minister for Education and Training and he did little to alter the existing operations and structures of the training authority prior to Finch's return as minister for a further year.

In response to national training policy, and acting on advice from the Northern Territory Employment and Training Authority board and advisory councils, Finch had also been active in realigning the Northern Territory Government training providers on the grounds that change would drive greater efficiency and quality through the vocational education and training system. He undertook these actions believing 'local ownership to be a critical element in successful delivery of any educational service' (Finch 1993, p. 2).

Figure 35. The Honourable Fred Finch handing over motorcycles for licensed training.
Source: Creator Bert Wiedemann, PH0730/1340, Northern Territory Government Photographer Slide Collection. Northern Territory Library.

In a statement delivered to the Legislative Assembly on 26 May 1993, Minister Finch (1993) previewed the progressive dismantling of the Northern Territory Open College prior to the start of the 1994 academic year. The Territory Training Centre in Stuart Park, the operations of the Adult Migrant Education Centre, the Top End regional operations of the Open College and its Palmerston Campus would all be transferred to the Northern Territory University Institute of TAFE. The funding for prisoner education that had previously been allocated to the Northern Territory Open College would be given directly to the Department of Correctional Services, and the Secondary Correspondence School would join the Schools Division of the Education Department. The Northern Territory Employment and Training Authority would be given an even greater role in quality control assurance, effective monitoring of outcomes and reporting outputs to the Northern Territory and Commonwealth governments.

Figure 36. Palmerston Campus.
Source: Courtesy of Charles Darwin University Library.

Finch also presided over the merger of Sadadeen Senior College and the Alice Springs College of TAFE to create Centralian College from the start of 1993. This new organisation would continue the Northern Territory's use of dual-sector education and training providers by catering for school students in years 11 and 12 as well as post-school vocational education and training students. Centralian College also provided a limited range of higher education courses under contract with the Northern Territory University. In 1994, Centralian College incorporated the Central Australian operations of the Northern Territory Open College as a result of the changes to delivery announced in Finch's May ministerial statement. In keeping with Finch's emphasis on local ownership, the Centralian College Council had considerable control over budget and operational issues and was, rather uniquely, even given the capacity to develop its own industrial award for lecturing staff. This distinctive award allowed for staff from school and TAFE backgrounds to be deployed both across programs and class times, making the college much more responsive to community and business priorities than traditional TAFE colleges or secondary schools had been.

Finch's *Ministerial statement: future organisation of vocational education and training services in the NT* also reaffirmed the Northern Territory's commitment to new public management principles. Responsibility for service delivery and all potential problems associated with dealing with the public, including the risk of failure, were contracted away from government and the minister. On the other hand, policy, funding and quality control were even more firmly centralised in executive government through the Northern Territory Employment and Training Authority which was directly responsible to the minister.

Despite a long-standing policy which separated relatively independent and responsive local delivery from centralised funding and policy considerations, Northern Territory ministers never seriously considered relinquishing their interests in the affairs of the colleges. The *Education Act* gave the minister considerable powers in relation to the conduct of the affairs of colleges, such as Centralian College or the Katherine Rural College. In particular, the minister had the power to appoint the chair of the college council as well as 10 of the 15 other members of council. In addition, the minister approved the appointment of the director of the college on the recommendation of the college council. Northern Territory Government ministers wanted to ensure that their philanthropy would be handled by people they knew and trusted to implement their express wishes: another example of self-identification. While provisions remain in the *Education Act* for the establishment of colleges, none have operated since 2003—the previous colleges have either been absorbed into Charles Darwin University as part of an ongoing consolidation of training provision starting with Finch's May 1993 ministerial statement or have been made subject to their own legislation as in the case of the Batchelor Institute of Indigenous Tertiary Education.

The Minister for Education and Training also maintained a strong suite of powers in vocational education and training at the Northern Territory University. By 1989, the university had consolidated its non-higher education programs into the Institute of TAFE, with its own board. The minister appointed five of the 10 members of this board. The other positions were occupied by a nominee from the Department of Education, a student, a staff member and the Director of the Institute of TAFE and, according to Berzins and Loveday (1999, pp. 180–181), 'the board was required to comply with the directives from the Minister for Education' as well as being responsible to the university council. Unsurprisingly, senior leaders in the Institute of TAFE 'found that this dual responsibility was a source of tension and conflict'. The Northern Territory Employment and Training Authority continued to be developed, including the removal of a source of continual irritation when the Department of Education training functions were transferred to the authority, and the Institute of TAFE and its board were disbanded in 1994. As part of a broader restructuring program, the Northern Territory University absorbed the Institute's administrative and academic functions, and leadership was provided through the appointment of Sabaratnam Prathapan as the Deputy Vice-Chancellor Vocational Education and Training—a role he would occupy from 1995 until May 1996.

By 1996, the Northern Territory Employment and Training Authority had overseen the implementation of the National Training Reform Agenda in the Northern Territory. The major reform initiatives included:

- the introduction and consolidation of a competency-based training system;
- national standards for vocational education and training qualifications;
- the creation of a market for training with public and private providers;
- new methods for the recognition of skills gained in Australia and overseas;
- the recognition of the National Training Board's roles;
- enhancement of pathways in the transition to work from school; and
- the establishment of the Australian National Training Authority.

Like Saville and Chard in the previous decade, Prathapan proved adept at moving across the organisational boundaries when he left the university and became the Chief Executive Officer of the Northern Territory Employment and Training Authority on 27 May 1996. He eagerly took up the task of institutionalising the national reforms. The *Annual Report 1996* (Northern Territory Employment and Training Authority 1997) notes that there were 109 declared vocations in the Territory and a large amount of more general vocational education being serviced by four public providers and 93 private training organisations under quasi-market conditions. The Authority's staffing had grown to 72 positions in five operational areas and they were supported by three Advisory Councils (the previous two planning functions had been consolidated into a single body), 12 Industry Training Advisory Boards and the Women's Reference Group.

Prathapan, as Chief Executive Officer of the Northern Territory Employment and Training Authority, was able to advocate for and defend policy positions that led to antagonism with his former employer, the Northern Territory University. The 1996 McInnes Review of the Northern Territory vocational education and training sector advocated for increased privatisation of the training system by introducing greater competition into the market from interstate providers and reinforcing the view that the authority did not support the integration of vocational education and training into the Northern Territory University (Berzins & Loveday 1999, p. 197). In spite of Minister Finch offering assurances of the future of the dual-sector arrangement in the Legislative Assembly in early 1997, the ongoing skirmishes over who controlled vocational education and training continued. On the one side, the Prathapan-led Northern Territory Employment and Training Authority saw the need for a more industry directed and market-driven training system. On the other, the university Vice-Chancellor, Ron McKay, vigorously defended the institution's independence and constantly raised the spectre of failure in the Territory's notoriously thin markets if the University's predominant share of vocational education and training was seriously diluted (Berzins & Loveday 1999, p. 198). Following the August 1997 election, the new minister, Peter Adamson, was able to reconcile the two parties to some extent. As will be shown later, by 1998 the Northern Territory Employment and Training Authority would be forced to give considerably more attention to its own future.

In spite of the continual debate over control of the training system and the importance of markets, each of the Authority's organisational structures and advisory mechanisms were in place to give effect to its clearly articulated main function: 'On behalf of the NT Government, NTETA purchases education and training services from registered providers to meet the needs of industry and the community' (Northern Territory Employment and Training Authority 1997, p. 7). In other words, this organisation was the vehicle, like private foundations used by the wealthy, through which the minister could exercise public philanthropy by using taxpayers' funds to serve a perceived public good. The authority structure also allowed the minister's office to monitor the pulse of the electorate while simultaneously providing access to the minister, and vice versa, as required.

Although frequently debated, from 1996–98 the operations of the vocational education and training system in the Northern Territory were not subject to significant institutional change except for the formation of Group Training NT when the operations of the Central Australian and Top End companies were merged due to the economic difficulties experienced by the Alice Springs-based organisation. The election of the John Howard-led Coalition Government in 1996 and its decision to retain the Australian National Training Authority reaffirmed the bipartisan approach to the principles articulated in the National Training Reform Agenda. Northern Territory registered training providers and the Northern Territory Employment and Training Authority both found themselves thrust into a reactive state of affairs, responding to a re-energised Australian National Training Authority and a very strong-willed and ideologically-driven Commonwealth Government minister, David Kemp. All training organisations were being challenged by increased exercise of Federal Government policy muscle accompanied by decreased funding that was euphemistically labelled 'growth through efficiency' (Northern Territory Employment and Training Authority 1999, p. 2).

Unlike the other states and territory, the Northern Territory was structurally and operationally well-placed to deal with the continued reform agenda as it had a complementary authority structure that worked well with the Australian National Training Authority's approach to policy and funding. With all of the registered training providers in the Northern Territory either from the private sector or operating at arm's-length from government under legislative provisions, the Northern Territory Cabinet maintained its position of having greater public policy freedom than did the other jurisdictions that felt obliged to maintain their state-owned and operated TAFE systems. The Northern Territory was frequently the first to move on major reforms and this responsive capacity 'paid handsome dividends for the Territory' according to former Chief Minister Shane Stone (Martin & Dewar 2012, p. 95).

During much of this period Peter Adamson served as the Northern Territory minister with responsibility for training, having replaced Finch in July 1997. In one of life's little ironies, Adamson was a former commercial television sports reporter who had worked at the then Channel 8 under the direction of Andrew Bruyn, the chairman of the Northern Territory Employment and Training Authority board; but now Adamson was the minister. Bruyn and the Authority's board were required to respond to his former employee's philanthropic priorities. During his nearly three years as minister, Adamson did not deliver a single ministerial statement on vocational education and training. Compared with the previous ministers, Adamson was unofficially considered by many public servants to be 'weak but nice'. He did not share either the capacity or desire to develop the reciprocal relationships with the various advisory councils and boards involved with training which the previous ministers had successfully used to advantage. Adamson's profile had been developed through the television screen, not in the suburban streets and small businesses where the electors live, shop and work. While it turns out he did understand the part of the job that allowed him to hand out public funds, it appears that he did not consider the philanthropic obligations of that privilege. Following the loss of his seat of Casuarina in the 2001 Northern Territory general election, Adamson stood for and won the office of Darwin Lord Mayor in 2002. Due to misappropriating Darwin City Council funds intended to be used for charitable donations, Adamson was charged, found guilty, fined $5,000 and served two months in prison (Lee 2007).

As described previously, the absence of institutional restructuring in the period 1996–98 did not diminish the enthusiasm of various parties in seeking greater control over the vocational education and training sector in the Northern Territory. Behind the scenes the groundwork was being laid for the seemingly inevitable next round of bureaucratic reorganisation. Adamson's disinterest and incapacity to make use of the vast advisory superstructure of the Northern Territory Employment and Training Authority opened the door for many to question the purpose and role for the various advisory councils and boards. In a case of unfortunate timing, the concerns about the cost, effectiveness and general operations of the Northern Territory Employment and Training Authority came to the attention of the Treasurer, Mike Reed, who was guiding a process to reduce Northern Territory Government expenditure that was called *Planning for Growth* (Personal communication, November 1998). Public servants readily euphemised Reed's review of government functions and expenditure as 'Pruning for Growth'.

Figure 37. Peter Adamson, Member of the Legislative Assembly, January 2001.
Source: Creator Northern Territory Government Photographer, PH0866/0088, Northern Territory Government Photographer Collection, Northern Territory Library.

Planning for Growth took place in the second half of 1998 and examined the operations of every Northern Territory Government agency. The arguments about education and training being different from the rest of the public service that had been so prominently used in the period before and immediately after self-government some 20 years earlier were raised yet again. The political potency of the separate nature of schooling and vocational education and training was not lost on the Treasurer. In September 1998, Reed completely bypassed Adamson and appointed a four-person task group to review the education system and to produce a report to Cabinet by 16 November. Walter Czernezkyj, the former principal of Katherine High School in Reed's electorate, was hand-picked by the Treasurer to be the chair of the task group. The future of the Northern Territory Employment and Training Authority was not included in the terms of reference given to the education review task group but considerable discussion took place behind the scenes nevertheless (Turnbull 1998).

The uncertainty created by *Planning for Growth* reignited the foundational arguments to do with the relationship between the Education Department and the vocational education and training sector—code for the control of staffing and budget. In addition, another long-standing debate over the merits of the alternative administrative structures for the management of training—an authority or a government department—resurfaced. As had happened with Minister Adamson, it appears that Prathapan, in his capacity as the Chief Executive Officer of the Northern Territory Employment and Training Authority, was pushed to the periphery of the government's decision-making process. The future of the Northern Territory Employment and Training Authority was not included in the terms of reference for the education system review. However, it is clear that the Commissioner for Public Employment (David Hawkes), Prathapan's deputy (Joyce Turnbull) and Czernezkyj were actively considering a detailed proposal for the 'transfer of NTETA functions to the Education Department' right down to detailed staffing arrangements that would reduce numbers from 75.5 to 32 (Personal communication, November 1998). Unlike the education review that incorporated an extensive and exhaustive Northern Territory-wide consultation with every possible interest group, the fate of the Northern Territory Employment and Training Authority was not being canvassed publicly.

At a Cabinet meeting held in late November 1998, the near-term destiny of the Northern Territory Employment and Training Authority was determined based upon the following parameters:

- continue as a separate entity but to be completely reviewed and restructured by the NTETA Board in a three-month time frame;
- retain current Chief Executive Officer;
- reduce staff from 78 to a maximum of 32;

- transfer property to the public service property management unit;
- retain the existing authority board;
- rationalise the Industry Training Advisory Boards;
- transfer corporate services to the Department of Corporate and Information Services;
- target budget savings of $4 million; and
- review the future of the organisation after a three-month period.

On 1 December, Reed (1998) presented Cabinet's decision in a brutally brief statement to the Legislative Assembly:

> The Northern Territory Employment and Training Authority is to be restructured so that it better reflects industry needs. Whilst it will remain autonomous it will be restructured, with roughly half the present staff and a correspondingly reduced budget.

During the Assembly debate that followed, Adamson reported that Cabinet had also decided to close Mataranka Station, operationally part of the Katherine Rural College, as a training facility and sell the property. As it turns out, this did not take place and the pastoral lease for this marginal cattle property was handed over to the Northern Territory University in 2001. Charles Darwin University announced that it would relinquish this lease in 2014 to consolidate operations at the renamed Katherine Rural Campus and increase delivery of agricultural training while students were on the job at cattle stations. The intention to divest training facilities that were part of the Northern Territory Training Network in 13 remote Indigenous communities as well as Katherine, Tennant Creek, Jabiru and Nhulunbuy was finally achieved in 2016. A number of options were canvassed such as transferring the facilities to the university, handing over responsibility to local councils in conjunction with Batchelor College or joining the training facilities with secondary schools. Up until 2016, the remote and regional town premises had remained with the training authority and direct government responsibility despite repeated approaches to the university and Batchelor Institute.

Prathapan's tenure as the Chief Executive Officer of the Northern Territory Employment and Training Authority did not survive the three-month review ordered by Cabinet and in April 1999 he was transferred to the Department of Transport and Infrastructure Development and permanently out of the vocational education and training sector.

He would be temporarily replaced by David Hawkes who took on the Chief Executive's role in addition to his main appointment as the Commissioner for Public Employment. Most of the day-to-day operations of the newly downsized authority were being guided by Joyce Turnbull during this period.

As part of the restructuring of the Northern Territory Employment and Training Authority, the principles of new public management through outsourcing were again in evidence. In May 1998, the Commonwealth Government opened its first New Apprenticeship Centre in the Northern Territory to support its training priorities as well as handling targeted national incentive and subsidy payments. This service was provided under contract by a consortium of seven Industry Training Advisory Boards: the Northern Territory Industry Training Bureau. In a unique partnership, and as part of the rationalisation of Northern Territory Employment and Training Authority operations, the legislated apprenticeship management functions that had been carried out by the authority were combined with the federal apprenticeship centre functions and put out to a second competitive tender. By December 1999, a 'one-stop shop' for apprentices throughout the Northern Territory was in operation due to a successful bid on the part of Group Training Northern Territory (Northern Territory Employment and Training Authority 2000, p. 13).

In a separate matter, the Northern Territory Government had decided to alter the status and name of Batchelor College with the support of the Labor Opposition. Having been established as a government agency in 1995, the moves to make it independent of the Northern Territory Public Service were initiated on 22 April 1999 with the introduction into the Legislative Assembly of the Batchelor Institute of Indigenous Tertiary Education Bill by Daryl Manzie on behalf of Adamson. The intention of the legislation, broadly based upon that of the Northern Territory University, was to make the new institute 'the main provider of higher education, and vocational education and training programs, for Aboriginal and Torres Strait Islander people from the Northern Territory and from other parts of Australia' (Manzie 1999). It was also noted that this change of name was a further step in the pursuit of university status when postgraduate and academic research profiles allowed.

Adamson's tenure as Minister for Tertiary Education and Training ended on 30 January 2000 and he was replaced by Chris Lugg. As with several other Northern Territory parliamentarians, Lugg's journey into a ministerial appointment had commenced with his active involvement as an official of the Country Liberal Party's organisational wing (Heatley 1998, p. 123). He won preselection for the Darwin rural seat of Nelson, was elected in August of 1997 and moved into the ministry two years later. Unlike Adamson, whose path to politics was built upon his high-profile media exposure, Lugg had literally worked in the political trenches and had built a close relationship with his constituents. He instinctively understood the dual obligations of responsiveness to the electorate and philanthropic behaviour expected of a minister in the Northern Territory.

Figure 38. The second Burke ministry, 1 August 2000.

This photo includes three ministers for training: Darryl Manzie, seated far left; Peter Adamson, standing far right; and the final Country Liberal Party Minister for Training in their first long period in power since self-government in 1978, Chris Lugg, seated far right.

Source: Creator Northern Territory Government Photographer, PH0866/0001, Protocol Collection, Northern Territory Library.

As a result of the *Planning for Growth* Cabinet decisions, the board of the Northern Territory Employment and Training Authority, still chaired by Bruyn, had been very active in restructuring the organisation based on the Rolfe Report that had been delivered in March 1999 (Lugg 2000, p. 5). Compared to the education system task group, Rolfe's study was much quicker, tightly focused and was never publicly or widely circulated. In response to recommendations contained in this review, new legislation was enacted in November 1999. The *Northern Territory Employment and*

Training Act 1999 provided Lugg with a considerably more streamlined organisation than that used by his ministerial predecessors. The previous three advisory councils had been eliminated from the new Act and the board membership reduced from 15 to 10 persons, each appointed by the minister. As before, there was no provision for the specific appointment of a person from a training provider to maintain a clear separation between policy/funding decisions and training delivery. The new Act required the board to consult with industry and to fund training as a result of that interaction. The downsized board was made subject to the direction of the minister. The chief executive officer, for legal purposes, was legislated to be 'the authority' and was also to take direction from the minister even when such actions contravened decisions that had been made by the board. Other sections of the legislation provided for recognition of national training packages/accredited courses, registration of training organisations, apprenticeship regulation (already outsourced), quality and compliance with the Act, as well providing for an Appeals Tribunal (Northern Territory of Australia 1999).

In May 2000, the Secretary of the Education Department, Walter Czernezkyj of the Education Review, was replaced by his mentor, the head of the Health Department, Peter Plummer. Shifting Czernezkyj from education into the position of the Chief Executive Officer of the Northern Territory Employment and Training Authority was seen as a serious demotion. The perceived inability to implement his own review's recommendations saw him moved from heading up the second-largest agency in the Northern Territory Government to being in charge of the 43 staff left after the restructuring of the authority (Northern Territory Employment and Training Authority 2000, p. 54). As a direct result of the election of the Labor Government in August 2001, Czernezkyj resigned on 27 January 2002 and was not replaced. He consequently left the Northern Territory and became the principal at Urrbrae Agricultural High School in Adelaide.

However, during his tenure as Chief Executive Officer, Czernezkyj was very sensitive and responsive to every ministerial utterance made by Lugg and the Northern Territory Government's plans for the 'role and direction' of the 'restructured' Northern Territory Employment and Training Authority (Lugg 2000, p. 1). The new minister resorted to a familiar tactic to place his stamp on the revamped authority by changing the words used in the system. He rejected the phrase vocational education and training (and its universally accepted acronym VET) in favour of returning to TAFE. Lugg justified his position by returning to the Country Liberal Party populism that had characterised the actions of many ministers:

> We have moved slightly away from the national trend to title the sector VET in the belief that the community is more comfortable with TAFE (Lugg 2000, p. 1).

When interviewed in 2012 about his time as the chair of the Northern Territory Employment and Training Authority Board, Andrew Bruyn also reinforced the significance of the preference for TAFE on the basis that small business and employers understood the simplicity of the term and the implication of attending 'tech colleges' for the off-the-job training component. Vocational education and training was seen to be yet another of the plethora of technical terms and acronyms that had become common in the training sector and served to alienate both employers and students. Minister Lugg was being responsive to both the electorate and advisory board that sat apart from and frequently proffered different views from those put forward by the technical experts of the public service.

The significantly leaner Northern Territory Employment and Training Authority continually adopted ever more practices associated with new public management during the period 2000 to 2001. The operations of the authority were recast along the lines of the 'funder–purchaser–provider model' that had come to dominate the delivery of health services in the Northern Territory. It seems likely that Czernezkyj's relationship with Plummer facilitated the transfer of this style of operation into the training sector. In addition, this method of public sector management provided a bureaucratically rational structuring and understanding of ministerial philanthropic behaviour. The minister assumed the role of funder by supplying resources resulting from his or her success in Cabinet meetings. The Northern Territory Employment and Training Authority already occupied the role of purchaser of training in a quasi-market serviced by both public and private organisations (for example, Northern Territory Employment and Training Authority 1998, p. 7). Finally, the Northern Territory's long-standing policy of separating delivery from policy ensured that there were a range of registered training organisations who would be the providers of program delivery by entering into resource agreements with the authority. By 2000, the concept of purchasing services from training providers had been extended beyond the apprenticeship services that were outsourced in the previous year to now include quality audit services and the industry advisory bodies. Lugg (2000, p. 5) described the extension of funder–purchaser–provider mechanisms in his ministerial statement to the Legislative Assembly:

> NTETA purchases advice about industry training from Industry Training Advisory Bodies or ITABS. In the future, NTETA will purchase advice in a more streamlined and focused manner, helping to improve the way in which training is directed.

The application of the funder–purchaser–provider model to the Industry Training Advisory Boards fundamentally changed their position in the training sector. They moved from being part of the vast advisory super-structure to now being a provider in some sort of marketplace. When implemented, the changes mooted by Lugg resulted in the winding up of the 11 Industry Training Advisory Boards. In the future, the Northern Territory Employment and Training Authority would only purchase industry advice from six Training Advisory Councils (Northern Territory Employment and Training Authority 2001, p. 3). As it turns out, there was only one funder and one purchaser in this 'market' for industry advice and only six providers were going to be supported.

After almost a decade of using an arm's-length statutory authority that had deep roots into almost every aspect of the training system, the logic of new public management and the impact of four ministers for training had produced a very different organisation from that envisaged by Stone in 1991. While the distinct separation between policy formulation and delivery had remained in place, almost every other function of the Northern Territory Employment and Training Authority had either been outsourced, downsized or re-rationalised. Stone (1991, p. 1) saw distinct benefits in having 'employer and employees all involved in making decisions' and having industry making 'the maximum possible input into policy development'. In order to remain in touch with the mood of the electorate, the vast advisory super-structure of the original Northern Territory Employment and Training Authority was carefully constructed by Stone (1991, p. 2) to 'advise government on a range of issues' and to 'be advisory to myself'. For the first minister for education and training, this new authority was not envisaged as a stripped down and utilitarian 'purchaser' of vocational education and training services and industry advice, rather its role was:

to establish the playing field on which providers meet the needs of the community, to advise government on the equitable use of funds and establish systems of accountability which increase public awareness of the efficient use of public moneys in the provision of vocational education and training (Stone 1991, p. 3).

In other words, the employment and training authority's purpose was to ensure that the minister understood the priorities of the industry and the community to guarantee that ministerial philanthropy was carefully targeted, not wasted, and that the public was well aware of the minister's responsiveness and largesse.

The changes to both the roles and functions of the Northern Territory Employment and Training Authority sanctioned by Reed, Adamson and Lugg produced exactly the type of 'processing bureaucracy' that the Commissioner for Public Employment, David Hawkes, had previously warned against. In place of the deep-seated involvement of nearly 200 industry-based individuals, a small band of policy and procurement experts interpreted the minister's needs. Quality assurance, apprenticeship support, training provision and industry advice were being purchased on behalf of the minister who was simultaneously being deprived of the mutually beneficial direct interaction with industry and the perceived kudos that flow from ministerial philanthropic behaviour. As described by Hawkes when interviewed, the Northern Territory Employment and Training Authority had become 'just another processing agency' which destroyed the capacity for ministers to keep in touch with the intimate political machinations of the miniscule Northern Territory electorates and to reap the rewards of electoral success.

The quasi-market that had been created for the provision of training had somewhat stabilised in the final two years of the Country Liberal Party's long dominance of government. There were four public providers and around 100 private providers, including a variety of not-for-profit and non-government organisations that were nevertheless reliant upon public funding. The role of the Northern Territory Employment and Training Authority was 'to purchase and fund training services delivered by providers in the Northern Territory' with about 75 per cent of the funding going to the public providers and 25 per cent to private providers (Northern Territory Employment and Training Authority 2001, pp. 27–31).

The former Katherine Rural College, now known as the Northern Territory Rural College, had always struggled to attract a critical mass of students or programs to be a viable concern, as the initial review had predicted at its inception. The inability to get out of Mataranka Station also contributed to the Northern Territory Government's decision to hand over responsibility for the operations of both the cattle station and the rural campus to the Northern Territory University commencing on 1 January 2001 (Northern Territory University 2001a, p. ii). This process of consolidation would be continued in 2003 with the creation of Charles Darwin University.

In the meantime, Batchelor Institute of Indigenous Tertiary Education, having received the Commonwealth's recognition as a higher education provider in 1988, continued its push towards achieving university status but found little overt support from either the Commonwealth Government or the Northern Territory University. The Commonwealth Government's financial contribution towards higher education offerings and the Northern Territory Government's support for vocational education and training were equally balanced, allowing for the dual-sector institute's operations to take place in many remote communities across the Northern Territory as well as interstate (Batchelor Institute of Indigenous Tertiary Education 2001).

Even with financial support from the Northern Territory Government, the Territory's largest provider of vocational education and training found itself in a precarious financial position in 1999. To plan a way forward, the Northern Territory University received funding from both the Territory and Commonwealth governments to commission an external consultancy conducted by KPMG (Webb 2014, pp. 27–28). In addition, the Northern Territory Government and the University Council formed a joint working party to make recommendations to council to bolster the institution's viability. 'The issues of resources for the university and stakeholder perceptions of the university lie at the heart of the strategic positioning project' (Northern Territory University 2001b, p. 3). The strategic positioning project and its nearly 50 recommendations would guide the university's direction through the final days of the Country Liberal Party's political domination in the Legislative Assembly.

In Central Australia, the turn of the century Centralian College's operation as the major regionally based provider of training was bolstered by easy access for secondary school students due to the dual-sector structure of the college. As had been the case since 1974, the competitive nature of the relationship with the Territory's largest training provider guided much of the planning and resource allocation conducted in Alice Springs. Centralian College had actively made steps to take training business away from the Northern Territory University by opening a branch of Training Solutions in the Darwin suburb of Parap. In particular, the college administration believed they had the full support of government ministers to target apprentices in the electrical and air-conditioning industries on the basis that increased competition would improve responsiveness to industry and increase the quality of program delivery. By the early 2000s, Centralian College and Training Solutions had taken over the provision of training for these vocations throughout the Northern Territory.

On the other hand, Centralian College and the Northern Territory University had entered into a contractual agreement for the provision of a limited range of higher education courses on the Alice Springs campus. The major offerings were in accounting and business in addition to a smaller effort in education. Otherwise, vocational education and training offerings by the two largest public providers remained geographically split, north and south, with the meeting point being in Tennant Creek where both organisations had staff operating out of the Northern Territory Employment and Training Authority training centre situated in the former Kargaru Primary School.

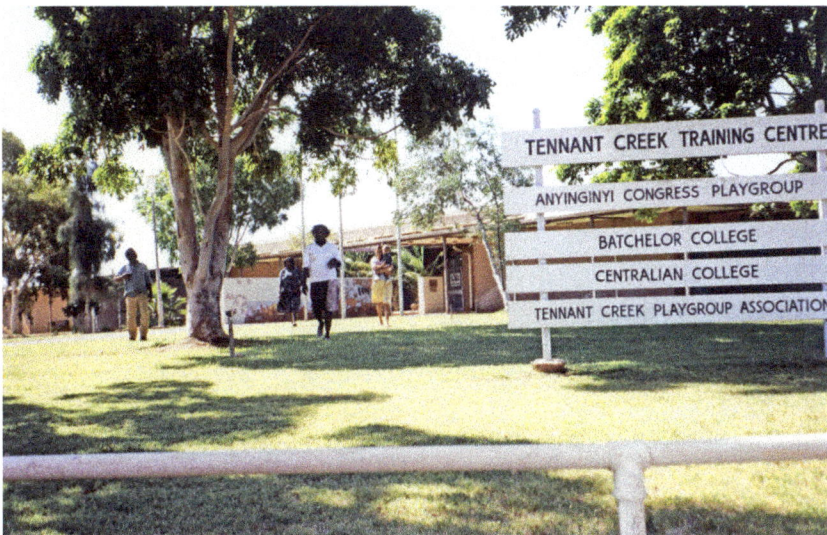

Figure 39. Former Kargaru School, November 1996.
Source: Creator Unknown, PH0705/0003, Batchelor College Annexe Collection, Northern Territory Library.

The Centre for Appropriate Technology had evolved into a non-government organisation with its own board and priorities, all but severing its ties with Centralian College as the two organisations moved in very different directions. The centre built and maintained its own relationships with both the ministerial offices and the Northern Territory Employment and Training Authority. It also astutely positioned itself to bid for major national contracts, established a separate trading company (CAT Projects) and became intimately aligned with the emerging Desert Knowledge movement.

The Institute of Aboriginal Development was embroiled in an impasse with the Country Liberal Party ministers and the Commonwealth Government that would only be resolved after Labor came to power in August 2001, and a delay of nearly five years. The institute had made a successful application to the Australian National Training Authority for capital works funding to upgrade older facilities and build a new library and teaching rooms on its Alice Springs campus located in South Terrace. Under direct instructions from the various ministers, the Northern Territory Employment and Training Authority would not release these funds unless the Institute for Aboriginal Development used them to build new facilities on the Sadadeen campus of Centralian College. The Northern Territory Government had decided that the future of the institute would be better guaranteed if it was co-located with the major public provider and did not duplicate an existing library, and that the new infrastructure would be better protected from the likely flooding at the Institute's current campus adjacent to the Todd River. In addition, the Commonwealth progressively developed the view that the money would be best spent by supporting the infrastructure needs of a proposed Desert Peoples Centre.

The serial changes to the Northern Territory Employment and Training Authority had also sown the seeds of its own demise. As with the Vocational Training Commission two decades before, the momentum to bring training policy back into a Northern Territory public service department had become irresistible, even to the Country Liberal Party. The authority's final annual report mooted the creation of a new government agency in the 2001–02 financial year: a department of employment and training. This organisation was to be created through the merger of the Northern Territory Employment and Training Authority and the Office of the Commissioner for Public Employment (Northern Territory Employment and Training Authority 2001, p. 2). However, with the installation of the

Northern Territory's first Labor Government as a result of the August 2001 general election, that plan was not implemented. Labor's initial minister with responsibility for vocational education and training was nevertheless also looking to the past to plan and structure the future.

Syd Stirling, a former teacher and employee of the Commonwealth Department of Employment, Education and Training, served as the Northern Territory minister responsible for training for five years until August 2006. When interviewed about the Labor Government's views on the merits of a departmental or authority structure for the control of vocational education and training in the Northern Territory, Stirling was direct and to the point:

> In relation to structural reform we had developed serious policy in the years 1999–2000. We had good educator and training experience in the caucus so we regarded ourselves as well equipped to overhaul what we considered a tired system that had virtually run itself with no strategic input from government and no accountability to anyone for results or lack thereof.

> I was very keen to get the previous NTETA, in operation when we were elected, integrated into a new Department of Employment, Education and Training.

> We had long held a view that NTETA lacked any strategic vision and was not as subject to Government policy direction as we would want given we had serious plans for growth in apprenticeship numbers and serious intent to do whatever was necessary to achieve the change and accountability required.

> We were seriously driven by what we saw as years of policy neglect. There was no focus from the Country Liberal Party and no view as to how things should work let alone be improved so we felt certain there was pretty much a blank canvas for us to imprint our plans upon. We were strongly supported by the Leader of the Opposition, Clare Martin, to bring these plans on.

> The final point was transferring Education to me from [Peter] Toyne once elected so that Education and Training sat with the Deputy Chief Minister — a deliberate elevation in the view of the community to underline its importance to the new Government.

In November 2001, the new Labor Government began implementing its policies with the transfer of the management of the Northern Territory Employment and Training Authority to the newly created Department of Education, Employment and Training—an organisation that mirrored the Commonwealth agency established by the Federal Labor Government minister, John Dawkins, two decades earlier to promote the reform of vocational education and training. Using exactly the same arguments that had guided the now opposition Country Liberal Party's rationale for spending public funds on TAFE, Stirling linked vocational education and training to the economic and social development of the Northern Territory. In a quite common display of bipartisanship that has come to define the training sector, human capital theory guided the policies and programs that justified Labor's allocation of public monies to train workers needed for the Northern Territory's growing economy and to promote social stability.

Figure 40. Students with Minister Stirling at a government-sponsored breakfast in Alice Springs, May 2003.

Source: Creator Northern Territory Government Photographer, PH0730/2127, Northern Territory Government Photographer Slide Collection, Northern Territory Library.

In August 2002, Stirling announced his government's intention to create a Ministerial Advisory Board for Employment and Training to replace the Northern Territory Employment and Training Authority Board. This new 13-member board would provide advice to the minister on the Territory's training profile and the related levels of compliance, promotion and expenditure used to achieve this profile. The composition of this advisory board would start to break down the strong separation of policy and service delivery that had been the hallmark of the previous employment and training authority. Membership would be subject to ministerial acceptance and would include:

- the chairperson;
- the chief executive officer;
- the chief executive officer of the agency with responsibility for industrial development;
- a vocational education practitioner;
- a nominee of the Commonwealth Government;
- three persons from outside the greater Darwin area;
- two chairs of training advisory councils;
- a nominee of the Aboriginal and Torres Straits Islander Commission;
- a nominee of the Trades and Labour Council; and
- a nominee of the Chamber of Commerce and Industry.

In addition, Labor decided to retain the six Training Advisory Councils to provide industry-specific advice but enhance their input through the use of labour market data provided by economists and other expert professional analysts. Lugg's attempts to rebadge the sector with the old term TAFE disappeared without a trace. However, that did not mean that Stirling readily accepted the technical jargon that had come to dominate the vocational education and training sector. When interviewed about his time as Minister for Employment, Education and Training, Stirling (2002) indicated that he 'never understood the language and acronyms associated with VET; these were tools of obfuscation'.

In addition to sharing with the previous government the reasons why the public should fund vocational education and training, the fresh Labor Cabinet also understood the beneficial nature of ministerial philanthropy. The composition of the ministerial advisory board represented the new government's constituency and provided the crucial direct relationship between the public and the minister, while promoting the greatest determinant of philanthropic behaviour: self-identification. The new Labor Cabinet consisted of people who had spent most of their recent working lives in the public and not-for-profit sectors. As a result, the novice ministers knew and understood how government bureaucracies operated and how to use them to achieve the desired social and economic agendas. In addition to the Chief Minister's high profile position as a television and radio presenter for the ABC, five of the other Cabinet members had been public servants and the final member had been a senior leader in non-government Indigenous organisations in the Northern Territory. The publicly funded bureaucracies and their methods of operating provided a comfortable and supportive environment for the newly elected government to exercise the mandate they had been given by the electorate after a quarter of a century in opposition. Unlike the Country Liberal Party, whose organisational roots and linkages lay in the small and medium-sized businesses of the Territory, the Labor Ministry was deeply connected to both the trade union movement and the public service bureaucracies.

As part of the planning that had taken place prior to the 2001 election, the Labor Party had been meeting with key individuals and organisations in every portfolio according to Stirling's interview in 2012. By drawing upon both his and Peter Toyne's educational expertise and contacts in training systems, they had decided that an independent statutory authority to direct vocational education and training was not going to meet the economic and social needs of the Territory as the new century dawned. According to Stirling:

> The best way to achieve and implement policy seemed to be to put it directly under the Department. We also had a view that the one Department should oversee education and training from preschool through to university and post-secondary VET programs.

The establishment of a portfolio of education, employment and training (changed to employment, education and training in November 2001) served a number of purposes. In addition to providing a familiar mechanism that fitted the minister's personal style and allowed for the necessary level of self-identification that would support philanthropic behaviour, there was also the more traditionally cited reason for organisational change: by having a different department structure the minister and government could be seen to be taking action and exerting their authority over the training system.

To accommodate the Territory's access to Commonwealth recurrent funding and capital resources, and to participate at the Ministerial Council as provided for in the Australian National Training Authority Agreement,

Northern Territory legislation had to be altered with the demise of the previous authority. The 'authority' for training in the jurisdiction was designated to be the Chief Executive Officer of the legislation's controlling agency (Northern Territory of Australia 2013, p. 11). Even more oddly, the current Act still retains references to the Australian National Training Authority even though it was unilaterally disbanded by the Commonwealth Government in 2005. For a variety of reasons, the final official separation of the employment and training functions from the Northern Territory Employment and Training Authority and their incorporation into the departmental structure did not occur until July 2003 (Northern Territory Department of Employment 2003, p. 5).

As an indication of the differing priorities for the deployment of vocational education and training held by the Labor Government, the combined agency was given a much broader remit than that accorded to the Northern Territory Employment and Training Authority by the previous government. The former overriding priority given to the provision of training for industry's needs was replaced by two key principles (Northern Territory Department of Employment 2003, p. 15):

- training for employment builds individual, community and industry capability; and
- equity in access stimulates opportunity and greater participation in the workforce.

These would be used to guide the operations of the new Department of Employment, Education and Training and left no doubt as to the significance, and related political advantage, assigned to vocational education and training by the Labor Government. 'We have put employment, education and training at the top of our agenda; we are prepared to stake the success of this government on how well we achieve in this area' (Stirling 2002, p. 27). The change in emphasis returned to envisaging equity as having access to training (rather than Stone's emphasis upon choice) and repositioned vocational education and training as having a much broader remit than being principally focused upon industrial skills production.

These two key principles allowed vocational education and training to be used as part of the solution to almost any problem the government wanted to address. In addition to the priority that had been previously accorded to industry, individuals and communities could now be singled out for improvement through the provision of training on the basis of increased equity and access. Framing the problems facing the Northern Territory in a manner that makes training an inevitable part of the solution also increases the groups in the electorate that could now be targeted for ministerial philanthropy. For example, Stirling (2002, pp. 2–5) cited some of the following groups as the intended beneficiaries of the public munificence that he controlled:

- the expansion of driver training and licensing to include youth in remote communities, trainees and other youth no longer at school;
- the extension of vocational education and training into rural and remote schools down to year 9 level through the Training for Remote Youth program;
- higher level vocational qualifications being obtained by Indigenous Territorians;
- the extension of the Northern Territory Futures Expo into regional centres;
- requiring major contractors on government projects to meet specified employment and training provisions on substantial projects;
- requiring the Northern Territory public service to increase local training and employment;
- encouraging Group Training Companies; and
- reducing the chances of exploitation of apprentices whilst on the job.

In addition to making its mark on the policy and bureaucratic arrangements for vocational education and training, the ambitious Labor Government was also very active in altering the delivery of training. While accepting the broad structure of a quasi-market, the public sector logics of better coordination, reducing duplication, breaking down silos and increased efficiency inevitably led to an examination of three public providers of vocational education and training. For such a small population, the logic and perceived advantages of having a single public training provider gained traction with the former public servants and not-for-profit employees who occupied the ministerial offices.

Cabinet directed Peter Plummer, the Chief Executive of the Department of Employment, Education and Training, to determine the potential for, and the best mechanisms to concentrate the public provision of, vocational education, higher education and research at the dual-sector university. Plummer had served on the Northern Territory University strategic positioning working group and was intimately acquainted with the operations of the university. Following the retirement of the Northern Territory University Vice-Chancellor, Ron McKay, due to ill health in 2002, Plummer's former mentor from Papua New Guinea, Ken McKinnon, was appointed to the position (Webb 2014, p. 31).

Figure 41. Peter Plummer, centre, served as the Chief Executive of three different Northern Territory Government agencies in addition to being the Principal of Batchelor College.
Source: Creator Patrick Nelson.

As was described at the time, McKinnon was in the Northern Territory to quickly accomplish a specific set of tasks without creating political waves. The process of consolidation of training that had commenced with Minister Finch's dismantling of the Northern Territory Open College in 1993 was to be continued by the Labor Government. As described by Webb (2014, p. 33), a reinvigorated university would be a partner in the Territory's social, cultural and economic development and:

> the formation of the new university was also aimed at remediating the existing fragmentation of education, training and research over a number of institutions and realising desired economies of scale and sustainability.

Stirling's venture into vocational education and training policy put an end to one very long-running debate and reinvigorated at least two others. The creation of Charles Darwin University in November 2003 lay to rest the question of the suitability of a university operating simultaneously as a major vocational training provider. For many in the Country Liberal Party and for the board members of the Northern Territory Employment and Training Authority, the status given to the sector in the university and the ability to influence its leadership as to the direction of vocational education and training were prime indicators of the university's capacity to respond to the needs of industry in the Northern Territory (Berzins & Loveday 1999, pp. 190–198). Arguments for and against the concept of a dual-sector tertiary education and training provider dated back to the establishment of the hybrid Darwin Community College, the refusal to countenance the expansion of advanced education courses at Alice Springs, and the only very recent renaming of the former Batchelor College in recognition of that organisation's ambitions in higher education. Nevertheless, the merger of Centralian College and the formal annexation of the Northern Territory Rural College with the Northern Territory University put an end to that particular debate, with only two public providers, both dual-sector, left in the jurisdiction. As described in recommendation three of the University's Strategic Positioning Project: 'In serving the people of the Northern Territory, the NTU will maintain a dual focus upon their intellectual and vocational needs' (Northern Territory University 2001b, p. 8).

On the other hand, the creation of a single Northern Territory Government department with responsibility for all policy and funding matters to do with education and vocational training immediately reignited debates over the relationship between the two sectors. The former board members of the Northern Territory Employment and Training Authority took every opportunity to speak against the absorption of training into the new department on the basis that training and employment functions of government were more effective when linked directly to industry and through a business-oriented department.

During his interview some 10 years after the abolition of the authority he chaired, Andrew Bruyn remained scathing of the decision because he believed that Labor's training policy was being set by the public service instead of ministers. In addition, Bruyn was of the view that the former close working relationship between the industry-dominated advisory bodies and the minister had been eliminated and that business people had to seek invitations to the minister's office in Parliament House through his or her advisors who carefully controlled access. Stirling confirmed the role of advisors when interviewed:

> At the NT level after I had driven what we considered the major changes in structural terms I was reliant on advisers for further policy refinement in terms of resources, incentives and packages designed to increase trade training numbers.

In addition, even very senior and experienced public servants saw the amalgamation as problematic. The former Commissioner for Public Employment, David Hawkes, opined when interviewed years later that 'there was not a lot of congruence between education and training' because 'it just confuses issues' and that such efforts 'are based upon political misunderstandings'. As will be shown, by the end of 2011 that debate continued throughout the entire period of Labor Government eventually resulting in the return of both employment and training functions to the Department of Business and Employment (Knight 2011).

The second argument resurfaced as part of the discussions being held in 2002–03 that would lead to the creation of two very different training organisations: the Desert Peoples Centre in Alice Springs and the Charles Darwin University. The gradual consolidation and reduction of the number of public providers that had taken place during the Country Liberal Party's time in government would continue during the Labor years. Given his former position as the principal at the then Batchelor College, as well as his deep knowledge of the university as a council member and through the strategic positioning project, Peter Plummer guided discussions to formally amalgamate training, higher education and research into a single new university structure. It was hoped to bring together the two institutions that still operated under the *Education Act* (Centralian College and the Northern Territory Rural College); Batchelor Institute; and the Menzies School of Health Research to create Charles Darwin University. For a variety of reasons, Plummer and the Northern Territory Government ministers could not persuade the council of Batchelor Institute of Indigenous Tertiary Education to become part of the new university. The major obstacle to amalgamation was the rekindled philosophical question of Aboriginal self-determination and self-management.

Some two decades after its policy dominance in the early 1980s (Northern Territory Archives Service 1980c), the reality was that the self-realisation, self-determination and self-management that had underpinned the planned community development approach to improve the lot of remote and regional Indigenous Territorians had not delivered the anticipated high levels of Aboriginal participation in the local workforces. In particular, neither the government departments of the 1980s nor the Northern Territory Employment and Training Authority relinquished responsibility for vocational training to the communities as envisaged. Those government agencies ensured that ministerial control of vocational education and training funding remained unchallenged. Cabinet's decision to create an environment where 'eventually all training would be contracted by communities' (Northern Territory Archives Service 1980c, p. 4) was never given a chance to succeed. In citing the Vocational Training Commission, Loveday and Young (1984, p. 13) reported that:

> If education and training are powerful tools determining how the community develops then responsibility for determining the training to go on in the community must rest with the people affected by it.

As history has shown, while the Northern Territory Government may have had a quite specific policy of 'Aboriginalising' both the workforce and decision-making at the local level, the ability to exercise ministerial philanthropy was just too important a tool to be relinquished to the sometimes capricious and/or politically motivated local councils. Arnott (2003, p. 55) laments the demise of community-based adult educators and the lack of Indigenous input and describes the post–Employment and Training Authority vocational training system thus: 'It is a centralised education and training process that keeps control of the funding and, to a large degree, the training outcomes'. Confirming the gulf that had opened between the policy intention of the 1980s and the training system's operations at the end of the century, the then director of the Northern Territory Employment and Training Authority, Joyce Turnbull (1999, p. 8), described how:

> the voice of industry and business at times seem (sic) stronger in the Territory than elsewhere. There is a clear tension between these goals [of statehood and economic development] and the needs of learners in remote areas, for whom conventional employment and lifestyle are neither likely nor desired.

However, the rhetoric associated with this approach to community development was firmly engrained in the planning and thinking of the Indigenous-controlled training organisations. In spite of the lack of employment outcomes and economic development in remote communities, a senior researcher at Batchelor College maintained that 'the aims of self-determination and self-management should be the basis of planning for education and training programs for Aboriginal people' (Coles 1993). A decade later these themes also dominated the discussions that eventually resulted in the establishment of the Desert Peoples Centre in Alice Springs. As noted in the early planning documents, 'the ultimate goal is driven by self-determination and self-management in order to achieve the best health and living conditions for Aboriginal Desert Peoples' (Ramsey 2002, p. 4).

During its final year of existence in 2001, the Northern Territory Employment and Training Authority made a grant of $300,000 to a consortium of the three key Aboriginal-controlled education and training providers in Central Australia (the Centre for Appropriate Technology, the Institute for Aboriginal Development and the Batchelor Institute of Indigenous Tertiary Education) for preliminary planning and feasibility studies for a Desert Peoples Centre that would be built in the new Desert Knowledge Precinct to the south of Alice Springs (Ramsey 2002, p. 12). The consortium had formally come into existence in 2000 following two years of discussions. In the words of the Northern Territory Employment and Training Authority (2001, p. 29):

> The main catalysts for the Centre have been the need to work together for scarce resources, the poor conditions of facilities and the need for a joint approach to Indigenous people's education and training.

As with the public providers, the Aboriginal-controlled organisations were being forced into consolidated bodies by the Northern Territory Government in the pursuit of increased efficiency and reduced duplication of capital infrastructure and training programs that would be funded from the public purse. The feasibility and scoping studies produced a comprehensive three-volume report that had one clear outcome in mind: 'the purpose of this document is to seek financial support for the establishment of a Desert Peoples Centre' (Ramsey 2002, p. 4). Of course, the purpose of such requests is to influence the philanthropic behaviour of the minister with responsibility for training. As will be shown, the comprehensive process of developing their funding proposal and the tenacity of the supporters of the new centre were highly successful. However, their approach was unequivocal in its commitment to the self-determination discussion that had been reopened. The possibility of joining with the other major training providers in the Northern Territory was explicitly rejected in all its forms including co-location:

> A consortium which included Centralian [College] as an equal partner would complicate and confuse the nature of the Desert Peoples Centre ownership and its educational environment. Ownership and governance would neither rest nor be seen to rest unequivocally with Aboriginal peoples (Ramsey 2002, pp. 19–20).

This question of ownership of the Desert Peoples Centre would have two immediate consequences. The first is that discussions around the amalgamation of the Northern Territory public providers to create a new university would come to exclude the Batchelor Institute, despite major efforts on the part of both the Australian and Northern Territory governments. The second effect had a much more immediate impact upon the creation of the Desert Peoples Centre itself.

As previously described, the Institute for Aboriginal Development, established by the Uniting Church in 1969 with the aid of Commonwealth Government funding, had been under the control of an Aboriginal Board of Management since 1971 and represented the longest history of self-management of the three consortium members (Loveday & Young 1984, p. 128). Having only recently won its years-long battle with the two governments over the release of capital infrastructure funds to redevelop its current campus, the Institute did not accept the logic of redirecting that money in support of the development of the Desert Peoples Centre at the greenfields site to the south of Alice Springs. In 2003, the Institute for Aboriginal Development was in a relatively strong position financially and organisationally. There were about 70 staff members employed in a wide range of education and training initiatives (including higher education offerings in conjunction with Latrobe University) and an income of some $5.4 million (Institute for Aboriginal Development 2004, pp. 17–19).

In order to protect its self-described role 'as the principal Aboriginal community-controlled education and training provider in Central Australia' the Board commissioned Marcia Langton and Zane Ma Rhea to undertake a review of the Institute's 'operations and more specifically, to examine its options about remaining in the Desert Peoples Consortium with the Centre for Appropriate Technology and the Batchelor Institute of Indigenous Tertiary Education' (Institute for Aboriginal Development 2004, p. 5). After extensive deliberations, the Institute for Aboriginal Development withdrew from the Desert Peoples Centre consortium and the annual reports from 2004 onwards make no mention of either the centre or any previous work done with the consortium. Quite simply, the board and staff of the institute were not willing to risk being drawn into partnership arrangements that might reduce or threaten their independence in the future—yet another example of the battles that have been fought over control of vocational education and training.

Unfortunately for the Institute for Aboriginal Development, the various funding streams that had traditionally supported community-based training organisations were progressively drawn more tightly into meeting the specified needs of industry or expanding vocational education and training into Northern Territory secondary schools, which had become a high priority for Minister Stirling. In a purposeful policy decision, the Northern Territory Government also decided to progressively reduce the funding of training for Adult and Community Education providers from 2007 onwards. The number of students that received public funding in this sector dropped from 822 in 2007 to zero in 2010 and no public funding has been allocated since (National Centre for Vocational Education Research 2011, Northern Territory Table 11; 2014, NT Tables). Along with other national changes to funding priorities, the Institute for Aboriginal Development suffered a precipitous decline in revenue; by 2013 it listed a staff of nine persons and no longer published financial statements in its annual reports (Institute for Aboriginal Development 2013). The chairperson of the Board of Management, Patricia Turner, stated: 'I am pleased to confirm that IAD is not insolvent, which means we can continue to trade, but we must secure ongoing funding to remain viable' (Institute for Aboriginal Development 2013).

With the benefit of hindsight, it appears that the Board of the Institute for Aboriginal Development misunderstood the real purpose of the Desert Peoples Centre. The newly incorporated association provided the bureaucratic mechanism to give effect to ministerial philanthropy in a way that was seen to protect the public's investment and reduce the political liabilities associated with handing over public money to community controlled organisations. While the minister still had significant control over Batchelor Institute, and the other three public providers of the time, by virtue of Northern Territory legislation, both the Centre for Appropriate Technology and the Institute for Aboriginal Development were incorporated associations operating independently of Northern Territory Government ministers. The bruising, multiyear battle over the release of the $2.6 million for the refurbishment of the Institute for Aboriginal Development campus had taught bureaucrats and ministers a very clear lesson on what can go wrong when control of funding decisions is lost. What should have been a strong political plus—following the well-rehearsed formula associated with repeated announcements of funding; handing over the cheque in front of the recipients; turning the first sod; and eventually unveiling the plaque on new building—was turned into a long-running series of negative media articles and public complaints made by the intended beneficiaries whose lives had been singled out for improvement. In addition, the new Institute for Aboriginal Development's publicly funded facilities now stood on land that was outside the control of the government.

The Northern Territory Employment and Training Authority did not provide the feasibility and scoping grant of $300,000 to the Desert Peoples Centre Consortium out of a deep felt endorsement of Aboriginal self-management. Rather, the real significance of creating yet another training organisation and increased complexity was to provide a structure that would allow ministerial philanthropy to be extended to these independent organisations. The proposed Desert Peoples Centre was an apparatus to safe-guard the public funds from the potentially unpredictable nature of decisions made by community-controlled organisations and ensure the government could still manipulate the use of government-funded infrastructure in a worst-case scenario. It is a matter of serendipity and political calculation that the proposed arrangement had the added advantage of being aligned with the long-running themes of self-management and community development. The Desert Peoples Centre consortium also ensured that the minister would be distanced from disagreements between individuals and organisations and provided a single point of reference for government officers to conduct negotiations or obtain feedback.

With the withdrawal of the Institute for Aboriginal Development from the consortium, the other two organisations proceeded with the project by submitting a revised business case for funding to the Northern Territory Government in 2003. In 2006, following the allocation of several years worth of vocational education and training capital infrastructure funding to construct other capital works for the broader Desert Knowledge Precinct, plans were made for erecting the first of what has now grown to more than 15 buildings that comprise the Desert Peoples Centre. Construction started in 2008 with the Desert Peoples Centre being officially opened by the Deputy Prime Minister, Julia Gillard, in 2010. The training programs currently on offer through the centre are provided by the Centre for Appropriate Technology and the Batchelor Institute, which have each retained their separate registered training organisation status. Batchelor Institute has moved most of its on-campus training to the Desert Knowledge Precinct, although library and accommodation services have remained at its Bloomfield Street site pending further funding being made available to transfer these functions. The Centre for Appropriate Technology has also retained its old Priest Street site as well as moving into the former CSIRO laboratories adjacent to the Desert Knowledge Precinct: the result of a $3 million gift from the Indigenous Land Corporation.

The Desert Peoples Centre had fulfilled its intended role. A succession of Northern Territory and Commonwealth Government ministers were able to furnish new capital training infrastructure to Indigenous-controlled organisations while protecting the long-term future of the public investment. On the other hand, neither of the two Indigenous-controlled organisations had to relinquish ownership of their existing assets on externally dictated terms or conditions.

The original proposal to have the Desert Peoples Centre operate as a registered training provider (Ramsey 2002, p. 3) did not materialise, partly because that was never the purpose intended for this incorporation. The centre provided a single point of contact for ministerial officers and bureaucrats to negotiate the terms and conditions that would open the doors to the public's largesse. Differences between various Indigenous interest groups had to be resolved before their proposals could go forward to the minister and, as evidenced by the fate of the Institute for Aboriginal Development, those who chose not to work inside the new structure lost access. In addition, the many millions of dollars that would eventually be spent on construction were not going to be just idly placed into the hands of independent organisations. The Northern Territory and Commonwealth Governments' insistence upon building at the new Desert Knowledge Precinct site, based upon the experiences with the Institute for Aboriginal Development stoush, meant that no party to the Desert Peoples Centre agreement could take control of the buildings either overtly or by de facto presence on their land. The Desert Knowledge Precinct occupies land leased to a Northern Territory Government statutory authority, Desert Knowledge Australia, and is subject to an Indigenous Land Use Agreement. In an act designed to ensure no loss of influence, the Northern Territory Government insisted that the Desert Peoples Centre be built on both a sub- and under-lease held by the Northern Territory Department of Employment, Education and Training in return for a peppercorn rent

(Zoellner 2014, p. 26). In other words, retaining control of the land upon which the Desert Peoples Centre sits ensures that the minister can not only justify the allocation of public funding, but regulate access if necessary.

As events have unfolded since the establishment of the Desert Peoples Centre, this seems to have been a prudent move. The Chair of the Centre for Appropriate Technology Board, Peter Renehan, described 2013 as follows: 'This has been a tumultuous year for CAT' due to the lack of certainty around its core funding, the loss of a major contract in Western Australia and the death of the Chief Executive Officer (Centre for Appropriate Technology 2014, p. 6). The 2013 income of $14.5 million for the organisation had dropped by over $11 million from $25.6 million in 2012, resulting in a deficit for the year of some $2.1 million (Centre for Appropriate Technology 2014, p. 36). The Centre for Appropriate Technology had steadily transitioned from a small and highly focused training organisation addressing the unmet needs of Indigenous people in Central Australia in 1980 to an association possessing high levels of knowledge on how to meet the complex needs of governments in the world of new public management. The Centre found that its expertise and skills were in demand right across Northern Australia and opened offices in Darwin, the Kimberley and far north Queensland to handle the contracting out of public service delivery aimed at social and lifestyle improvements in remote Indigenous communities. The movement into this arena of other non-government organisations and the private sector has had a serious impact upon the business model used by the Centre for Appropriate Technology, as has the withdrawal of Northern Territory vocational education and training funding for the adult and community education sector.

Similarly, Batchelor Institute of Indigenous Tertiary Education, the other partner in the Desert Peoples Centre, has also described how it faces an unsustainable trend in its fiscal future. Batchelor Institute (2014, p. 44) continues to rely upon the Northern Territory and Australian governments for over three-quarters of its income. As noted by the Director, Adrian Mitchell:

> However, with the high costs of delivering remote training and the ever increasing burden of maintaining ageing infrastructure, the biggest challenge facing the Institute is still its long term financial viability and in 2013 expenditure on Vocational and Education and Training exceeded funding provided by the Northern Territory Government by over $2 million (Batchelor Institute of Indigenous Tertiary Education 2014, p. 3).

By early 2003, the powerful emotional attraction of the reignited debate over self-determination expressed through an unambiguously Aboriginal-controlled education and training organisation, when combined with the long-established goal of becoming Australia's first Indigenous University, precluded the Batchelor Institute of Indigenous Tertiary Education from ever seriously considering the many approaches made for it to become part of Charles Darwin University. Furthermore, the Northern Territory University's historic perceived lack of responsiveness to Indigenous self-determination (Berzins & Loveday 1999, pp. 201–203) and its low profile in Central Australia also contributed towards Batchelor Institute's efforts to develop the Desert Peoples Centre instead of pursuing the offers of both the Commonwealth and Northern Territory Governments to join the other public providers in the new, amalgamated university. Similarly, the matter of Indigenous self-determination ensured that neither the Institute for Aboriginal Development or the Centre for Appropriate Technology were ever considered for inclusion in the mergers required to consolidate vocational training, higher education and research in a novel and contemporary post-school organisation.

Regardless, the same rationale of consolidation and efficiency that had spawned the Desert Peoples Centre as a benevolent apparatus was also driving much of the activity that resulted in the creation of Charles Darwin University in the early 2000s. The increasing level of open competition between Centralian College, Batchelor Institute and the Northern Territory University in the quasi-market for training presented both the Northern Territory Employment and Training Authority and its minister with a seemingly endless set of problems. Every allocation of funding or buildings would be met by a chorus of criticism from the other two institutions that had missed out. Instead of reaping political and community rewards for philanthropic behaviour, ministers were having to constantly defend their decisions, while those in receipt of the public munificence treated this as 'only getting our fair share' or even being 'short-changed'. By creating a single institution with a Territory-wide remit, the arguments over relative priorities and consultation with the community and industry would fall back upon the university and the minister would be freed to make final choices with a focus upon the best political perceptions of any particular decision. In addition, the single institution made negotiations over resource agreements a much simpler activity for the newly created Department of Employment, Education and Training.

As with Indigenous self-determination the proposal to amalgamate all of the public providers into a single institution headquartered in Darwin reopened the debate over the so-called 'Berrimah Line'. This fictional boundary at Darwin's former southern outskirts represented the bureaucrats' perceived lack of understanding of the real needs and aspirations of Territorians who resided outside the capital city. While not hotly contested in 2002–03, all of the previous arguments were brought out—dating all the way back to the Darwin Adult Education Centre handing back control of Adult Education in Alice Springs to the South Australian Education Department in the days prior to self-government. In late 2002, the Centralian College council was cognisant of the long-running debates over local decision-making and the counter arguments of economies of scale associated with being part of a much larger entity, when it considered Minister Stirling's invitation—relayed through the Chief Executive of the Department of Employment, Education and Training, Peter Plummer—to amalgamate with the Northern Territory University, the Menzies School of Health Research and the Northern Territory Rural College to form a new university.

During the previous year, the council had commissioned David Rolfe, who had previously reviewed the Northern Territory Employment and Training Authority, to assist with an exercise in scenario planning regarding the future viability of Centralian College in the face of emerging financial and operational pressures and a stagnant training market. The final report made for rather grim reading: in three years time, college operations would be about the same but stretched to the limit; in five years there would be severe financial, information technology systems and staffing difficulties; and within 10 years the college would be broke. Several ways forward were suggested including amalgamation with other providers either in the Northern Territory or even interstate. In the end, council decided that the Central Australian community would be best served by having a formal university presence in Alice Springs and Tennant Creek.

As a result of the amalgamation and the agreement of both parties, the Centralian senior secondary school was progressively returned to the Department of Employment, Education and Training while the ownership of the entire Sadadeen campus was eventually transferred to Charles Darwin University. The newly created university had staff permanently based in Yulara in the far southwest of the Territory, Alice Springs, Tennant Creek, Mataranka Station, Katherine township, the rural college campus just north of Katherine, Jabiru, Nhulunbuy, Palmerston and at Casuarina.

The three Mobile Adult Learning Units that had been operated by Centralian College were now also capable of being deployed throughout the Territory when and where climatic and road conditions allowed.

As a salutary side note and vindication of Centralian College's previously mentioned fiscal scenario planning exercise, the financial fate of Batchelor Institute of Indigenous Tertiary Education provided a timely example of the limitations of small specialist training providers. Centralian College and Batchelor Institute had a similar scale of income and expenditure—quite modest when compared to that of the Northern Territory University. Batchelor Institute's decision to reject the opportunity to be a part of the new university eventually led to its near bankruptcy (Ravens 2009) in the time frame predicted in Rolfe's report to the Centralian College Council. By October 2009 the Northern Territory and Commonwealth Governments had to provide some $6.4 million to Batchelor Institute to support continued operations (Masters 2009). As noted previously, the institute continues to struggle with financial viability, while its higher education joint venture with Charles Darwin University—the Australian Centre for Indigenous Knowledges and Education—has put even further pressure on its ability to maintain a positive fiscal environment.

After 12 months of extensive consultations, negotiations and relationship building, the legislation to create Charles Darwin University was passed by the Northern Territory Legislative Assembly in November 2003. In spite of the consistent reluctance of Batchelor Institute's council to take any action that would be seen to undermine the principle of Aboriginal self-determination, there have been concerted attempts to bring the only other public provider into the university. For example, in the face of persistent rumours that he was considering the removal of the institute's higher education provider status, the Commonwealth Minister for Education, Brendan Nelson, made available a $3 million grant in 2006 to fund the development of a formal partnership agreement between Charles Darwin University and Batchelor Institute of Indigenous Tertiary Education. The partnership compact was carefully negotiated over many months and operated from 2007–09. The externally financed relationship did not result in the marriage that had been hoped for, despite the institute's parlous financial state. The core matter of Indigenous control and the mixed messages being sent through the actions of both the Northern Territory and Commonwealth Governments dumping millions of dollars into the Desert Peoples Centre buildings ensured that there would be no change from the long-standing public policy position of having a specialist Indigenous tertiary education and training provider operating alongside a dual-sector 'mainstream' institution catering for the entire Northern Territory population.

As a consequence of Minister Stirling's efforts to shepherd through the consolidation of vocational education and training at Charles Darwin University and Batchelor Institute, ministerial philanthropic ambition has a rather streamlined mechanism for the delivery of training that has ostensibly met the needs of the next seven ministers following in the role. With one or two minor exceptions that will be described later, the basic structure of the quasi-market in 2014 consisted of the two public providers (with their quite distinct missions), a highly variable number of interstate providers and 46 Northern Territory-based enterprise and private registered training organisations (Department of Industry 2014). The principal–agent contractual relationship inherent in new public management still operates and allows the Northern Territory Government to dominate policy and funding decisions. By contracting away the messiness of dealing with service delivery and the risk of failure, ministers can carry out their philanthropic activity guided by their close relationship to the voters, their political acumen and the calculation of electoral success that comes from handing out public funds.

Figure 42. Batchelor Institute of Indigenous Tertiary Education, 2011.
Source: Creator Darren Clark, PH0875/0038, Darren Clark Collection, Northern Territory Library.

Chief Minister and Minister for Education and Training, Paul Henderson's response to the financial crisis at Batchelor Institute in 2009 is a classic example of the benefits of this philanthropic mechanism. In a demonstration of 'all care but no responsibility', Henderson is reported to have stated (Ravens 2009):

> We've been working very closely with Batchelor and the Australian Government in terms of a way forward. A financial audit has been carried out, a management team has been appointed and certainly we are discussing with the board of Batchelor about a business plan.
>
> The NT government does not have the capacity to enforce an administrator on the institute. It is an independent board and it manages its own affairs. Closure is not an option. My absolute drive (is) to improve secondary education in remote communities and Batchelor needs to be a key part of that. Certainly, I will continue to work with (federal Education Minister) Julia Gillard to that effect. Batchelor is an important institution and it has to stay.

Of course, after carefully setting the scene, Henderson was able to demonstrate the power and benefits of ministerial philanthropy by 'working with' the Commonwealth minister to find nearly $6.5 million to save this organisation with which he had self-identified (by wishing to improve the lives of remote Indigenous people) but had also distanced himself from direct ministerial responsibility for its financial problems. When interviewed about his principal motivation for becoming Chief Minister, Henderson replied, '[I] really felt like I could take the Territory forward' (Martin & Dewar 2012, p. 171). And being able to use a minister's public philanthropy associated with the vocational education and training system provided a powerful tool to realise his vision for an improved society.

As we have seen, the vocational education and training public policy tool has two interacting parts—centralised policy/funding and dispersed delivery. The stabilisation of delivery that accompanied the establishment of Charles Darwin University and the Peoples Desert Centre returned attention to the Northern Territory Government's policy and funding arrangements. Stirling's Ministerial Advisory Board for Employment and Training commenced in 2002–03 and met nine times in the 2003–04 financial year. This advisory board then met less frequently in each of the following two years (six and four times respectively) and finally ceased operating in February 2006 (Department of Employment 2006, p. 91) although provision for the board remained in the relevant legislation. Unlike the Northern Territory Employment and Training Authority, the Ministerial Advisory Board did not have control over expenditure or public policy as these roles had been carried out by professional experts in the Department of Employment, Education and Training. The steady decline in the number of meetings and eventual winding up of this advisory committee suggests that its contribution was decreasingly relevant to the minister's preferred method of working within government bureaucracies and his own capacity to identify the groups that would produce the most benefit from public philanthropy.

In order to bring the processes of government back into alignment with the determinants of ministerial philanthropy, particularly direct relationships and self-identification, the Northern Territory Government and Minister Henderson developed a new training advisory mechanism to replace the previous board—Employment and Training round tables:

> The round tables provide an opportunity for industry stakeholders to engage in dialogue directly with government on employment and training issues affecting the Northern Territory (Department of Employment 2006, p. 91).

The round tables were to meet six times a year in the major population centres of the Northern Territory. As with the ministerial advisory board, over a period of several years the round table meetings slowly ground to a halt and were quietly discontinued. In the final years of the Labor Government in the Northern Territory, there was no formal advisory mechanism or structured relationship between government ministers and those involved in the vocational education and training; thus distancing the minister from employers, students and training providers.

Following Stirling's departure from the ministry in 2007, three different persons held the training portfolio—Marion Scrymgour, Paul Henderson (twice) and Chris Burns. When interviewed and asked about the role of ministerial advisors, Syd Stirling stated that their role was to 'help guide the minister to ensure that public servants achieve implementation of our policies'. In the absence of a direct relationship with the training community, the Labor Government became almost totally reliant upon their ministerial advisors and the department to guide policy and funding. The bringing 'in-house' of vocational education and training policy had two major impacts. The first was the reduction in electoral advantages that can be had from the exercise of ministerial philanthropy. In yet another display of the bipartisanship which has been repeatedly demonstrated in vocational education and training, the Labor Government's attention to the area mirrored that of the Country Liberal Party when they were coming to the end of their period in power. As with Fred Finch's departure a decade earlier, the ministers that followed Syd Stirling did not exhibit the same intuitive understanding and capacity to operate as a ministerial philanthropist. While the technique would not be abandoned, as evidenced by the lifeline Henderson threw to Batchelor Institute, the use of vocational education and training as a form of public philanthropy was not being used to full advantage.

The second effect was to revitalise the public service battles over budgets and personnel associated with departmental structures and responsibilities. In Labor's final term of government, the 'super-department' of employment, education and training would be progressively dismantled. In 2008, the employment function was removed from the 'super-department' and re-integrated into the Department of Business with Kon Vatskalis serving as the minister and returning to a similar situation that had existed in the years prior to the establishment of the Northern Territory Employment and Training Authority in 1992. The final dissolution was announced by the Minister for Business and Employment in September 2011. In a media release, Rob Knight (2011) told the public of 'changes to adult training in the Territory to ensure the best employment outcomes for industry and individuals' by combining 'adult training with the employment function of the Department of Business and Employment'. Knight also indicated that vocational education and training for school students would remain with the Department of Education and Training. Labor's excursion through a 1980s-style super-department and its consequent dismantlement provides support for the interview observations of the former Commissioner for Public Employment, David Hawkes. He believed that vocational education and training was an uncomfortable fit with the broader education portfolio. Those charged with the responsibility for running schools are seldom seen to possess a deep knowledge of the overarching needs of the economy or how to best gather and use views of business to support ministerial ambition.

The separation of employment and training functions from the broader education portfolio came about because one of the principal concerns of both industry and the training sector actually came to fruition. The major objection to Stirling creating the 'super-department' was that the vocational education and training function would become subordinated to the needs of the school system. While Stirling had been able to manage that potential problem, his successors were to find the task impossible. As with most of the Labor members of the Legislative Assembly, Marion Scrymgour and Chris Burns had professional backgrounds in academia and not-for-profit organisations (ABC News 2012). Scrymgour also had worked in local government, at the Northern Land Council and in Indigenous health delivery programs. Yet, again, these ministers had little in common with industry and business interests and were much more comfortable with a trusted band of advisors and working within the confines of the various bureaucratic organisations. There is little evidence to demonstrate that either had any formal and sustained vocational training advisory mechanisms or relationships with industry. It seems likely that these characteristics severely limited their capacity to behave like wealthy philanthropists and reap the electoral rewards. Both would retire from politics at the August 2012 election.

Scrymgour had been elected as part of the Clare Martin-led sweep into government in 2001 and served in a number of ministerial roles. As part of the internal party power play that saw Paul Henderson topple Martin from the chief ministership, Scrymgour replaced Stirling as both the Deputy Chief Minister and Minister for Education and Training in November 2007. In the 15 months that Scrymgour served as minister, vocational education and training was considered to have been treated with benign neglect by her office. She made little reference to the sector in the Legislative Assembly and this was in passing when discussing the *NT Jobs Plan* or vocational training being used in secondary schools. Her time was totally consumed by school education matters that included a long-running, bitter industrial dispute with teachers, an unfriendly media, some rather crucial mistaken statements/actions and impatience with the education bureaucracy. In October 2008, almost a year after becoming minister, Scrymgour was the subject of an extraordinary attack in the Legislative Assembly launched by the Leader of the Opposition, Terry Mills, when he moved 'that this Assembly express a want of confidence in the Minister for Education and Training' (Department of the Legislative Assembly 2008, p. 1).

Figure 43. Marion Scrymgour (left) being sworn in as a member of the ninth Northern Territory Legislative Assembly on 16 October 2001.

Also being sworn in is Jodeen Carney, Member for Araluen, and seated, to the far right, is the first Labor Party Chief Minister of the Northern Territory, Clare Martin.

Source: Creator unknown, PH0753/0011, 9th Assembly Collection, Northern Territory Library.

While Mills used the full range of confected political outrage that is frequently on display in this venue, his major complaints seemed to revolve around three issues: the minister delving into operational issues to deal with individual teachers; teachers' strike action over enterprise bargaining matters; and the sacking of Margaret Banks, the Chief Executive Officer of the Department of Education and Training. Scrymgour (Department of the Legislative Assembly 2008, pp. 9–11) launched a spirited defence of her actions by admitting her mistake of referring in the media to Banks having 'retired' rather than 'resigned'. She then confirmed that the Chief Executive Officer had been sacked: 'simply put, she was advised her services were no longer required. I simply felt that there was no appropriate sense of urgency being generated at the top level' to address the poor educational outcomes being achieved in remote Indigenous community schools. The Labor Government had allocated quite significant resources to the Education Department and the minister was not seeing the sorts of results she felt ought to be visible.

Figure 44. Margaret Banks, the Chief Executive of the Department of Employment, Education and Training, introducing Minister Scrymgour, at the far left, during the January 2006 scholarships and bursaries awards ceremony held at Parliament House.
Source: Creator Patrick Nelson.

The minister's urgent focus upon remote schools produced the predicted outcome of merging education and training—vocational education and training was given low or minimal political priority; became disconnected from industry; and was effectively being driven by employment policy. While Scrymgour survived the want of confidence motion, she was seriously damaged. Chief Minister Henderson acted in February 2009 by giving her a demotion in Cabinet, which resulted in her resignation from the ministry in June of that year.

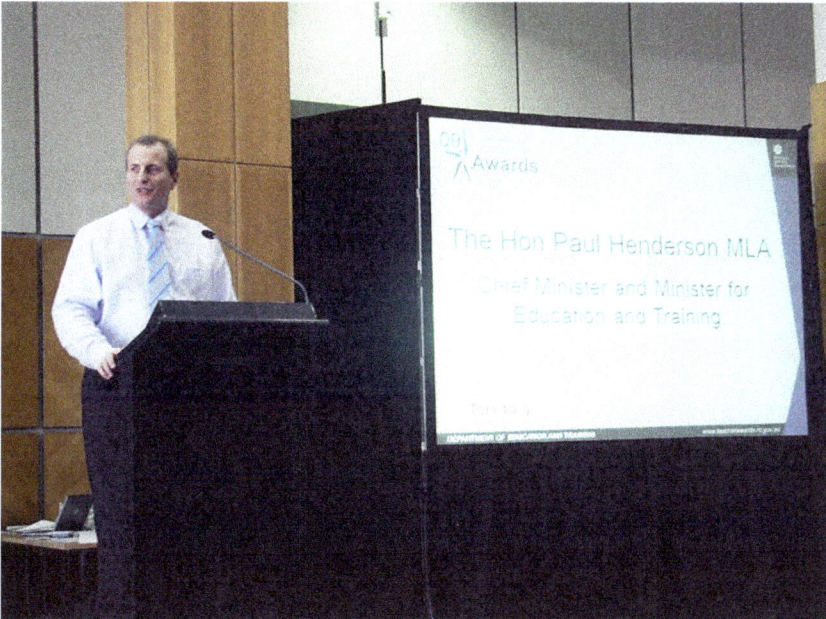

Figure 45. Minister Henderson preparing to present prizes at the Teaching Excellence Awards ceremony at Parliament House, October 2009.

Source: Creator Patrick Nelson.

Henderson resumed the education and training portfolio following Scrymgour's departure. He immediately attempted to raise the profile of training by recommencing the ministerial round tables and promoting the various 'investments' in vocational education and training being made by his government as a way of harnessing the benefits of ministerial philanthropy that he better understood and used when compared to Scrymgour and Burns. One of his first actions was to make a ministerial statement to the Legislative Assembly on 10 February 2009 to try to limit the damage done to the government's reputation because of the previous minister's disengagement with the training sector and the subsequent leadership vacuum created (Henderson 2009). In outlining his government's achievements, Henderson reported to Parliament that the Northern Territory had the highest vocational education and training participation rate in the nation, which had been achieved through a number of initiatives including:

- Work Wear and Work Gear assistance to apprentices to buy tools and equipment;
- 1,700 incentives paid to employers of apprentices and trainees;
- Work Ready program for secondary school students;
- 600 Territorians adding new skills through the $1.5 million Build Skills program;
- a variety of Indigenous pre-employment programs operating around the Territory;
- training for the emerging oil and gas industry and planned developments;
- a Productivity Places Program Pilot for higher level qualifications; and
- Vocational Education and Training Program for remote schools costing $500,000.

Henderson would remain Minister for Education and Training until December 2009, when Chris Burns assumed the role. As with Scrymgour before him, there is little evidence that Burns had an affinity with the training sector or those employers who would benefit from the public investment directed at building the Northern Territory's skill base. During the almost two years that Burns had responsibility for vocational training, he was totally reliant upon his ministerial advisors and departmental advice. There was no formal industry-led advisory body in place and a number of observers at the time believed that Burns was isolated from the sector and its major issues. He made no major ministerial statements dedicated to vocational education and training to the Legislative Assembly while giving the sector brief mention in relation to growth in jobs and school-based vocational programs.

Figure 46. Minister Burns, second from right, overseeing the celebration of a Charles Darwin University lecturer's 40 years of teaching.

From left to right: CDU Pro Vice-Chancellor of VET John Hassed, long-serving horticulture lecturer Liz Hagan, NT Minister for Education and Training Chris Burns and Baz Levarde.

Source: Creator Unknown. Office of Media, Advancement and Community Engagement, Charles Darwin University.

The overall workload expected of Burns would have significantly contributed to this lack of attention to vocational education and training's philanthropic potential. In addition to the two other ministerial portfolios held by Burns, he was also the Leader of Government Business in the Legislative Assembly. Scrymgour's quitting the ministry in February was followed by her resignation from the Australian Labor Party in June of 2009. She was joined by Allison Anderson who resigned from the ministry and the party in August. This left the party without sufficient seats to form government. Scrymgour was lured back into the Labor Party leaving the numbers on the floor of the Legislative Assembly equally balanced and the fate of government in the hands of the Darwin rural area independent, Gerry Woods. He negotiated a complex deal to support Labor's tenuous hold on power in return for the establishment of the Council of Territory Cooperation as a committee of the Legislative Assembly with wide-ranging powers to examine most any issue of interest and a promise of leadership stability; and high levels of consultation on the legislative program. As the Leader of Government Business, Burns had to manage every detail of the operations of parliament to avoid any possibility of being forced to an early election by an emboldened Country Liberal Party. Burns was simply too busy fending off political disaster to actually take advantage of the benefits of philanthropic behaviour.

One other significant action was undertaken by the Northern Territory Government in 2011 when it delegated its powers to register and regulate training organisations to the national regulator, the Australian Skills and Quality Authority. This removed the final major potential point of political pain that would face a philanthropically-minded minister. Acting under the authority of Northern Territory legislation, the minister makes the ultimate decision about the future operations of registered training organisations that are accused of not meeting the required standards. While the public understands, sometimes even demands, the theoretical basis for the enforcement of regulations, the final decision to close down a provider, putting trainers out of work and disrupting students' study, seldom receives positive publicity for the minister. Again, through the application of new public management, government and the minister can contract away operational responsibility for failure, the drudgery of quality audits and the potential for electoral damage. Northern Territory ministers have been given almost total freedom to act philanthropically with the one exception that will be described shortly.

The Northern Territory Government also had taken a series of decisions in 2010 to defund the adult and community education sector while consolidating its support for the delivery of vocational education and training through a historically stable set of recurrent resource agreements with:

- Charles Darwin University;
- Batchelor Institute of Indigenous Tertiary Education;
- the Centre for Appropriate Technology;
- the Institute for Aboriginal Development;
- Seafood and Maritime Industries Training; and
- Nungalinya College.

Private and enterprise providers have to negotiate access to both user choice funding for apprentice and trainee training with the Department of Business. They can also bargain for access to a range of other specialised programs that are normally carefully targeted at regional areas or specific groups of residents that have been identified for special treatment—frequently described as disadvantaged.

In addition, three government agencies have a long history of being registered training providers to meet specialist enterprise needs:

- Police, Fire and Emergency Services provide their own entry level and advanced training for firefighters and those who will undertake policing duties;
- The Department of Health and Community Services provides dedicated training programs in a narrow range of community health areas; and
- The Department of Correctional Services both provides training for its own staff to become corrections officers and for prisoners in a limited number of lower level qualifications that can be provided in the prison environment.

The rather purist separation of delivery functions from policy, regulation and funding also meant that the potential for conflict of interest in the Department of Education (in all of its incarnations) was best avoided if it was not a registered training organisation. For those schools that wished to access contestable public vocational education and training monies in addition to their normal government grants, the option has always been open to become a registered training provider since the early 1990s when that mechanism was established. The special relationship between the Alice Springs town schools and the dual-sector Centralian College meant that developing a partnership agreement was a much simpler and less onerous means to access formally recognised vocational education and training for secondary-aged students. On the other hand, most secondary schools in the Top End became registered training organisations either directly or by association with the Catholic Education Office or Northern Territory Christian Schools Limited.

As time has gone by, only the Christian Schools Limited, Nhulunbuy High School and Taminmin High School have maintained their status as a registered training organisations. With the transfer of the training function to the Department of Business and Employment in 2011, the major sources of conflict were somewhat mediated. However, in 2014, the Department of Education and Training established a small registered training organisation offering three low level qualifications aimed at remote school students. The rationale for the department being a training provider is based upon arguments of market failure in remote areas. The public policy advantages associated with a funder–purchaser–provider model have been dissipated due to the fact that the same departmental officers who operate the registered training provider are also the administrators of vocational education and training funding allocations that provide for school-based training. In other words, the very existence of the departmental training organisation makes the same agency both a purchaser and provider with the potential to move into other training areas relatively easily. By definition, this also makes the minister responsible for outcomes, problems, failures and managing conflicts of interest associated with the delivery of services. The benefits of both new public management and ministerial philanthropy are dissipated because the minister is simultaneously responsible for all three roles—funder, purchaser and provider—when his department takes on the role of registered training provider.

In 2005, the issue of vocational education and training in secondary schools also furnished the setting for a constitutionally bold move on the part of the Commonwealth Government. Although the Commonwealth had operated schools in its territories prior to self-government, by following the principles of new public management, it had gradually divested itself of direct ownership of schools and made much greater use of carefully targeted funding interventions through state and territory governments to achieve national public policy outcomes. The Howard Coalition Government had determined through an extensive polling campaign that many voters were nostalgic about the days when the state education systems had technical high schools, and sensed an opportunity for electoral advantage as it entered its fifth term in office.

State-owned specialist technical schools had been progressively converted to comprehensive high schools and/or senior colleges in most states and territories throughout the 1970s and 1980s. The Federal Coalition Government went to the October 2004 general election with a commitment to open 24 Australian Technical Colleges around Australia, if elected. Once returned to office, the Australian Government proceeded to pass legislation to finance this policy in 2005 and subsequently identified another four geographical areas that would receive such a college. In defending the need for the colleges, the Federal Minister for Vocational and Further Education, Andrew Robb, described these new institutions and the Commonwealth's intervention into state affairs as an important step because 'it does mean that we are getting back to where the technical high schools that were closed 20 and 30 years ago, the one huge mistake in education around the country, is being corrected' (*The World Today* 2007).

Darwin was identified by the Commonwealth as one of the areas that would benefit from the operations of an Australian Technical College and the initiative was warmly received by the Northern Territory minister, Syd Stirling. The entire process of establishing these Commonwealth-funded colleges provides a textbook example of ministerial philanthropy. Local industry-dominated consortia from each identified area were 'invited' to apply to the Department of Education, Science and Training to establish and operate the college either using existing facilities or overseeing the building of a new college using Commonwealth funds. The task of justifying the need for secondary school-aged training, developing the business case, devising risk mitigation strategies, forming operational budgets and forward planning were all left to the local community groups. If their application was successful, these local consortia would take responsibility for running a secondary school. The principal–agent contractual arrangement at the core of new public management remained a cornerstone of this scheme. This freed the Commonwealth minister to hand out the public's money on the basis of an electorally safe, self-described need guided by a process that forced potential competitors to actually come together and present a united front that was less likely to find fault with the final funding decisions. This example of Commonwealth ministerial philanthropic activity, mirroring the technique used to such great electoral advantage in the Northern Territory, is described as follows:

> The department assessed the proposals and advised the minister on the ratings of proposals for each region. The selection of successful applicants was a decision of the Government. On 15 July 2005, the minister announced the first 12 successful applicants to establish colleges. Applicants from regions where two proposals were rated as 'suitable and best' were asked by DEST to combine their proposals to provide a single, strong proposal for the region (The Auditor-General 2007, p. 71).

Not surprisingly, there were complaints that the vast majority of regions targeted to receive an Australian Technical College coincided with marginal federal electorates (The World Today 2007). The exercise of ministerial philanthropy seeks to both direct society in a particular direction and seek electoral advantage. This was certainly the case for Darwin, which had been identified as a potential site in July 2005. After extensive negotiations that included the personal interventions of the local federal member and the then Commonwealth minister, a funding agreement was signed on 26 September 2006. The Australian

Technical College Darwin commenced operations as both a registered training organisation and school in 2007 with a few dozen students in a limited range of industry areas.

The local Member of the House of Representatives, Dave Tollner, took a very high level of personal interest in bringing the college to fruition as he was intended to be a major electoral beneficiary. The Darwin bid for the operating rights for the college had been subject to proposals from several groups and the process to negotiate 'a single, strong proposal' was perceived by the politicians to be taking too long. Tollner enlisted the help of the federal minister, Gary Hardgrave, to come to Darwin and give the locals some encouragement. The minister's robust and hard-line approach was not all that well received. However, his actions did assist moves forward when he unilaterally eliminated any possibility of approving a proposal that included Charles Darwin University, the largest provider of vocational education and training in the Northern Territory and experienced provider of secondary school training, as either a partner of the consortium or as a site for college buildings. Many commentators at the time attributed the minister's position to an ideological predisposition against the word 'university'. Hardgrave's other major claim to fame, before being sacked from ministerial duties by Prime Minister Howard in January 2007, was his failed attempt to change the name of the sector. In seeking to exert his authority over the vocational education and training sector, the minister decided that 'vocational and technical education' would be used. As with Northern Territory Minister Lugg's attempt to revert to TAFE, Hardgrave misunderstood the implications of reordering the simple sequence of words for literally millions of voters and the impact upon hundreds of thousands of web pages, application forms, official documents and reporting formats.

Hardgrave's ambition to exert control over the sector badly miscalculated the political risks of rebadging the entire sector and unintentionally served to limit the political advantages associated with the massively expensive program to revise technical high schools. His ministerial career was yet another casualty of the skirmishes waged over the control of vocational education and training. For the period 2005–09, the total funding for Australian Technical Colleges was estimated to be some $585 million with about $473 million coming directly from Commonwealth appropriations that would be spent on a projected 8,400 students spending the full-time equivalent of two years at the colleges (The Auditor-General 2007, p. 77). This works out to about $35,000 per student per year, which was more than double the $16,000 per student spent in the Northern Territory—Australia's most expensive jurisdiction (Department of Employment 2006, p. 55). When asked in a personal conversation about this cost differential, Hardgrave's successor, Andrew Robb, rationalised that the cost was never about the delivery of training but about forcing the states and territories to reintroduce technical education into secondary schools and that the strategy had been successful with South Australia, for example, re-establishing vocational secondary schools. Unfortunately for the Federal Coalition Government, their attempt to tap the public's favourable memories and turn it to electoral advantage miscarried. Dave Tollner lost his seat and the Coalition failed in its bid for re-election in 2007.

The Australian Technical College Darwin was developed as a cooperative hybrid model in anticipation of low numbers of senior students who would be prepared to move to a completely separate school and away from their local secondary college or school. Extensive training infrastructure in several existing public and private schools was either upgraded or purpose-built using funds from the Australian Technical College's program. A head office and some generic training facilities were established in Stuart Park, somewhat ironically, within view of the very first Northern Territory Government training establishment dedicated to preparing young people for traditional trades employment—the Skills Training Centre. With the election of the Rudd Labor Federal Government in 2007, the funding for the Australian Technical Colleges was diverted to a program known as Trade Training Centres in Schools and the operations were progressively handed over to state and territory education providers. The Australian Technical College Darwin headquarters was closed as the Department of Education and Training assumed responsibility in late 2009, while the infrastructure that had been provided was quietly absorbed into the individual schools.

The dismantling of the Australian Technical Colleges program by the Rudd Labor Government did not detract from the positive political calculations associated with the provision of vocational training facilities for secondary school-aged students. The Labor Opposition had taken a more flexible policy to the 2007 election—it could potentially include each and every secondary school in the nation. Ministerial philanthropy from the federal minister could be targeted at individual post codes and even particular suburbs through the Trade Training Centres in Schools program. Under this program, the Northern Territory received six grants, each of which was in the expansive rural and remote safe Labor seat of Lingiari that occupies the entire jurisdiction except Darwin. With the defeat of Labor in 2013, the Abbott Coalition Government still sensed the potential benefits of such a funding source and performed the politically irresistible relabelling of the program to allow for the provision of Trades Skills Centres in both clusters of or at individual secondary schools.

When describing what her government did well, former Chief Minister Clare Martin replied that she was the 'proudest of what we did in growing jobs and training' (Martin & Dewar 2012, p. 163). Her Labor successors continued with this theme by stating 'training is a hallmark of the Territory Government' (Department of Business and Employment 2012, p. 10). A retrospective account of the 11 years of Labor Government paints a rather less rosy picture. The number of people in training and the expenditure on training flatlined in the Labor years (Zoellner 2012). The four Labor ministers repeated the journey of the previous Country Liberal Party following self-government by changing the administrative arrangements from an authority to a department and eventually separating training from the education function. Their focus was more on restructuring agencies and providers, less on the advantages of philanthropic behaviour. In the end, they paid the ultimate electoral price.

In August 2012, the Country Liberals once again tasted success at the ballot box after 11 years in opposition. Their campaign was constructed upon a mix of the 'it's time' factor, a focus upon taking previously 'unwinnable' bush seats from Labor and a return to the Country Liberal's own concoction of populism and liberalism. Members of the so-called 'old guard' of the party such as Graeme Lewis and Col Fuller—who would go on to become Cabinet Secretary after the election—made major strategic contributions before and after the campaign. While the Country Liberals went to the election with the pledge to re-establish an employment and training authority, they have yet again demonstrated the same bipartisan comfort by retaining similar policy settings in vocational education and training. The Country Liberals inherited a department of business and employment from the Labor Government which was rebadged as the Department of Business post-election. The employment and training functions were left in this economic agency by the new government. Some progress has been made towards the pre-election commitment to re-establish a 'training authority' with the appointment of several senior business and industry figures to an interim Northern Territory Employment and Training

Authority Advisory Board in September 2014. This group was headed up, again, by Andrew Bruyn, the board chair of the former Northern Territory Employment and Training Authority.

After several changes in the early Cabinets following the 2012 election, Dave Tollner—the former federal member who had demonstrated such a keen interest in the Australian Technical College—became the Minister for Business and gained responsibility for vocational education and training as well as Desert Knowledge Australia and its precinct containing the Desert Peoples Centre. Tollner is much more aligned with the private sector than public service bureaucracies—a characteristic of the previous Country Liberal Party Government and ministers that had overseen a near doubling of the resources allocated to vocational education and training for the two decades following self-government (Zoellner 2012).

At the time of writing, Tollner was having a rest from his relationship with vocational education and training. Having made some very injudicious comments about a Country Liberal staff member, he returned to the back bench in response to the adverse public reaction and the immediate impact such events make in the Territory's intimate political environment. The business, training and employment ministerial duties were taken on for several months by the Chief Minister, Adam Giles, in addition to the other 10 ministries he took over when Tollner resigned his Cabinet duties. Clearly, by allocating this huge workload to a single individual as in the case of Minister Burns, the possibility of managing the personal relationships and self-identification that will allow a minister to take advantage of philanthropic opportunities is severely limited.

In December 2014, ministerial responsibilities were reassigned with yet another repetition of earlier Country Liberal Party approaches. Alice Springs-based Robyn Lambley was made the Minister for Education as well as Employment and Training. This mirrors the early 1990s arrangements exercised by Shane Stone. It also placed the responsibilities for business and industry in a different portfolio, repeating the structures used by the Northern Territory Government 25 years earlier.

8

Late 2015 and September 2016 postscript

Some hopes and dreams can last for centuries due to their seductively powerful, 'common sense' appeal. The economically minded, democratic and philanthropically inclined British colonists from 1860s South Australia would be very comfortable—if disappointed in the glacial progress—with the ongoing intentions to develop the northern half of the 'great central state' functioning as an advanced market democracy, producing wealth and trading with Asia (Cross 2011). The Northern Territory Government's strategic planning document *Framing the future* repeats the century and a half old mantra citing the desire to 'strengthen the Territory's role as the gateway between Australia and Asia' by creating 'an economy that unlocks the potential of our regions' supported by the 'ongoing training and skills development of Territorians' (Northern Territory Government 2013, p. 5).

The predominant metaphors of settlement and improvement, indeed the extension of British civilisation itself, into new environments provided the basis for an irresistible desire on the part of European settlers to make the traditional owners of the Northern Territory into objects that needed to be developed into productive citizens. Vocational training was first imported into the Territory as part of the philanthropically inspired project of social and economic advancement as an extension of the settlement and development undertaken by the early South Australian colonists. As described by Elsey (1986, p. 12), adult education is one of the most common sense and widely accepted ways to bring about social change because it has traditionally adopted a social problem focus. It provides a simplistic commitment to welfare through learning. This social change conception of vocational education and training has its roots in traditional British 'philanthropic concerns of the intellectual middle class' (Elsey 1986, p. 17).

This benign philanthropy is built upon notions of:

- service to the community;
- rational administration;
- legislation and social planning;
- universal voting; and
- development of public health and education services.

This sympathetic desire on the part of the wealthy to improve the lot of others is deeply intertwined with the operations of market capitalism as first described by the father of modern economics, Adam Smith, in the mid-eighteenth century:

> The rich only select from the heap what is most precious and agreeable. They consume little more than the poor, and in spite of their natural selfishness and rapacity, though they mean only their own conveniency, though the sole end which they propose from the labours of all the thousands whom they employ, be the gratification of their own vain and insatiable desires, they divide with the poor the produce of all their improvements. They are led by an invisible hand to make nearly the same distribution of the necessaries of life, which would have been made, had the earth been divided into equal portions among all its inhabitants, and thus without intending it, without knowing it, advance the interest of the society, and afford means to the multiplication of the species (Smith 1759, pp. 508–509).

The late nineteenth-century views of the wealthy Scottish-American industrialist, Andrew Carnegie, demonstrate the application of Smith's theory—of the necessary linkage between capitalism and philanthropic behaviour—in support of the argument used in this analysis of the behaviour of the Northern Territory Government ministers since self-government. Carnegie (1889) proposed that surplus wealth could be disposed of either by leaving it to family members, bequeathing it for public purposes or administering it during the lifetime of those who garnered the fortune. According to Carnegie, the rich would best benefit the nation's people and society by attending to the distribution of their wealth during their own lifetime thus dignifying their own lives:

> The man of wealth thus becoming the mere agent and trustee for his poorer brethren, bringing to their service his superior wisdom, experience and ability to administer, doing for them better than they would or could do for themselves. Those who, would administer wisely must, indeed be wise, for one of the serious obstacles to the improvement of our race is indiscriminate charity. In bestowing charity, the main consideration should be to help those who will help themselves. Individualism will continue, but the millionaire will be but a trustee for the poor; intrusted for a season with a great part of the increased wealth of the community, but administering it for the community for better than it could or would have done for itself (Carnegie 1889, pp. 15 and 18).

Education and training were particularly important areas targeted by Andrew Carnegie and other philanthropists, such as the Rockefellers, for the administration and distribution of their wealth in ways they believed would most improve society. 'Through conditional grant making, and by emphasising efficiency, sustainability and governance, these American philanthropic organisations [foundations] sought to modernise the practices and proclivities of universities and academics in the English-speaking world' (Harvey et al. 2011, p. 175).

In the Northern Territory, vocational education and training has been assigned an almost identical role to that described by Carnegie's interpretation of philanthropy. Training is conceived of as a mechanism to solve economic and social problems and needs to be wisely administered by high-minded ministers who depend upon public sector expertise to give effect to their visions and plans for improvement.

Personal services such as training can be provided for by both public and private means. At the heart of advanced democratic economies lie two competing principles—individualism and collectivism. The first deals with the civic right to public goods while the second refers to the right of the state and its ministers 'to plan, control and ration resources in the interests of all' (Elsey 1986, p. 24). The Northern Territory's modern quasi-market for vocational education and training is still premised upon the harmonisation of mild socialism and an open marketplace, using mechanisms that had originally been aimed at the Indigenous population, later extended to unruly European elements of society and finally made available to everyone in the form of an 'entitlement' to training (Council of Australian Governments 2012):

> Government in playing a leading part in social welfare provision bases its policies on democratic consultation with a variety of political, economic and social interests and works in partnerships with other providing bodies (Elsey 1986, p. 30).

The problems of poverty and deprivation that become amenable to philanthropic interventions on the part of ministers are framed in ways that assume poverty and disadvantage to be a result of personally acquired deficiencies. The solution to these problems is an emphasis 'on acquiring new skills and changing attitudes' (Elsey 1986, p. 71).

When asked during interviews, senior policy makers and politicians from the Northern Territory provided the following examples of why they deployed the problem-solving capacity of vocational education and training during their time in office:

- The former Deputy Chief Minister and Minister for Education and Training Syd Stirling believed, 'Training changes behaviours to a desirable state of affairs. It helps those being trained to understand why things need to be done in a certain way'.

- Additionally, Col Fuller—the last Secretary of the Department of Chief Minister in the initial 26 year-long run of Country Liberal Party governments—was characteristically brash in his description of the importance of training to governments: 'Training can rehabilitate those who break the rules or do not conform to social norms'. However, he also linked the need for control with economic development by stating 'the main problem being addressed by training is one of skill shortages. Particularly in the early days of the Northern Territory, there was a need to build a critical mass of businesses and population'.

- Supporting this view, the former Commissioner for Public Employment and Secretary of the Department of Labour and Administrative Services, David Hawkes, repeated his view that training is 'the only answer if people are not behaving as they ought to—you have to train them' and 'training is necessary to ensure longer term workforce needs are satisfied. Training needs to respond to satisfy skill needs across the economy otherwise major gaps will occur'.

- Furthermore, the Chair of the Northern Territory Employment and Training Authority at the time of its demise in 2001, Andrew Bruyn, opened his interview by stating his belief that training 'fixes problems that are deemed as someone's fault' and 'fixes issues for those at the bottom of the socio-economic ladder'.

Vocational education and training is a form of philanthropy that started as a tool of Northern Territory missionaries in their efforts to 'improve' the life of Aborigines but has become a mainstream political mechanism with broad application to the entire population to structure social behaviour and support an advanced market democracy. The minister with responsibility for training is given the temporary control over the training system and its resources by the community with the expectation that the public's largesse will be used efficiently and effectively to support the continued economic and social development of the Northern Territory.

As described throughout this book, some ministers are better at this task than others, if only because they have a superior understanding of both the potential benefits and the electoral obligations of behaving like a wealthy philanthropist. It is doubtful that any of these ministers of the Crown would describe themselves as sharing the traits of Andrew Carnegie or John D Rockefeller, however, this examination of their behaviour and motivations suggests that they have much in common. There is a shared desire to use time-limited access to financial resources to improve society in ways that they recognise and have experienced—ensuring the continued survival of a capitalist economy by assisting all responsible citizens to participate in work, either through direct employment or entrepreneurial endeavours. 'Even the poorest can be made to see this, and agree that great sums gathered by some of their fellow-citizens and spent for public purposes, from which the masses reap the principal benefit, are more valuable to them than if scattered among them through the course of many years in trifling amounts' (Carnegie 1889, p. 12).

In 2015, Minister Robyn Lambley joined the group of more than two dozen ministerial philanthropists since self-government who have successfully mastered the intensely personal political hothouse and been given responsibility for training. It is instructive to examine the motives for entering politics that she provided in her maiden speech to the Northern Territory Legislative Assembly delivered on 19 October 2010:

The people of Araluen have spoken, and it is with enormous pride that I stand before the Northern Territory parliament as the new member for Araluen. Humbly, I confess I am not a polished politician as many of my esteemed new colleagues. I am an average person who has had the great fortune to benefit from the unbelievable opportunities the Northern Territory has had to offer.

Like many of us, I arrived in Alice Springs with little more than a suitcase, a yearning sense of adventure, and a bucket full of enthusiasm. Almost 17 years later, I am proud to say the Northern Territory is my home, where I met my husband, where my two children were born, where we have established our family business, and where I have lived the greater part of my life. It is an intensely proud and humble Territorian who speaks to you today with her hand on her heart.

The Northern Territory has been good to my family and me, and for this reason I am before you today. I believe we all have a responsibility to try to put back into our community what we get out of it, to reciprocate, to give, and to enable. We have a responsibility to serve our community, and particularly those less fortunate than ourselves. This principle is intrinsic to why I have decided to embark on a path in politics. My vision for the Northern Territory is to enable all Territorians, to provide others with the opportunities I have been afforded, and to serve people as they have served me.

Not all problems require an intervention by government. Not all problems require public resources and public servants to fix them. The community can be enabled and empowered to respond to needs. Governments do not have to be instrumental in providing everything and finding the solution for everything. Neighbourhood Watch is an example of community action. A free-market democracy means, theoretically, government does not need to be big or intrusive in most areas.

The converse side to my lifelong interest in social justice is my business acumen. My parents, grandparents and great-grandparents were all successful, to varying degrees, as business owners. I was raised valuing the importance of financial independence, and the freedom and strength of being self-employed. I was also raised understanding the worry, endless headaches and demands of business.

Business is key to the future of the Northern Territory. Private enterprise is by far our biggest employer. In the electorate of Araluen, 70% of residents are employed and supported by private enterprise. We need to do everything we can to promote and create all manner of business in the Territory. A robust, open economy is far preferable to one which is propped up by government and managed by public servants who have no experience of business, who have never had the experience of risking everything they have to make a quid. We need to listen to the business sector and work with them.

This extended excerpt is not intended to suggest that Minister Lambley is unique in her motivations or intentions. The purpose is, in fact, the complete opposite: her words serve as an exemplar of the characteristics of those vocational training ministers that have gone before and highlight their philanthropic disposition. It also returns us to the main thesis that has been developed in this history of vocational education and training in the Northern Territory. If one seeks to influence training policy and resource allocation, an understanding of the drivers of ministerial decision-making is required. Put simply, these ministers act like wealthy philanthropists and their decisions are driven by the most important factor that influences giving behaviour—self-identification with the intended recipient of the public's munificence.

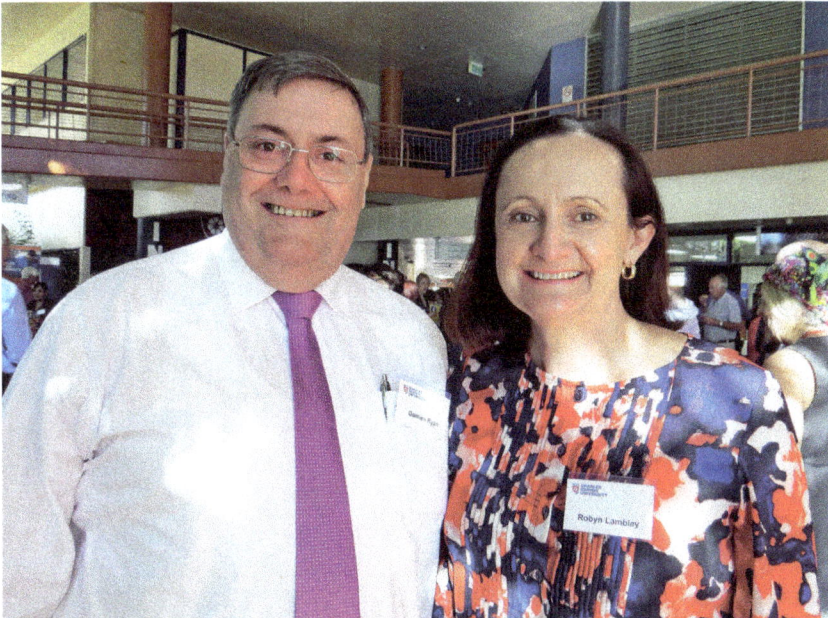

Figure 47. Robyn Lambley, Member of the Legislative Assembly, with the Mayor of Alice Springs, Damien Ryan, joining in the celebrations at the Alice Springs campus of Charles Darwin University recognising 25 years of university-level education in the Northern Territory, June 2014.

Source: Creator Patrick Nelson. Office of Media, Advancement and Community Engagement, Charles Darwin University.

The new Minister for Employment and Training clearly described the type of society and economy that she believed would be the best for the future of the Northern Territory and its residents and it was remarkably similar to that held by virtually all of her predecessors. Once the ministers gained access to the resources, they have each wanted to change society and the world to more closely conform to their views of how life should be lived by the population. Some have seen a larger role for government, others less so, but the difference between them is slight. This world-changing desire is a trait they have in common with the super-rich philanthropists. In their analysis of Andrew Carnegie's philanthropic behaviour, Harvey et al. (2011) describe how dominant economic actors have abundant power (defined as command of resources) and their governing position is gained not through passivity, but inevitably requires victory in a succession of contests for control. The action of the wealthy philanthropist is:

> a world-making process through which already successful entrepreneurs use their power to accumulate more power, extend their social and political influence and increase their capacity to shape society according to their will (Harvey et al. 2011, p. 5).

What did the new minister, with her self-described philanthropic pedigree, find in the vocational education and training portfolio in 2015? Perhaps controversially, this account would suggest that not much has changed over the years since the Kangan Report in 1974 except that there are considerably more people in training—with more than 2500 students commencing apprenticeships or traineeships in the Northern Territory in 2013 in over 500 declared occupations (Department of Business 2015). At the national level, the Commonwealth Government was conducting a number of reviews into vocational education and training in the name of consistency and the most efficient use of public funds—the responsibility for vocational education and training had been removed from the industry portfolio and returned to a Department of Education and Training and the endless debate over state versus federal government responsibility for training had been dusted off yet again (Department of Prime Minister and Cabinet 2014).

Closer to home in the Northern Territory, the merits of boards/ commissions/authorities, as opposed to departmental structures under direct ministerial control, were being reconsidered. The related, sometimes heated, debate of which department's experts should be framing vocational education and training policy and allocating public funding on behalf of the minister continued to thrive. The minister also inherited a quasi-market for the provision of training and assessment services that has become well-established since 1992. Her government was the major 'customer' in this market financing a variety of about 50 private providers as well as the two public providers which operate at arm's-length from government to train Territorians. This arrangement fuels another seemingly irreconcilable contest over the appropriate balance of public funding between the two sectors. Feeding this discussion is the interrelated issue of how can the minister best interact with and obtain advice from business and industry in a manner that recognises the unique, intensely personal nature of the Northern Territory's political landscape. Finally, the minister noted her concerns about the limits of government intervention and seeks assurance that the largesse she distributed would produce the type of society, economy and democracy with which she self-identified.

Unfortunately for Minister Lambley, and in a demonstration of the battles one must wage to remain a public philanthropist, she lost her Cabinet position as a result of her part in the February 2015 botched attempt to remove Adam Giles as the Country Liberals' Parliamentary Leader and Chief Minister. This type of instability has been a feature of the Country Liberals since they returned to the Treasury benches in August 2012. Lambley actually had two brief stints as Minister for Education and Training, while Dave Tollner served for the longest period of time from March 2013 until August 2014. Four other ministers occupied the position for short periods of time culminating in the current occupant, Peter Styles, being set to achieve a new record if he remains minister up until the scheduled August 2016 Legislative Assembly general election. In total, there were 15 Country Liberal ministries in the period August 2012 to August 2016.

Regardless of the particular, rather circular, responses to these questions that remain permanently on the agenda, the ministers have always had two mechanisms upon which they rely to give effect to their ambitions. The Northern Territory Government has shifted vocational education and training between departments or statutory authorities in accordance with the minister's preferences, sense of electoral advantage and political skills. Regardless of which bureaucratic structural arrangement is in use, the operational role has remained the same. The department or authority fulfils the same function as does a wealthy philanthropist's foundation. The technical expertise required to implement the minister/philanthropist's objectives is provided through these organisations.

In addition, these bodies can serve as buffers between givers and receivers, protect the reputation of the philanthropist, identify potential recipients displaying those desirable characteristics required in a market democracy and take steps to ensure the financial resources are not squandered or mishandled.

The leaders of these departments/foundations/authorities are generally eager to provide their minister/philanthropist with the 'best' outcome and will fight over the capacity to influence giving behaviour. The middle managers are frequently ambitious and will seek to promote their organisation as being best-positioned to meet ministerial wishes. Having multiple agencies that are competing with each other—as well as arm's-length training providers from which to choose—gives Northern Territory Government ministers increased policy flexibility and access to a wider variety of data and information with which to both plan their interventions into the behaviour of the population but also monitor the outcomes.

A new minister would have soon found out that she or he had access to the second, and most useful, tool in the vocational education and training policy repertoire—the review—which has frequently been used by those who have gone before. A number of Northern Territory specific reviews impacting upon vocational education and training have been described in the preceding chapters. Australia-wide, the National Centre for Vocational Education Research lists over 100 relevant 'landmark reviews' into vocational education and training since the mid-1960s. Well-constructed reviews provide the minister with considerable electoral and organisational advantages. The first step involves the appointment of the person to lead the review. This individual must not only have the confidence of the minister, but also understand the views and motivations that have prompted the commissioning of the review. The review must have access to expert advice, large amounts of data and a schedule of interviews and consultations that meet the political imperatives that characterise the electorates of the Northern Territory. As a general rule, involving greater numbers of people and organisations in the review better serves the political and personal ambitions of the minister. The results of the review are most useful when presented as a series of recommendations that can be separately implemented and carefully worded in ways that leave room for interpretation by ministerial minders. Reviews also serve another important purpose in that they also 'buy time' as they provide the appearance of action, yet protect the minister from having to make either an immediate or firm decision resulting in unintended consequences.

Reviews have frequently been used to focus the public policy debate upon the public sector bureaucratic structures, on the potential threat to vested interests that might result from changes in the status quo and the personalities of those individuals who are implementing government programs. This has allowed the real drivers of vocational education and training—ministers acting as wealthy philanthropists—to remain comfortably masked by the actions of senior bureaucrats, affording the ministers even greater latitude to create the sort of world they hold dear.

This contemporary account of the development of vocational education and training in the Northern Territory has found that the motivations of those who wish to improve the circumstances of their fellow citizens have remained remarkably consistent over time, as have the organisational and policy options available to philanthropically-minded ministers. Knowing that Northern Territory Government ministers are motivated and behave in ways that are nearly identical to those demonstrated by wealthy philanthropists helps one to understand what has happened in the Northern Territory's training arena since self-government and, consequently, the best means of influencing the future direction of vocational education and training. This creates a new space for novel methods of presenting information and future policy options to decision-makers.

This account of the philanthropic use of vocational education and training invites us to avoid the fallacy of considering the present as a point of arrival but rather to acknowledge that we are at a point of departure (Burawoy 2013).

Postscript

During the final sitting day of the Northern Territory's 12th Legislative Assembly in July 2016, the first major overhaul to the legislation governing vocational education and training since the early 1990s was passed. The *Training and Skills Development Act* (Legislative Assembly of the Northern Territory 2016) maintained the focus upon nationally recognised training used to support employment and economic growth. The role of the minister is clearly defined as well: 'The Minister is responsible for the administration and management of VET in the Territory' (Legislative Assembly of the Northern Territory 2016, p. 6).

In a 'back-to-the-future' scenario, the new Act provides for the establishment of a nine member Northern Territory Training Commission 'to provide high level strategic advice to the Minister, prepare a VET investment framework and an annual VET investment plan' (Legislative Assembly of the Northern Territory 2016, pp. 6–7). Mr Andy Bruyn, the former chair of the Northern Territory Training and Employment Authority, was appointed by Minister Styles as the inaugural chairperson of the Commission which is 'subject to Ministerial direction' and 'must give effect to a direction' (Legislative Assembly of the Northern Territory 2016, p. 8). This statutory authority does not have a mandate to operate at the national level nor the capacity to employ its own staff; it will be supported by the Department of Business whose Chief Executive Officer is a member of the Commission. The activities of the Training Commission are further constrained by legislated provisions that insist 'the CEO or a delegate must attend all meetings of the Commission' and:

> an act or decision of the Commission at a meeting of the Commission is not valid if the CEO or the CEO's delegate is not in attendance when the act is done or the decision is made (Legislative Assembly of the Northern Territory 2016, p. 9).

In his media release announcing the changes to the administration of vocational education and training in the Northern Territory, Minister Styles (2016) also announced that Northern Territory Government resources that had been allocated to the six remaining Training Advisory Councils would be 'redirected' to a new incorporated body, the Industry Skills Advisory Council Northern Territory. This arm's-length organisation will engage directly and intimately with industry to provide contemporary advice to the Department of Business on the skills needs of employers and businesses in relation to the economic growth of the jurisdiction, as well as liaising with a number of federal bodies to ensure the formal qualifications being delivered in the Northern Territory are nationally recognised and up-to-date. All employees of the advisory councils were employed by the new council. In addition, the membership of the board of directors of the Industry Skills Advisory Council was drawn from the directors of the former training advisory councils and an independent chairperson, Don Zoellner. The Industry Skills Advisory Council commenced operations on 1 July 2016.

On 27 August 2016, a Northern Territory general election was held at the end of the four-year fixed-term of parliament. While the final results are yet to be determined at the time of writing, there is the distinct possibility that the Country Liberal Party will only hold two seats in the 25-member assembly. Minister Styles was not re-elected, while the former training minister, Robyn Lambley, was re-elected as an independent member as was former Chief Minister, Terry Mills. The Labor Party was overwhelmingly elected along with at least four independents. On the final day of August 2016, Labor leader Michael Gunner was sworn in as Chief Minister, the first one to have been born in the Northern Territory. With the exception of two ministries, Gunner temporarily assumed all other ministerial portfolios and will make final appointments as the results of the election are finalised. The one certainty is that the Northern Territory is destined to have a spanking new person in the role of public philanthropist with responsibility for the distribution of the public's vocational education and training funds.

References

ABC News 2012, 'Northern Territory Votes: Retiring MPs', Australian Broadcasting Corporation, viewed 2 October 2014, www.abc.net.au/elections/nt/2012/guide/departingmps.htm.

Acting Minister for Territories 1960, *The skills of our Aborigines*, Commonwealth Government Printer, Canberra.

Alexander, F 1959, *Adult education in Australia: An historian's point of view*, Melbourne, FW Cheshire.

Andrew, E 1977, *Technical and Further Education Council for the Northern Territory*, Northern Territory Legislative Assembly Hansard 2 March 1977, viewed 20 March 2014, parliament.nt.gov.au/__data/assets/pdf_file/0007/366532/PR17-Debates-1-March-1977-17-March-1977.pdf.

Anon. 1937, 'The future of the territory: Report of the Northern Territory investigations committee', *Queensland Country Life*, 9 December 1937, p. 1.

Archer, R 2012, 'Hands on and hands up', paper presented to NCVER VET Research Conference, Adelaide.

Arnott, A 2003, 'Learning from the past: Implications for effective VET delivery of adult education services in the Northern Territory', *Australian Journal of Adult Learning*, vol. 43, no. 1, pp. 43–72.

Australian Bureau of Statistics 2011, 'About the ABS', Australian Bureau of Statistics, viewed 17 November 2011, www.abs.gov.au/websitedbs/Corporate.nsf/Home/About+the+ABS.

Australian Committee on Technical and Further Education 1974, *TAFE in Australia: Report on needs in Technical and Further Education (Kangan Report)*, Australian Government Publishing Service, Canberra.

Australian Public Service Commission 2007, *Changing behaviour: A public policy perspective*, The Australian Government, Canberra.

Australian Workforce and Productivity Agency 2013, *Future Focus: 2013 national workforce development strategy*, Department of Industry, Innovation, Science, Research and Tertiary Education, Canberra.

Bacchi, C 2009, *Analysing policy: What's the problem represented to be?* Pearson, Frenchs Forest.

Baker, G 2012, 'Indigenous workers on Methodist Missions in Arnhem Land: A skilled labour force lost', in N Fijn, I Keen, L Christopher & P Michael (eds), *Indigenous participation in Australian economies II*, ANU E Press, Canberra.

Barry, A, Osborne, T & Rose, N (eds) 1996, *Foucault and political reason: Liberalism, neo-liberalism and rationalities of government*, University of Chicago Press, Chicago.

Batchelor Institute of Indigenous Tertiary Education 2001, *Batchelor Institute of Indigenous Tertiary Education Annual Report 2000*, Batchelor Institute of Indigenous Tertiary Education, Batchelor.

—— 2014, *Batchelor Institute of Indigenous Tertiary Education Annual Report 2013*, Batchelor Institute of Indigenous Tertiary Education, Batchelor.

Becker, G 1993, *Human capital: A theoretical and empirical analysis with special reference to education*, Third edn, University of Chicago Press, Chicago. doi.org/10.7208/chicago/9780226041223.001.0001.

Bekkers, R & Wiepking, P 2007, *Generosity and philanthropy: A literature review*, VU University, Amsterdam.

Bennett, D 1982, 'Education: Back to the drawing-board', in G Evans & J Reeves (eds), *Labor essays 1982: Socialist principles and parliamentary government*, Drummond Publishing, Richmond.

Beresford, CE 1977, *Pre-employment survey: A report of pre-employment requirements in the Northern Territory*, Department of Education NT Division, Darwin.

Berzins, B & Loveday, P 1999, *A university for the territory*, Northern Territory University, Darwin.

Bill & Melinda Gates Foundation 2014, *What we do*, Bill & Melinda Gates Foundation, viewed 8 April 2014, www.gatesfoundation.org/ What-We-Do.

Blakely, S 2013, *My giving pledge*, Spanx, viewed 19 November 2013, image.email.spanx.com/lib/fefb1d70736607/d/1/Saras-Letter.pdf.

Brennan, D 1994, *The politics of Australian childcare: From philanthropy to feminism*, Cambridge University Press, Cambridge.

Brody, B 1987, 'The role of philanthropy in a free and democratic state', in E Paul, F Miller Jr, J Paul & J Ahrens (eds), *Beneficence, philanthropy and the public good*, Basil Blackwell, Oxford. doi.org/10.1017/ s0265052500000558.

Burawoy, M 2013, 'Ethnographic fallacies: Reflections on labour studies in the era of market fundamentalism', *Work, Employment and Society*, vol. 27, no. 3, pp. 526–36. doi.org/10.1177/0950017012460316.

Burchell, G, Gordon, C & Miller, P (eds) 1991, *The Foucault effect: Studies in governmentality*, University of Chicago Press, Chicago.

Butlin, N, Barnard, A & Pincus, J 1982, *Government and capitalism: Public and private choice in twentieth century Australia*, George Allen and Unwin, Sydney.

Carnegie, A 1889, *The gospel of wealth*, The Carnegie Corporation of New York, viewed 8 November 2014, carnegie.org/publications/ search-publications/pub/272/.

Centre for Appropriate Technology 2014, *Centre for Appropriate Technology annual report 2013*, Centre for Appropriate Technology, Alice Springs.

Chard, G 1983, *Enhancing the vocational preparation of youth in the Northern Territory*, Northern Territory Department of Education, Darwin.

Coles, P 1993, *Educational and vocational training needs of the Aboriginal labour market in rural and remote areas of the Northern Territory*, Australian Government Publishing Service, Canberra.

Commonwealth of Australia 1946, *Parliamentary debates (Hansard) session 1945–46 third session of the Seventeenth Parliament second period (from the 6th March 1946 to the 9th March 1946)*, Government of the Commonwealth of Australia, Canberra.

Coombs, HC 1994, *From Curtin to Keating: The 1945 and 1994 white papers on employment: A better environment for human and economic development*, North Australia Research Unit, The Australian National University, Darwin.

Council of Australian Governments 2012, *National partnership agreement on skills reform*, Commonwealth of Australia, Canberra.

Coutsoukis, P 1999, 'The reconstruction of corporate social involvement and some of its potential impacts on non-profits', paper presented to Fall Conference of the New England Sociological Association, Boston, 6 November 1999.

Cross, J 2011, *Great central state: The foundation of the Northern Territory*, Wakefield Press, Adelaide.

Cummin, IR 1986, *The apprenticeship system in the Northern Territory*, Northern Territory Department of Business, Technology and Communications, Darwin.

Daly, S 2012, 'Philanthropy as an essentially contested concept', *Voluntas*, vol. 23, pp. 535–57. doi.org/10.1007/s11266-011-9213-5.

Darwin Community College Planning Committee 1970a, *First report of the Darwin Community College planning committee*, Department of Education and Science, Canberra.

—— 1970b, *Second report of the Darwin Community College planning committee*, Department of Education and Science, Canberra.

Dawkins, J 1988a, *A changing workforce*, Australian Government Publishing Service, Canberra.

—— 1988b, *Industry training in Australia: The need for change*, Australian Government Publishing Service, Canberra.

—— 1989, *Improving Australia's training system*, Australian Government Publishing Service, Canberra.

Dawkins, J & Costello, R 1983, 'Education: Progress and reality', in G Evans & J Reeves (eds), *Labor essays 1983: Policies and programs for the Labor Government*, Dove Publishing, Blackburn.

Dawkins, J & Holding, A 1987, *Skills for Australia*, Australian Government Publishing Service, Canberra.

Department of Business 2015, *Fact Sheet 2014*, Northern Territory Government, viewed 16 January 2015, www.dob.nt.gov.au/training/vet/Pages/fact-sheet-2014.aspx.

Department of Business and Employment 2012, *NT employment strategy 2012–2015*, Northern Territory Government, Darwin.

Department of Education and Science 1969, *One hundred years of education in the Northern Territory*, Commonwealth of Australia, Darwin.

Department of Education Northern Territory Division 1974, *Department of Education: Northern Territory Division annual report 1973*, Department of Education: Northern Territory Division, Darwin.

—— 1977, *Report for 1976 Department of Education: Northern Territory Division*, Department of Education: Northern Territory Division, Darwin.

—— 1978, *Report for 1977 Department of Education: Northern Territory Division*, Department of Education: Northern Territory Division, Darwin.

Department of Employment, Education and Training 2006, *DEET annual report 2005–06*, Northern Territory Government, Darwin.

Department of Industry 2014, 'Skills', Australian Government, viewed 18 September 2014, training.gov.au/.

Department of Industry and Small Business 1985, *Proceedings of a seminar on traineeships: 30 April 1985*, Department of Industry and Small Business, Darwin.

Department of Prime Minister and Cabinet 2014, *Reform of federation white paper: Roles and responsibilities in education part B: Vocational education and training and higher education*, Issues paper 4, Australian Government, Canberra.

Department of the Legislative Assembly 2008, *Debates: Eleventh Assembly first session 21/10/2008: Parliamentary record no. 2*, Northern Territory of Australia, viewed 2 October 2014, parliament.nt.gov.au/parliamentary-business/hansard-debates-and-minutes-of-proceedings/full-text-transcripts/full_text_transcripts_listing/nest_content?target_id=346211&parent_id=358649.

Department of Trade, Australian Council of Trade Unions (ACTU) & Trade Development Council (TDC) 1987, *Australia reconstructed: ACTU/TDC mission to western Europe: A report by the mission members to the ACTU and the TDC*, Australian Government Publishing Service, Canberra.

Deveson, I 1990, *Training costs of award restructuring: Report of the Training Costs Review Committee, Volume one*, Australian Government Publishing Service, Canberra.

Dollery, B & Wallis, J 2003, *The political economy of the voluntary sector*, Edward Elgar, Cheltenham.

Donovan, P 1983, *Gsell, Francis Xavier (1872–1960)*, Australian Dictionary of Biography, National Centre of Biography, The Australian National University, viewed 10 April 2014, adb.anu.edu.au/biography/gsell-francis-xavier-6502.

Economic and Statistical Branch 1961, *Development in the Northern Territory: Notes on expenditure, investment and achievements during the ten years to 30th June 1961*, Department of Territories, Canberra.

Editor 1985, 'The right bus', *NT News*, 19 October 1985, p. 6.

Education Advisory Group 1978, *Report of the Education Advisory Group on matters relating to the structure of educational administration for a self-governing Northern Territory*, Northern Territory Government, Darwin.

Elsey, B 1986, *Social theory perspectives on adult education*, University of Nottingham Department of Adult Education, Nottingham.

Evans, G & Reeves, J (eds) 1980, *Labor essays 1980: Policies and programs for the Labor Government*, Drummond Publishing, Richmond.

Everingham, P 1981, 'Introductory address', in R Herr & P Loveday (eds), *Small is beautiful: Parliament in the Northern Territory*, Australasian Study of Parliament Group and the North Australia Research Unit of The Australian National University, Canberra.

Falk, I, Arnott, A, Blohm, R, Grenfell, M, Guenther, J & Wallace, R 2004, *Creating effective pathways to employment and training for the employment disadvantaged in the Northern Territory*, Department of Employment, Education and Training, Darwin.

Finch, F 1993, *Ministerial statement: Future organisation of vocational education and training services in the NT*, Northern Territory Legislative Assembly, Darwin.

Fisher, D 1983, 'The role of philanthropic foundations in the reproduction and production of hegemony: Rockefeller Foundations and the social sciences', *Sociology*, vol. 17, no. 2, pp. 206–33. doi.org/10.1177/0038 038583017002004.

Fosdick, R 1989, *The story of the Rockefeller Foundation*, Transaction Publishers, New Brunswick.

Freire, P 1996, *Pedagogy of the oppressed*, Penguin Books, London.

Giese, N 1990, *The Darwin Institute of Technology: A historical perspective*, Northern Territory Library Services, Darwin.

Goozee, G 2001, *The development of TAFE in Australia*, Third edn, National Centre for Vocational Education Research, Leabrook.

—— 2013, *From Tech to TAFE: 1949–1997*, Retired New South Wales TAFE Officers' Association, Sydney.

Gordon, C 1991, 'Governmental rationality: An introduction', in G Burchell, C Gordon & P Miller (eds), *The Foucault effect: Studies in governmentality*, University of Chicago Press, Chicago.

Harris, T 1987, *Ministerial statement: Northern Territory University*, Northern Territory Legislative Assembly, Darwin.

Hart, AM 1970, 'A history of the education of full-blood Aborigines in South Australia with references to the Northern Territory', MA thesis, University of Adelaide, Adelaide.

Harvey, C, MacLean, M, Gordon, J & Shaw, E 2011, 'Andrew Carnegie and the foundations of contemporary entrepreneurial philanthropy', *Business History*, vol. 53, no. 3, pp. 425–50. doi.org/10.1080/000767 91.2011.565516.

Hay, I & Muller, S 2013, 'Questioning generosity in the golden age of philanthropy: Towards critical geographies of super-philanthropy', *Progress in Human Geography*, pp. 1–19.

Heatley, A 1979, *The government of the Northern Territory*, University of Queensland Press, St Lucia.

—— 1990, *Almost Australians: The politics of Northern Territory self-government*, The Australian National University North Australia Research Unit, Darwin.

—— 1998, *The territory party: The Northern Territory Country Liberal Party 1974–1998*, Northern Territory University Press, Darwin.

Henderson, P 2009, *Ministerial statement: Framework for training workforce*, Northern Territory Legislative Assembly, Darwin.

Herman, A 2003, *The Scottish Enlightenment: The Scots' invention of the modern world*, Fourth Estate, London.

High schools and secondary colleges working party 1985, *High schools and secondary colleges in Alice Springs: A report to the Minister for Education*, High schools and secondary colleges working party, Alice Springs.

Higher Education Planning Group 1988, *Higher Education in the Northern Territory*, Northern Territory Government, Darwin.

Hill, M & Hupe, P 2002, *Implementing public policy: Governance in theory and practice*, Sage Politics Texts, Sage Publications, London.

Industry and Employment Advisory Council 1986, *Annual report 1986*, Industry and Employment Advisory Council, Darwin.

Industry Commission 1998, *Microeconomic reform in Australia: A compendium from the 1970s to 1997 research paper*, Australian Government Publishing Service, Canberra.

Institute for Aboriginal Development 2004, *Institute for Aboriginal Development Annual Report 2003*, Institute for Aboriginal Development, Alice Springs.

—— 2013, *Institute for Aboriginal Development Annual Report 2012–2013*, Institute for Aboriginal Development, Alice Springs.

Jaensch, D 1981, 'Political representation in a unique polity', in R Herr & P Loveday (eds), *Small is beautiful: Parliament in the Northern Territory*, Australasian Study of Parliament Group and the North Australia Research Unit of The Australian National University, Canberra.

Jordan, I 1999, *Brief History of the Baptist Ministry to the Indigenous people of Central Australia*, Australian Baptist Missionary Society, Adelaide.

Joynt, RD 1918, *Ten years' work at the Roper River mission station, Northern Territory, Australia, August 1908 to August 1918: A short history of the Roper River Mission written by the Rev. R. D. Joynt, pioneer missionary to the Roper Aborigines*, Church Missionary Society of Australia and Tasmania, Melbourne.

Katherine Rural College Planning Committee 1976, *Katherine Rural College Planning Committee Report*, Australian Government Publishing Service, Canberra.

Kemp, D 1998, 'The VET market', in C Robinson & R Kenyon (eds), *The market for vocational education and training*, National Centre for Vocational Education Research, Leabrook.

Kirby, P 1985, *Report of the Committee of Inquiry into Labour Market Programs*, Australian Government Publishing Service, Canberra.

Knight, R 2011, *Maximising opportunity through employment and training NT*, Northern Territory Government, Darwin.

Lee, N 2007, 'Former Darwin Lord Mayor sentenced to two months jail', ABC Radio, viewed 3 May 2016, www.abc.net.au/local/stories/2007/09/05/2024601.htm.

Legislative Assembly of the Northern Territory 2016, *Training and Skills Development Act*, Northern Territory of Australia, Darwin.

Loveday, P & Young, E 1984, *Aboriginal adult education: TAFE in the Northern Territory*, The Australian National University, North Australian Research Unit, Darwin.

Lugg, C 2000, *Ministerial statement: The Northern Territory Employment and Training Authority*, Northern Territory Legislative Assembly, Darwin.

Lyons, M 2001, *Third sector: The contribution of nonprofit and cooperative enterprises in Australia*, Allen & Unwin, Crows Nest.

Manne, R & Feik, C (eds) 2012, *The words that made Australia*, Ebook Introduction, Black Inc. Agenda, Collingwood.

Manzie, D 1999, *Batchelor Institute of Indigenous Tertiary Education Bill*, Northern Territory Legislative Assembly, Darwin.

Martin, C & Dewar, M 2012, *Speak for yourself: Eight Chief Ministers reflect on Northern Territory self-government*, Charles Darwin University Press, Darwin.

Masters, E 2009, 'Batchelor Institute scales back learning centres', ABC News, viewed 18 September 2014, www.abc.net.au/news/2009-12-02/batchelor-institute-scales-back-learning-centres/1165602.

Mathers, R 1982, *Report on accreditation policy and practice for TAFE courses in the Northern Territory*, Department of Technical and Further Education South Australia, Adelaide.

McDonald, K & Scaife, W 2011, 'Print media portrayals of giving: Exploring national "cultures of philanthropy"', *International Journal of Nonprofit and Voluntary Sector Marketing*, vol. 16, no. 4, pp. 311–24. doi.org/10.1002/nvsm.430.

McDowell, J, Oliver, D, Perrson, M, Fairbrother, R, Wetzlar, S, Buchanan, J & Shipstone, T 2011, *A shared responsibility: Apprenticeships for the 21st century* Department of Employment, Education and Workplace Relations, Canberra.

Minister for Territories 1958, *Assimilation of our Aborigines*, Commonwealth Government Printer, Canberra.

National Archives of Australia 1961a, *Alice Springs School*, Northern Territory Administration, Darwin, F1 1940/61.

—— 1961b, *Education Board*, Northern Territory Administration, Darwin, File number 65/2663.

—— 1961c, *Education Enquiry Committee, Northern Territory Administration, statements and enquiries received*, Northern Territory Administration, Darwin, Item F1 60/2005.

—— 2014a, *Commonwealth Government records about the Northern Territory: Education*, Australian Government, viewed 10 April 2014, guides.naa.gov.au/records-about-northern-territory/part2/chapter13/13.2.aspx.

—— 2014b, *Commonwealth Reconstruction Training Scheme administrative records – fact sheet 178*, Australian Government, Canberra.

National Centre for Vocational Education Research 2011, *Australian vocational education and training statistics: Students and courses 2010*, National Centre for Vocational Education Research, Adelaide.

—— 2013a, *Australian vocational education and training statistics: Students and courses 2012*, National Centre for Vocational Education Research, Adelaide.

—— 2013b, *Historical time series of apprenticeships and traineeships in Australia from 1963*, National Centre for Vocational Education Research, Adelaide.

—— 2014, *2013 students and courses: Australian vocational education and training statistics*, National Centre for Vocational Education Research, Adelaide.

Northern Territory Archives Service 1964, *Report on an investigation into curriculum and teaching methods used in Aboriginal schools in the Northern Territory to the Honourable CE Barnes, MP, Minister of State for Territories March 1964*, Northern Territory Administration, Darwin, Series NTRS 1874, Historical Society of the Northern Territory Inc, collection of historical documents and items 1877–ca 1977.

—— 1971–2003, *Cabinet Submission Number 13: Technical and Further Education Council for the Northern Territory*, Cabinet Decision Number 13, Northern Territory Department of the Chief Minister, Series Number NTRS 2575/P1, Volume One.

—— 1974–1987, *Department of Education (1974) submission to Joint Parliamentary Committee on the Northern Territory*, Northern Territory Education Division, Peter Loveday, Series Number NTRS 1041, Records Related to Northern Territory Constitutional Development.

—— 1977–1979, *Chief Minister departmental memoranda to Majority Leader and the Chief Minister (PAE Everingham) 1977–1979*, Northern Territory Government, Darwin, NTRS 784 Box 15 – Folder Educational General.

—— 1977–2003a, *Cabinet Paper Number 14: Apprentices Board*, Cabinet Decision Number 14, Northern Territory Department of the Chief Minister, Series Number NTRS 2575/P1, Volume One.

—— 1977–2003b, *Cabinet Submission Number 459: Education administration*, Cabinet Decision Number 529, Northern Territory Department of the Chief Minister, Series Number 2575/P1, Volume 17.

—— 1977–2003c, *Cabinet Submission Number 978: Funding of technical and further education projects*, Northern Territory Department of the Chief Minister, Series Number 2575/P1, Volume 50.

—— 1980a, *Allow non-Darwin member of Industrial Training Commission*, Northern Territory Government, Series NTRS 2575, Box 20, Item 51, Cabinet Decision 1162.

—— 1980b, *Establishment of a Northern Territory University*, Northern Territory Government, Series NTRS 2575, Box 20, Item 49, Cabinet submission 959.

—— 1980c, *An integrated approach to Aboriginal communities*, Northern Territory Government, Series NTRS 2575, Box 21, Item 52, Cabinet Decision 1013.

—— 1980d, *Northern Territory Industries Training Commission*, Northern Territory Government, NTRS 2575, Box 21, Item 54, Cabinet Decisions 1242 and 1243.

—— 1980e, *Skills Training Centre in Darwin*, Northern Territory Government, NTRS 2575, Box 23, Item 58, Cabinet Decision 1353.

—— 1980–1982a, *Minister for Education correspondence related to education (JM Robertson) 1980–1982*, Northern Territory Government, NTRS 1052 Box 7 Item E21.

—— 1980–1982b, *Northern Territory Post-School Advisory Council Annual Report for 1980 to the Honourable the Minister for Education*, Northern Territory Government, Darwin, NTRS 1052 Box 10 Minister for Education correspondence relating to education (JM Robertson) 1980–1982.

—— 1981, *Minister for Education correspondence relating to education (JM Robertson 1980–1982)*, Northern Territory Government, Series NTRS 1052 Box 11.

—— 1981–1988, *Records relating to the Northern Territory University Planning Authority Advisory Committee*, Peter Loveday, Series Number 845, Re-organisation of post-school education in the Northern Territory.

—— 1982a, *Amendments to the Industries Training Act 1979*, Northern Territory Government, Series 2575, Box 47, Item 110, Decision 2553.

—— 1982b, *Employment prospects for Northern Territory youth*, Northern Territory Government, Series 2575, Box 50, Item 116b, Decision 2686.

—— 1982c, *Industries Training Bill amendments and drafting notes*, Northern Territory Government, Series 2575 Box 49, Item 115a, Decision 2636.

—— 1982d, *Northern Territory Post-School Advisory Council Annual Report 1981*, Northern Territory Government, Series 2575, Box 46, Item 108a, Decision 2483.

—— 1983a, *Alice Springs Apprenticeship Scheme*, Northern Territory Government, Series 2575, Box 53, Item 121b, Decision 2825.

—— 1983b, *Ministerial statement on school leavers*, Northern Territory Government, Series 2575, Box 65, Item 138, Decision 3266.

—— 1983c, *Northern Territory Post-School Advisory Council Annual Report 1982*, Northern Territory Government, Series 2575, Box 53, Item 121a, Decision 2383.

—— 1984–1991a, *Community College of Central Australia: General correspondence*, Office of the Public Service Commissioner, Series Number NTRS 1770/P1, Item Number 87/1967.

—— 1984–1991b, *Economic Planning Advisory Council*, Office of the Public Service Commissioner, Series Number NTRS 1770/P1, Item Number 87/2102.

—— 1984–1991c, *Joint TAFEAC/IETAC Meeting 23rd October 1990 Capricornia House Lindsay Street Darwin*, Office of the Public Service Commissioner, Series Number NTRS 1770/P1, Item Number 90/0879.

—— 1984–1991d, *Report of the Committee of Inquiry into Labour Market Programs: The Kirby Report*, Office of the Commissioner for Public Employment, Series Number NTRS 1770/P1, Item Number 85/0071G.

—— 1984–1991e, *Review of the Industries and Employment Training Act*, Office of the Public Service Commissioner, Series Number NTRS 1770/P1, Item Number 89/1279.

—— 1984–1991f, *E and T: Review of Industries and Employment Act*, Office of the Commissioner of Public Employment, Series Number NTRS 1770/P1, Item Number 87/0849.

—— 1984–1991g, *TAFE Advisory Council (TAFEAC)*, Office of the Public Service Commissioner, Series Number NTRS 1770/P1, Item Number 87/0585.

—— 1985–1989, *General history files on 'Higher Education, Economic and Political Change' and its implications for higher education 1986*, Northern Territory Department of Education, Series Number NTRS1261, ID Number 2001/0301 Part 31.

—— 1985–1990, *Department of Education confidential secretariat records 1985–90 report of the training costs review committee*, Northern Territory Department of Education, Series Number NTRS1314, ID Number 2001/0296 Part 9.

—— 1 June 1987–26 October 1987, *Ministerial File TAFE, administration, finance and staffing*, Northern Territory Department of Education, Series Number NTRS 550/Part 3, ID Number 102ML Part 3.

—— 2 November 1988–30 December 1988, *Ministerial file TAFE, administration, finance and staffing*, Northern Territory Department of Education, Series Number NTRS550/Part 6, ID Number 102ML Part 6.

—— 20 May 1988–28 November 1988, *Ministerial file TAFE, administration, finance and staffing*, Northern Territory Department of Education, Series Number NTRS550/Part 3, ID Number 102ML Part 5.

Northern Territory Department of Education 1985, *1985 review and reorganisation of the Northern Territory Department of Education*, Northern Territory Government, Darwin.

—— 1992, *Technical and Further Education Handbook 1992*, Northern Territory Government, Darwin.

Northern Territory Department of Employment, Education and Training, 2003, *Northern Territory Department of Employment, Education and Training annual report 2002–03*, Northern Territory Department of Employment, Education and Training, Darwin.

Northern Territory Employment and Training Authority 1993, *Annual report 1992*, Northern Territory Department of Education, Darwin.

—— 1994, *Northern Territory Employment and Training Authority annual report 1993*, Northern Territory Department of Education, Darwin.

—— 1996, *Northern Territory Employment and Training Authority annual report 1995*, Government Printer of the Northern Territory, Darwin.

—— 1997, *Northern Territory Employment and Training Authority annual report 1996*, Northern Territory Department of Education, Darwin.

—— 1998, *Northern Territory Employment and Training Authority annual report 1997*, Government Printer of the Northern Territory, Darwin.

—— 1999, *1999 VET plan*, Northern Territory Employment and Training Authority, Darwin.

—— 2000, *Northern Territory Employment and Training Authority annual report 1999–2000*, Northern Territory Government, Darwin.

—— 2001, *Northern Territory Employment and Training Authority annual report 2000–2001*, Northern Territory Employment and Training Authority, Darwin.

Northern Territory Government 1984, *Submission of the Northern Territory Government to the Committee of Inquiry into Labour Market Programs*, Northern Territory of Australia, Darwin.

—— 2013, *Framing the future blueprint draft*, Northern Territory Government, Darwin.

Northern Territory Industries Training Commission 1981, *What is the Industries Training Commission (ITC)?*, Northern Territory Industries Training Commission, Darwin.

Northern Territory Industry Training Commission 1981, *Annual report 1980–81*, Northern Territory Industry Training Commission, Darwin.

Northern Territory of Australia 1948, *Northern Territory Legislative Council Debates: First session 1948 (Second Meeting)*. Commonwealth of Australia, Canberra.

—— 1960, *Welfare Ordinance 1953–1960*, Northern Territory Legislative Council, Darwin.

—— 1987a, *Annual report 1986/87 Public Service Commissioner for the Northern Territory*, Northern Territory Government, Darwin.

—— 1987b, *Department of Industry and Small Business annual report: A partial report for the period 21 December 1984 to 30 June 1985*, Northern Territory Government, Darwin.

—— 1988a, *Annual report 1987/88 Public Service Commissioner for the Northern Territory and Department of Labour and Administrative Services*, Northern Territory Government, Darwin.

—— 1988b, *Department of Business, Technology and Communications annual report 1985/86*, Northern Territory Government, Darwin.

—— 1989, *Annual report 1988/89 Public Service Commissioner for the Northern Territory and Department of Labour and Administrative Services*, Northern Territory Government, Darwin.

—— 1992, *Annual report 1990/91 Public Service Commissioner for the Northern Territory and Department of Labour and Administrative Services*, Northern Territory Government, Darwin.

—— 1999, *Northern Territory Employment and Training Act 1999*, Northern Territory Government, Darwin.

—— 2013, *Northern Territory Employment and Training Act*, Northern Territory Government, Darwin.

Northern Territory Open College 1987, *Development of community education centres in Aboriginal communities in the Northern Territory*, Northern Territory Department of Education, Darwin.

Northern Territory University 2001a, *Northern Territory University Annual Report 2000*, Northern Territory University, Darwin.

—— 2001b, *Strategic positioning for the future*, Northern Territory University, Darwin.

Northern Territory Vocational Training Commission 1984, *Annual report 1983–84*, Northern Territory Vocational Training Commission, Darwin.

Ostrower, F 1995, *Why the wealthy give: The culture of elite philanthropy*, Princeton University Press, Princeton.

Patterson, T 2001, *A Social History of Anthropology in the United States*, Berg Publishers, Oxford.

Pattinson, D 1980, *The Community College of Central Australia: An educational specification*, Northern Territory Department of Education, Darwin.

Perron, M 1992, *Address by Chief Minister Marshall Perron re the outcomes of the meeting of the Heads of Government Canberra 11 May 1992*, Northern Territory Legislative Assembly, Darwin.

Polonsky, M, Shelley, L & Voola, R 2002, 'An examination of helping behaviour – some evidence from Australia', *Journal of Nonprofit & Public Sector Marketing*, vol. 10, no. 2, pp. 67–82. doi.org/10.1300/J054v10n02_04.

Pope, K 1986, *Sudden death in Northern Territory's Public Service*, Administrative and Clerical Officer's Association, Darwin.

Price, AG 1930, *The history and problems of the Northern Territory Australia*, University of Queensland, Brisbane.

—— 1949, *White settlers and native peoples: An historical study of racial contacts between English-speaking whites and aboriginal peoples in the United States, Canada, Australia and New Zealand*, Georgian House, Melbourne.

Productivity Commission 2014, *Report on Government Services 2014*, Australian Government, Canberra.

Ramsey, G 2002, *Desert Peoples Centre: Volume one - our statement*, Desert Peoples Centre, Alice Springs.

Ravens, T 2009, 'Batchelor College in NT "won't close"', *Sydney Morning Herald*, viewed 18 September 2014, news.smh.com.au/breaking-news-national/batchelor-college-in-nt-wont-close-20090820-erpf.html.

Reed, M 1998, *Ministerial statement: Planning for Growth: Health, education, power and water authority and review of progress to date*, Northern Territory Legislative Assembly, Darwin.

Robertson, J 1982, *Industries Training Amendment Bill*, Northern Territory Legislative Assembly Hansard 13 October 1982, viewed 20 March 2014, parliament.nt.gov.au/__data/assets/pdf_file/0003/367203/PR10-Debates-12-14-October-1982.pdf.

Rose, N 1996, 'Governing "advanced" liberal democracies', in A Barry, T Osborne & N Rose (eds), *Foucault and political reason: Liberalism, neo-liberalism and rationalities of government*, University of Chicago Press, Chicago.

Russell, D 2014, 'How to save the Australian public service', *The Age*, 1 April 2014, p. 20.

Schervish, P 1998, 'Philanthropy', in R Wuthnow (ed.), *The Encyclopedia of Politics and Religion*, Congressional Quarterly Inc, Washington.

Schervish, P, Coutsoukis, P & Havens, J 1998, *Social participation and charitable giving revisited: A replication of a multivariate analysis*, Boston College Centre on Wealth and Philanthropy, Boston.

Schervish, P, Herman, A & Rhenisch, L 1986, 'Towards a general theory of the philanthropic activities of the wealthy', paper presented to Annual Spring Research Forum of the Independent Sector, New York, 13–14 March 1986.

Schuyt, T, Bekkers, R & Smit, J 2010, 'The philanthropy scale: A sociological perspective in measuring new forms of pro social behaviour', *Social Work and Society International Online Journal*, vol. 8, no. 1, pp. 1–7.

Shimpo, M 1985, *Young Aboriginals and employment: A survey of socio-cultural factors, education and training facilities affecting the employment of young Aboriginals in the Northern Territory*, Northern Territory Department of Education, Darwin.

Slim, W 1954, 'Preface', paper presented to Northern Australia: Task for a nation – 20th summer school of the Australian Institute of Political Science, Canberra, 30 January to 1 February 1954.

Smith, A 1759, *The theory of moral sentiments*, University of Oxford Text Archives, Oxford. doi.org/10.1093/oseo/instance.00042831.

Sri-Pathimanathan, C 1985, *Apprentice recruitments and some policy aspects concerning apprentice training in the Northern Territory*, Department of Industry and Small Business, Darwin.

Stirling, S 2002, *Ministerial statement: Northern Territory employment and training strategy to 2005*, Northern Territory Legislative Assembly, Darwin.

Stone, S 1991, *Northern Territory Employment And Training Authority Bill (Serial 89) & Education Amendment Bill (Serial 90): Presentation and second reading, debate adjourned*, Northern Territory Legislative Assembly, Darwin.

—— 1992, *Ministerial statement: A new era in vocational education and training*, Northern Territory Legislative Assembly, Darwin.

Strike, TM 1981, *An introduction to the philosophy of Aboriginal adult education in the Northern Territory*, Adelaide College of Advanced Education, Adelaide.

Styles, P 2016, *Training and skills paves the way for NT VET sector*, Northern Territory Government, Darwin.

Tangentyere Council 1984, *Employment and training needs of Aboriginal town campers in Alice Springs*, Tangentyere Council Incorporated, Alice Springs.

Tannock, P 1975, *The government of education in Australia: The origins of Federal policy*, University of Western Australia Press, Perth.

—— 1976, 'The development of the Federal Government's role in education', in G Harman & C Selby Smith (eds), *Readings in the economics and politics of Australian education*, Permagon Press, Sydney.

Technical and Further Education Commission 1976, *Report for the triennium 1977–1979: First report of the Technical and Further Education Commission*, Australian Government Publishing Service, Canberra.

The Auditor-General 2007, *Audit report no. 3 2007–08 performance audit: Australian Technical Colleges Programme: Department of Education, Science and Training*, Australian Government, Canberra.

The Legislative Council for the Northern Territory 1962, *Report from the Select Committee on the educational needs of the people of the Northern Territory*, Commonwealth Government Printer, Canberra.

The Parliament of the Commonwealth of Australia 1974, *Constitutional development in the Northern Territory: Report from the Committee on the Northern Territory*, Australian Government Publishing Service, Canberra.

The World Today 2007, 'Australian Technical Colleges under attack', ABC Radio, viewed 22 September 2014, www.abc.net.au/worldtoday/content/2007/s1946012.htm.

Thompson, J 1999, *The making of the Northern Territory University*, Northern Territory University Press, Darwin.

Thorpe, T 2005, 'Remote delivery – not just education work!', paper presented to Australian Corrections Education Association, Darwin, 9–11 October 2005.

Trade Training Working Group 1997, *Apprenticeships at the crossroads: A report on apprenticeship training in the Northern Territory*, Trade Training Working Group, Darwin.

Turnbull, J 1998, *Response to transfer of NTETA functions to the Education Department paper*, Northern Territory Employment and Training Authority, Darwin.

—— 1999, 'David and Goliath: A contrast in dimensions', *Training Agenda*, vol. 7, no. 3, p. 8.

Tuxworth, I 1985, *Censure of the Chief Minister Debate*, Northern Territory Legislative Assembly Hansard 28 February 1985, viewed 20 March 2014, parliament.nt.gov.au/__data/assets/pdf_file/0009/367443/PR05-Debates-26-February-7-March-1985.pdf.

Uibo, M 1993, 'The development of Batchelor College 1972–1990: An historical account', MA thesis, Northern Territory University.

Urvett, M 1982, *Development of public educational services in the Northern Territory 1876–1979: Research working paper number 82.8*, University of Melbourne Centre for the Study of Higher Education, Parkville.

Urvett, M, Heatley, A & Alcorta, F 1980, *A study in transition: Education and policy-making in the Northern Territory*, Centre for the Study of Higher Education at the University of Melbourne, Parkville.

Webb, C 2014, *An eventful journey: The evolution of Charles Darwin University*, Charles Darwin University, Darwin

Weller, P & Sanders, W 1982, *The team at the top: Ministers in the Northern Territory*, The Australian National University, North Australian Research Unit, Darwin.

Whitelock, D (ed.) 1973, *The vision splendid: Adult education in Australia: W. G. K. Duncan's 1944 report with commentaries*, University of Adelaide, Adelaide.

—— 1974, *The great tradition: A history of adult education in Australia*, University of Queensland Press, St Lucia.

Whyatt, B 1977, 'Apprentice's presentation night address 25 February 1977', in CE Beresford (ed.), *Pre-employment survey: A report of pre-employment requirements in the Northern Territory*, Department of Education NT Division, Darwin.

Wilson, H & Estbergs, E 1984, *The Northern Territory Chronicle*, Second edn, Northern Territory University Planning Authority, Darwin.

Wolf, C 1989, *Markets or governments*, MIT Press, Cambridge.

Working party on vocational training for Aboriginals in the Northern Territory 1973, *Report of the working party on vocational training for Aboriginals in the Northern Territory*, Department of Aboriginal Affairs, Darwin.

Zoellner, D 2012, 'Do not pass go, do not collect $200: The priority given to vocational education and training research and policy', paper presented to Australian VET Research Association annual conference, Canberra, 11–13 April 2012.

—— 2013a, 'At the leading edge: Enacting VET in the Northern Territory', paper presented to Australian Vocational Education and Training Research Association 16th annual conference, Fremantle, 3–5 April 2013.

—— 2013b, 'If vocational education and training is the answer, what was the question?: Theorising public policy and the behaviour of citizens', PhD thesis, Charles Darwin University, DOI 10.13140/ RG.2.1.4555.9522.

—— 2014, *A strategic review of Desert Knowledge Australia*, Charles Darwin University, Alice Springs, DOI 10.13140/RG.2.1.1672.3684.

www.ingramcontent.com/pod-product-compliance
Lightning Source LLC
Chambersburg PA
CBHW040151270326
41926CB00079B/4620